The Call of Bilal

ISLAMIC CIVILIZATION AND MUSLIM NETWORKS
Carl W. Ernst and Bruce B. Lawrence, editors

Highlighting themes with historical as well as contemporary significance, Islamic Civilization and Muslim Networks features works that explore Islamic societies and Muslim peoples from a fresh perspective, drawing on new interpretive frameworks or theoretical strategies in a variety of disciplines. Special emphasis is given to systems of exchange that have promoted the creation and development of Islamic identities—cultural, religious, or geopolitical. The series spans all periods and regions of Islamic civilization.

A complete list of titles published in this series appears at the end of the book.

The Call of Bilal

ISLAM IN THE AFRICAN DIASPORA

Edward E. Curtis IV

The University of North Carolina Press   Chapel Hill

*This book was published with the assistance of the
Anniversary Endowment Fund of the University of North Carolina Press.*

© 2014 The University of North Carolina Press
All rights reserved
Manufactured in the United States of America
Set in Charis by codeMantra, Inc.
The paper in this book meets the guidelines for permanence and durability
of the Committee on Production Guidelines for Book Longevity of the Council
on Library Resources. The University of North Carolina Press has been a
member of the Green Press Initiative since 2003.

Cover illustration: Sheik Abdul Hameed Ahmad, Bahia, Brazil, 2013. Photograph by
Renato Brito Semanovschi.

Library of Congress Cataloging-in-Publication Data
Curtis, Edward E., 1970–
The call of Bilal : Islam in the African diaspora / Edward E. Curtis IV.
    pages cm. — (Islamic civilization and Muslim networks)
Includes bibliographical references and index.
ISBN 978-1-4696-1811-1 (pbk : alk. paper) — ISBN 978-1-4696-1812-8 (ebook)
1. Islam—Africa. 2. African diaspora. 3. Muslims—Non-Islamic countries.
4. Bilal ibn Rabah. I. Title.
BP64.A1C87 2014
297.089′96—dc23
2014013130

18 17 16 15 14   5 4 3 2 1

For my daughter, Alia May

CONTENTS

Acknowledgments, xi

1 Introduction, 1

2 The Heirs of Bilal in North Africa and the Middle East, 21
Healing, Spirit Possession, and Islam in the Village

3 African Muslims in Europe, 53
Mandinga, Murids, and British Black Muslims

4 Siddis and Habshis in South Asia, 85
Shrines of the African Saints and Life-Cycle Rituals in the Village

5 Islamic Jihad or Just Revolt?, 111
African Muslims in Latin America and the Caribbean

6 African American Muslims in the United States, 135
Making Physical and Metaphysical Homelands

Conclusion, 167
Echoes of Bilal across the African Diaspora

Notes, 177

Bibliography, 193

Index, 209

ILLUSTRATIONS

Shrine of Bilal in Jordan, xvi
A male leader summons spirits that possess the bodies of female dancers, Bizerte, Tunisia, 2008, 20
Cover of Poetic Pilgrimage's CD *The Starwomen Mixtape* (2010), 52
Sidi Malang Mohamad blesses a woman, Kapalsadi village, Bharuch district, Gujarat, India, February 2004, 84
Jamaʿat al-Muslimeen leader Yasin Abu Bakr surrenders to Trinidad and Tobago authorities on August 1, 1990, 110
Nation of Islam rally, 1964, 134

ACKNOWLEDGMENTS

Let me begin by expressing my appreciation for the project's research associate and my friend Jeremy Rehwaldt. Before I sat down to write the book's first draft, I tested out ideas and talked them through with Jeremy. Our collaborative process provided me with immediate feedback and, just as important, helped me avoid the absolute isolation that, at least for me, actually makes writing harder. In addition to being my conversation partner, Jeremy researched and drafted sections of the chapter on African-descended Muslims in Europe. Finally, Jeremy copyedited the manuscript before I submitted it to the University of North Carolina Press.

I am grateful to Sylvester Johnson, who read this manuscript in a couple of different forms, schooled me on some things that I had not adequately addressed, and inspired me to pursue the project. Sylvester, with whom I cofounded the *Journal of Africana Religions*, is one of the most supportive, brilliant, and helpful colleagues that I have ever known. No one familiar with Sylvester and his work will be surprised by these remarks since he collaborates with many others to pursue pathbreaking projects in Africana and religious studies. I am lucky to work with and learn from him.

I thank the many institutions that made it possible for me to do my research and to write the book. First and foremost, thanks go to my supportive academic home, the Indiana University School of Liberal Arts in Indianapolis. As holder of the Millennium Chair of the Liberal Arts, I have been able to maintain a strong research agenda while being rewarded for my efforts to engage community members and the broader public in my work. I so appreciate being a part of this community. Financial support for the project also came from the Carnegie Corporation of New York, which funded a year's research leave from 2008 to 2009. The work that I did that year on the transnational history of Islam in the United States informed and inspired this current project. Much of the actual writing of *The Call of Bilal* was supported by a regular sabbatical granted by my school and by a grant from the IU New Frontiers in the Arts and Humanities program. Of course, none of these parties is responsible for what I have written.

I tested out ideas from the book in various venues, and I thank audiences at Indiana University–Purdue University Indianapolis, the American Academy of Religion, and the Association for the Study of the Worldwide African Diaspora for those opportunities. A portion of my chapter on black Muslims in North Africa and the Middle East appeared in "The Ghawarna of Jordan," *Journal of Islamic Law and Culture* 13, nos. 2–3 (2011): 193–209, and I am happy to acknowledge the journal for permission to use that material here. The article was the product of my research in the southern Jordan Valley, and many people and institutions made it possible, especially the American Center of Oriental Research, Barbara Porter, Jean Bradbury, Hani Elayyan, Sarah Harpending, Nofeh Nawasra, Ana Silkatcheva, Rabeeʿ Zureikat, and residents of Ghor al-Mazraʿa and Ghor el-Safi.

Several colleagues were willing to write letters of support for this project; thanks go to Judith Weisenfeld, Ebrahim Moosa, Carl Ernst, Stephen Angell, and my dean, William Blomquist. Other colleagues went out of their way to provide helpful feedback, answer my questions, or support my research in other ways. Robert Rozehnal responded to my chapter on Siddi and Habshi Muslims in Pakistan and India with important questions and suggestions for improvement. Pashington Obeng answered additional questions about their religious lives in rural Karnataka via e-mail and phone and even contacted some of his informants on my behalf. Mauro Van Aken talked to me about his research in the Jordan Valley, giving me additional insight into the sociology of the *dabka*, or line dance. As usual, members of the American Academy of Religion's Study of Islam Section e-mail subscription list came to my aid with bibliographical information. When it came time to publish the book, I received wonderful guidance from those colleagues who reviewed the manuscript anonymously. My departmental colleague Kelly Hayes shared a helpful critique of an early version of chapter 2. Another departmental colleague, David Craig, was always willing to listen to me and give me support, and my chair, Peter Thuesen, did the same while also writing on behalf of the project.

I am grateful that I had the opportunity to work once again with my editor, Elaine Maisner, and with Alison Shay, Paula Wald, and the entire staff of UNC Press. Julie Bush improved the book with her splendid, meticulous copyediting. And in Indianapolis, departmental staff member Debbie Dale offered both good cheer and lots of administrative assistance with the various business-related components of the project.

People from all over the African diaspora helped me obtain the illustrations for the book. Amy Catlin-Jairazbhoy generously supplied the photograph of Sidi Malang Mohamad blessing a woman in Gujarat, India. Richard Jankowsky put me in touch with Matthieu Hagene, who shared a photograph of a Stambali ceremony in Tunisia. Muneera Rashida and Sukina Abdul Noor, the members of Poetic Pilgrimage, let me reprint their *Starwomen Mixtape* cover. Judy Raymond and Mark Lyndersay gave me the image of Yasin Abu Bakr surrendering to Trinidad and Tobago authorities. João José Reis located a photograph of Nigerian-born Shaykh Abdul Hameed Ahmad, a Muslim religious leader in Bahia, Brazil.

Most of all, I am thankful that while I was completing this book, I had a whole other life that I shared with Regan Zwald and our children, Zayd and Alia. Having written books for both Regan and Zayd, I am glad that I can dedicate this one with all my love to my daughter, Alia.

The Call of Bilal

1

INTRODUCTION

> I was shown paradise. . . . I heard the noise of the steps before me, and, lo, it was that of Bilal. —Prophet Muhammad[1]

After a band of Muhammad's followers left Mecca in 622 C.E. for the Arabian town that would come to be known as Medina, the city of the Prophet, the community of Muslims grew to include not only the Prophet's followers from Mecca but many from Medina as well. These Muslims would gather at the appointed times—sunrise, midday, midafternoon, dusk, and after sundown—to perform the *salat*, the Muslim prayer that includes the prostration of the body in the direction of Mecca. According to the stories in the hadith literature, which chronicles the words and deeds of the Prophet Muhammad and his companions, the Prophet decided that Muslims needed some sort of announcement that the prayers were about to begin. Many methods were considered—lighting a fire, blowing a horn, raising a flag, and using a bell or clapper. All were eventually rejected. Instead, a man named Bilal ibn Rabah was asked to call Muslims to prayer using only his voice. According to Islamic tradition, Bilal was a tall man whose thin beard barely covered his cheeks. Some said that he "had sparkling eyes, a fine nose, and bright skin" and that "he was also gifted with a deep, melodious, resonant, and vibrant voice."[2]

Bilal climbed to the roof of the tallest house around the mosque in Medina. From there he summoned the believers to prayer, saying,

(opposite)
Shrine of Bilal in Jordan. Although Bilal ibn Rabah was likely buried in Damascus, Syria, there is also a shrine dedicated to his memory in the Amman area of Jordan. Black Jordanians do not generally regard Bilal as a patron saint or racial ancestor in the same way that black Muslims in South Asia and many parts of Africa do. Instead he is seen mainly as an honored companion of the Prophet Muhammad. Courtesy of Bilal Dweik.

God is Great [or Greatest]! God is Great!
God is Great! God is Great!
I witness that there is no god but God.
I witness that there is no god but God.
I witness that Muhammad is the Messenger of God.
I witness that Muhammad is the Messenger of God.
Come to prayer.
Come to prayer.
Come and thrive.
Come and thrive.
God is Great! God is Great!
There is no god but God.[3]

With great constancy Bilal continued to issue the *adhan*, or call to prayer, every day, with few breaks, for the rest of the Prophet's life. Perhaps the greatest of these recitations was in 630 C.E., from the top of the Kaʿba, the sacred house of worship that was, according to Islamic tradition, originally built by Abraham. After conquering Mecca without a battle, the Prophet Muhammad entered the sacred house and then, emerging from the inside, asked Bilal to issue the call to prayer. It was likely the climax of Bilal's career.[4]

From the viewpoint of Arabian tribal society, Bilal was an unlikely candidate for this position of honor. Also called Ibn Hamama, Bilal was born into slavery in Mecca, perhaps to a master named Umayya bin Khalaf. Bilal's mother was African, perhaps from Ethiopia. Bilal also had dark or black skin, but it would be several centuries before blackness became synonymous with slavery in the Middle East. While there seemed to have been at least some prejudice against dark-skinned people, slaves could also be brown or white. In the seventh century, slavery in the Middle East, as in many other parts of the world, was a multiracial affair.[5] It was largely the social stigma attached to Bilal as a former slave that made Muhammad's decision to name him prayer-caller a countercultural one.

One of Muhammad's very first followers, Bilal had earned a position of honor in the community after enduring great hardship. When it was discovered that he had converted to Islam, Bilal was punished and even tortured by Umayya bin Khalaf and other nobles. It was not the place of a slave, said Umayya, to reject the gods of Mecca. According to Islamic tradition, Bilal reacted to his torture—which included being crushed under a heavy stone—by at first shouting and then finally only whispering,

"Ahad," the One, meaning that there was only one God.⁶ He was eventually rescued by Abu Bakr, another of the Prophet's earliest followers and the man who would become the first caliph of Islam after Muhammad's death. Abu Bakr purchased Bilal's bond and manumitted him.⁷ Even then, as one of Muhammad's earliest followers, Bilal also suffered the fate of early Muslims who struggled to make ends meet in the face of persecution in Mecca.⁸

Bilal became the Prophet's constant companion, and hadiths record that he performed several functions besides calling Muhammad and those around him to prayer. In 624 C.E., for example, during the very first celebration of ʿId al-Fitr, the holiday marking the end of the Ramadan month of fasting, Bilal planted an ʿanaza, or spear, on the spot from which the Prophet would lead the congregational prayers. This spear indicated the direction of the Kaʿba, the sacred house in Mecca toward which Muslims were told to pray.⁹ He was also a personal servant and steward to Muhammad, to whom he would bring water for the performance of the ablutions necessary before making prayers.¹⁰ And Bilal accompanied Muhammad into every battle he fought, eventually tracking down and killing his former tormenter, Umayya.¹¹ Bilal sometimes acted as the Prophet's treasurer. After the congregational prayers on the days of ʿid, the Prophet directed the women in attendance to give their *sadaqa*, or charitable donations, to Bilal, and they took off some of their jewelry and flung it on Bilal's garment.¹² In other instances, Bilal distributed some of the Prophet's gold, silver, food, and clothes to believers in need.¹³

In the time of the second caliph, Umar, Bilal moved to Syria, where he joined the military campaign to subdue the Levant. He died sometime between 638 and 642 C.E., no more than a decade after the death of the Prophet, and was buried somewhere in Syria. According to some sources, he had refused on almost all occasions to recite the adhan after the death of Abu Bakr, the man who freed him. There were exceptions, including the occasion of his own visit to Medina, when Hasan and Husayn, the Prophet's grandchildren, asked him to perform the adhan.¹⁴

The paradox of Bilal's low social status in pre-Islamic terms and his high social status in post-Islamic terms generated important ethical lessons that outlived Bilal himself. One such lesson came by way of the Qurʾan. When, one day, a delegation of Meccan nobles came to see Muhammad, they balked at the presence of Bilal and other former slaves in Muhammad's company. They asked Muhammad to dismiss these lower-class people or to see them separately. On this occasion, Muhammad recited the Qur'anic verse that directed him and other Muslims to "expel not . . . those who worship their Lord day and night, seeking only God's pleasure," no matter what social stigma they may suffer (6:52).[15] Muhammad also challenged the social and ethnic hierarchies in his farewell sermon, forbidding division between Arab and non-Arab in Islam. According to Aisha, the Prophet's daughter, Muhammad also said, "If a slave having some limb of his missing and having dark complexion is appointed to govern you according to the Book of God the Exalted, listen to him and obey him."[16]

THE HEIRS OF BILAL

This is not a book mainly about Bilal ibn Rabah, but his story is one that reverberates among African and African-descended Muslims and often symbolizes their experiences. Bilal's "up from slavery" tale prefigures the ways in which later Muslims of African descent would claim his heritage as proof of their legitimate role as moral leaders for Muslims worldwide. His role in early Islam as a prayer-caller also mirrors the creative activity of later African-descended Muslims who made instruments named after him, traced their spiritual lineage to him, and invoked his name in spirit possession ceremonies. In some locales, Bilal became a saint whose intervention could be called upon when someone was in need of help or healing. In other places, Bilal represented a historical connection to the very origins of Islam, evidence that people of African descent have always heard and responded to the Prophet's message.

Bilal's experiences as a slave alert us to the pivotal role that slavery and later racism would come to play in the experiences of most African-descended Muslims in the diaspora. In some places, such as the Middle East and Africa, fellow Muslims enslaved Bilal's heirs.[17] In other places, including Europe and the Americas, non-Muslims stole the freedom of Muslims of African descent.[18] Even after slavery was officially abolished in many countries, the descendants of slaves or those who were perceived to look like them were often subjected to both de jure and de facto racial discrimination. As this book will demonstrate, the religious practice and thought of most Muslims in the African diaspora has responded directly to or has reflected the influence of the centuries-old trade in African human beings, the racialized societies that engaged in and were constituted by such trade, and the political consequences of slavery and racism.

Finally, Bilal's story reminds us that there has been an African presence in Islamic religion dating from the very origins of the faith. African Muslims were present and played a variety of roles in the expansion of the early Islamic state. They served in the armies of Caliphs Abu Bakr, Umar, Uthman, and Ali and later in those of the Umayyad and Abbasid empires that conquered various cities in Europe, Africa, and Asia. African Muslims helped to fashion the Sunni and Shiʿa Islamic traditions that would become representative of most Muslims' religious practices in the region. Some of the earliest leaders of Islam also had African relatives; to cite one prominent example, the paternal grandmother of Caliph Umar was Ethiopian.[19] It was also African people who created the institutions, networks, governments, and religious technologies essential to the Islamization of Africa itself. By the seventh century, Arab armies emerging from the Arabian Peninsula had established garrisons across North Africa. Military conquest did not mean forced conversion, however, and it took several centuries before the majority of Berbers and other North Africans indigenized the faith and professed their belief in Islam.[20]

Similarly, West Africans were largely responsible for the growth of Islam in their region. Beginning in the eleventh century, Manding speakers and others traversed the Sahara, establishing commercial networks with Muslims in the Maghrib, or North Africa. Using elements of *fiqh*, or Islamic jurisprudence, to govern business transactions, some of these traders converted to Islam. Over many centuries, aspects of previously existing African religions were also blended with beliefs in Muhammad's prophetic example and the efficacy of the Qurʾan to create a form of Islam that became popular among a larger group of West Africans. For most, the role of Sufi masters, those who commanded special knowledge and had cultivated a special relationship with God, was key to the practice of Islam in the region. Powerful West African leaders such as Mansa Musa, Sunni Ali, and Askia Muhammad also patronized various Muslim institutions, especially schools and seminaries.[21]

Likewise, it took centuries for Islam to spread in East Africa, and East Africans themselves were largely responsible for making Islam an indigenous East African religion. Muslims from Arabia and Egypt established a presence in the Horn of Africa by the 800s, but it was only from the twelfth to the fifteenth century that Swahili became the language of a large-scale Islamization along the entire East African coast. Unlike Islam in West Africa, however, Islam in East Africa remained a largely coastal phenomenon until the 1800s when more and more groups in the interior converted to the faith.²²

From the Middle Ages until today, Muslims from the African continent have been on the move as travelers, pilgrims, merchants, scholars, performers, nomads, sailors, and mystics.²³ Before the twentieth century, millions of them were enslaved, forcibly settled in communities across Eurasia, the Americas, and the African continent itself. Their diaspora, or dispersal, became global. From the time of the North African conquest of Iberia in 711 C.E. until today, Muslims of sub-Saharan African descent have moved around in, lived in, and influenced Europe, and contemporary communities of black Muslim migrants are having an important impact on the national life of European countries such as Great Britain, France, Germany, and Italy. When, in the late 1700s and 1800s, the North African and Middle Eastern middle and upper classes sought slaves, they increasingly turned to sub-Saharan Africa.²⁴ Distinct diaspora communities of sub-Saharan or black Africans have existed in the Arabic-speaking countries of North Africa and the Middle East ever since. Over a longer period of time, East African warriors, workers, concubines, merchants, and others came around the Horn of Africa and across the Indian Ocean to what today is India and Pakistan. Many of them became known as Siddis, a word related perhaps to the Arabic word *sayyid*, meaning a relative of the Prophet Muhammad or simply "Master" or "Mister."²⁵ Finally, the slave trade over the Atlantic brought well over a million Muslims to the New World, and while enslaved Muslims in North and South America did not generally pass on their Islamic identity to their children or grandchildren, the number of African-descended Muslims in North America, South America, and the Caribbean rose again in the twentieth century as a result of both conversion and the immigration of free Africans to American shores.²⁶

This book will explore the religious practices of all of these Muslims of African descent—those who have heard, at least symbolically, the call of Bilal. The book's main goals are (1) to offer the first synthetic account of Islam in the global African diaspora, (2) to create a portrait of the diverse ways in which Islam is practiced by people of African descent, and (3) to explore how those practices of Islam are influenced by the experience and interpretation of diaspora. Such a globe-trotting overview is made possible only by the expansion of scholarship produced mainly in the last decade or so about African-descended Muslims in the diaspora. While this book includes some of my own ethnographic and archival research, it relies even more on the scholarship of others. My hope is that readers of this book will gain an expanded view of the ways that African-descended people practice Islam—so that for U.S. readers, for example, the term "black Muslim" conjures images not only of Malcolm X and Louis Farrakhan but also of the devotees of Bava Gor in South Asia, the female trancers of the Stambali in Tunis, and the followers of Ahmadu Bamba in Paris.

The concept of an Africana Muslim diaspora is useful to this synthesis because it invites the analysis of similarities and differences among its subjects, and this book builds on recent efforts to further our understanding of the African diaspora. It emphasizes both ruptures and links among African-descended people. The growth of studies focusing on various diasporas has been, quite literally, exponential in the past two decades.[27] With the growth of diaspora studies have come competing definitions of the word "diaspora" and disputation over how it applies to people of African descent.[28] Scholar William Safran's influential 1991 theory of diaspora argues that it is fundamentally defined by the identification of a group with a homeland—diasporic people, he says, make myths about and maintain memories of the homeland, care about its destiny, and dream of returning to it one day.[29] The problem with such a definition, answered some critics, was that it excluded a lot of dispersed populations. What happens, for example, when we try to understand dispersed groups of human beings who do not consider a "homeland" to be an essential part of their identification with the rest of the group? Sociologist Paul Gilroy argues, for example, that modern black communities in the Atlantic world were brought together not by a shared belonging to Africa but by their shared experience of racial oppression.[30] In some cases, anthropologist James Clifford claims, diasporic *routes* may be more important than diasporic *roots*. That is, instead of being rooted in a central location and dreaming of returning there, a dispersed community might be connected to one another in other ways. "Transnational connections linking diasporas," Clifford asserts, "need not be articulated primarily through a real or symbolic homeland. . . . Decentered, lateral connections may be as important as those formed around a teleology of origin/return."[31] So instead of a diaspora centering all of its hopes and dreams on a homeland, dispersed people might actually put their collective hopes in one another, in multiple places, in global institutions, in various networks, in their race, or in their religion.[32]

Another challenge posed by many studies on diaspora is that, focused as they are on national, transnational, and other kinds of political meanings and identities, they do not always take into account the multiple religious dimensions of diaspora.[33] This lack of attention to religious meanings is strange, given that diaspora has been so associated in the English language with the Galut, the forced exile of Jews from Roman Palestine in the first century. For many Jews, the Galut was not only a political exile but also a religious event interpreted as divine punishment for collective sin and as a divine promise of redemption and restoration, not only for Jews but perhaps for the whole world. Still other Jews insisted that the Galut could be understood only in a "metaphysical-ontological domain." In this view the Galut was "the shattering in the divine being when part of the divine . . . is driven away and alienated from its true place." It is the "cosmic exile of the divine."[34] As these definitions of the Jewish diaspora after 70 C.E. suggest, analyzing a diaspora through a religious studies lens requires a broad array of categories through which one can view the meanings of physical dispersion.

Using the approaches of religious studies invites us to look beyond earthly territory and focus on the idea of space more generally. Sacred space, whether on the earth or in some other realm or plane, can be a meaningful component of diasporic practice.[35] Some theories of diaspora are limited in their ability to explain otherworldly views of human scattering despite the fact that, for many humans, religious maps of dispersion possess cosmological and metaphysical dimensions.[36] These maps of diaspora need not refer to physical territory.[37] Diaspora can mean the scattering of groups of people in spaces and places that go beyond this earth—as religious people imagine that they have been transported to the heavens and sometimes back. Furthermore, human experiences of diaspora are often created using more than words and images. Maps of human scattering can also be embodied, felt, ritualized, and experienced in ways that are as concrete to religious practitioners as those found in any atlas.

If that is so, understanding Islam in the African diaspora requires a definition of diaspora that helps to analyze the multiple meanings of Africa, religious and political, to Muslim practitioners. I propose, simply and provisionally, that diaspora be understood as a physical scattering of human beings across time and space that has political, economic, social, cultural, psychological, religious, and emotional meanings. This definition focuses on two components: the physical dispersion of humans and the meaning that they and others assign to such movement. For some, this definition will be too broad. But for me, its very inclusiveness and flexibility means that the dispersal of African-descended Muslims must be defined in reference to specific historical and contemporary phenomena. Surely there is and can be no one definition of this important theoretical concept; allowing only one definition would cut off the important conversations that need to take place. The important thing is that each scholar makes clear what he or she means when using the word. In any case, this study regards the African diaspora as a question to ponder rather than as a given. The book's origins lie in a curiosity about what has happened as Muslims and followers of other religions from Africa have been scattered across the continent itself and around the world. Answers to questions about the meaning of that diaspora—the "so what" question—can be assayed only through careful analysis of specific data.

This book's particular concern is the role of Islam in the making of diasporic consciousness and experience. *The Call of Bilal* brings to light both explicit and implicit debates about the relationship between identification with an African diasporic identity and Islamic practice. It shows that even among black Muslims who explicitly claim an African Islamic ancestry or origin, some will name certain Islamic traditions as having African influences while others will not attribute any African influences to their Islamic practice. These latter black Muslims, living in various places, may see any cultural practice, African or not, as an impermissible innovation, a cultural accretion corrupting the "pure" religion of Islam. They do not necessarily see themselves as part of any African diaspora but rather as members of the global Muslim community, a lateral diaspora. Moreover, when a diasporic identity is claimed by someone, that person need not do so primarily to express political solidarity with all others who share in that diasporic identity. The idea of belonging to the global community of Africans can be deployed in different ways in different circumstances. Identity making is often as much a product of local, regional, and national exigencies as it is the impulse to be part of some global community. "Local agencies and situations mediate the global, transforming global rhetoric and phenomena to service specific locations," Prita Sandy Meier writes.[38] African identity, like all identities, is often used strategically to enforce or challenge social hierarchies and political institutions. Islamic identities work in the same ways, and this study pays a great deal of attention to the diversity of Islamic identities and practices among its subjects.

I have organized the book in chapters that focus on certain regions of the African diaspora. Of course, the story of Bilal's heirs could be told using a completely different narrative structure. For example, one might organize the book around certain Islamic religious practices such as prayer and the Ramadan fast or around thematic approaches such as John Renard's "seven doors to Islam" or John Bowen's "new anthropology of Islam."[39] I have chosen to organize the story of the African Muslim diaspora inside of regions with the hope that such a structure will reveal the truly global nature of Islam among African-descended people and the ways that the social, political, and cultural histories of these regions often influence and shape the forms of Islam that are practiced there. But I also pay attention to how Islamic practices and Muslim people move across, around, and above such boundaries. At times, region is not the only or even the most important context in which to explain Islamic practice among African-descended people. Instead, this work pays attention, as needed, to the local, national, regional, and global contexts. It explores religious practice and identity making from all of these different vantage points: from the point of view of the globe, as ideas, goods, and people travel across various temporal and spatial boundaries; from the vantage point of the nation, as national politics, laws, and other structures shape and constrain the forms of religion that are practiced; and from the perspective of the local—a town, a neighborhood, a street, a shrine, a home, or a room. Perhaps most important, the book insists on seeing space beyond terrestrial terms, from the point of view of individual and collective experiences that live inside the spirit world, the world unseen, and the heavens above.

This book demonstrates that there is no one, single, definitive pattern of Islamic practice in the African diaspora beyond an acknowledgment, sometimes more theoretical than practical, of what are often called the five pillars of Islam. Like most of the world's 1.6 billion Muslims, no matter what their race or ethnicity, African and African-descended Muslims almost universally profess their belief that there is one God and that Muhammad is God's messenger. Though quantitative data confirming the universal nature of these beliefs do not exist for the African diaspora, polling data from Africa itself are perhaps suggestive. According to a 2012 Pew poll that interviewed thirty-eight thousand Muslims in thirty-nine different countries around the globe, most Muslims on the African continent told interviewers that the five pillars are incumbent on all Muslims.[40] These pillars include the profession of belief in God and Muhammad's prophetic mission, daily prayer (salat), the dawn-to-sunset fast of the month of Ramadan (*sawm*), annual alms for the poor and needy (*zakat*), and, if one is able, the pilgrimage to Mecca. But when asked whether they themselves actually observe these practices, the differences among Africans—and Muslims worldwide—are noteworthy. For example, 91 percent of Ghanaian Muslims said that they prayed five times per day, while only 32 percent of Muslims in Mozambique reported doing so.[41] In addition to differing rates of ritual observance, Muslims in Africa and around the globe often disagree about various Islamic doctrines. The Qur'an makes clear, for example, that God created angels, including the angel Gabriel. While majorities of Muslims around the world profess their belief in angels, there are significant differences in the size of the majority that does so. In Tunisia, for example, 99 percent of Muslims interviewed said that they believed in angels; only 57 percent of Senegalese Muslims said that they believed in them.[42] Muslims in Tunisia are also more likely to believe in the existence of the "evil eye" than most Africans who live south of the Sahara: while 90 percent of Tunisians said that the evil eye can cause real harm to people, only 20 percent of Kenyan Muslims agreed.[43]

Just as African and African-descended Muslims vary by ritual observance rates and by doctrinal belief, they are also divided along sectarian lines. Like most Muslims, the vast majority of African and African-descended Muslims are Sunni, meaning that they follow the Sunna, or the traditions of the Prophet Muhammad, and the authoritative interpretations that emerged through hundreds of years of fiqh, or Islamic legal interpretation and ethical analysis. But shared Sunni identity often means little in terms of how Muslims actually practice their religion. While Sunnis share common religious texts (the Qur'an and the hadith), interpretations and uses of such texts differ greatly. Some African-descended Muslims identify as Shiʿa Muslims, meaning that they are aligned with communities that have cohered around the belief that Ali, the son-in-law and cousin of Muhammad, and his descendants are the rightful leaders of the Muslim community. In addition to both Sunni and Shiʿa Muslims of African descent, there are relatively new religious movements among African-descended people; some are associated with the messianic thought of South Asian leader Ghulam Ahmad or the American prophet Elijah Muhammad. Such groups represent an important but relatively small number of African-descended Muslims in the contemporary world.

One of the major contemporary dividing lines inside Sunni Islam—one that was less important in premodern times—is between Sufi and non-Sufi interpretations of Islam. Put too simply, Sufism is synonymous, for many Muslims, with Islamic spirituality. Sufis are Muslims who practice pietistic and sometimes mystical forms of Islam generally meant to bring Muslims closer to God and often to the Prophet Muhammad, the Prophet's family, and Islamic saints. For many premodern Muslims, being Sunni and Sufi were synonymous, even if practitioners themselves did not label themselves as such; they saw no contradiction between the two. Sufism includes formal organizations, called *tariqas*, or orders, in which one becomes the student of a spiritual master (a shaykh or pir) in order to learn how to traverse the difficult path toward knowing God more intimately. Sufism also refers to the popular religious acts performed at the shrines of Islamic saints, who are believed to possess *baraka*, spiritual power, and perhaps the ability to intercede on the practitioner's behalf on matters both material and spiritual with God. Other popular Sufi practices include the use of talismans or other forms of spiritual healing and protection. Finally, Sufi themes can be identified in some of the world's most famous poetry, such as that of Rumi; in Islamic philosophy; and in Islamic visual art.[44]

But some modern, reform-minded Muslims, sometimes labeled "fundamentalists" or "revivalists," have rejected many if not most Sufi practices as impermissible innovations to Islam. According to them, Sufism violates doctrinal boundaries determined by the Qurʾan, the Sunna, and the practices of the *salaf*, or the pious ancestors of Muhammad's era. This innovative, modern reading of Islam rejects traditional Islamic practices such as the veneration of Muslim saints and devotional singing or dancing.[45] Determining which traditions can be justified as authentically religious and which are cultural innovations has become a major question in the modern practice of Islam, and it is a question important to Islam among African-descended Muslims. The tensions between tradition and reform and between religion and culture are sometimes gendered, with women representing and defending cultural practices associated with African people against the so-called pure Islam of men. In some cases, the Islam practiced by women *and* men of African descent is associated both with femininity and with cultural "tradition"—and challenged by non-African people as an example of cultural ignorance and a corruption of Islam. The coding of African Islam as impure is, as we shall see, just one example of how race and racism have had a deep impact on the practice of Islam among African-descended people.

DEFINING BLACK AND AFRICANA IDENTITY

Even if African-descended Muslims do not have one way of practicing Islam, they often live as Muslims in societies that are, to a greater or lesser degree, racist. This is, at the very minimum, one way in which all of the contemporary subjects of this study are linked. We inhabit a world that was built, in significant ways, through the social production of racialized identities and practices. This is true not only in the part of the world shaped by the Atlantic slave trade but also in all places that were caught up in a world dominated and constituted by the European imperium; in the modern world, most people became racialized.[46] Ideas of racial hierarchy took root among the colonizers and the colonized, and the so-called black African was almost always understood to be at the very bottom of the civilizational order of the human species. Racialization became a method governing imperial territories and various minorities in the colonizers' homelands. By the late nineteenth and early twentieth centuries, whites—those seen as coming from Aryan, Nordic, or Caucasian racial stock—were "deemed naturally superior and therefore uniquely suited to rule over inferior races," according to historian Zachary Lockman.[47] In a formulation made famous by Edward W. Said, this knowledge about nonwhite races provided justification for the imperial powers that sought to dominate them.[48] Colonial governance structures based on ideas of white superiority subsequently distributed resources and power along lines of race. And even after explicitly racist ideas were opposed or eschewed, contemporary globalization reproduced the racial hierarchies that had accompanied the birth of modernity.[49]

Throughout this modern world of racialization and imperial domination, certain stereotypes, prejudices, and "knowledge" about an ideal-typical person called a "Negro," or black African, circulated. As philosopher Lewis Gordon puts it, "Although there are people who function as 'the blacks' of particular contexts, there is a group of people who function as the blacks everywhere. They are called in now-archaic language—*Negroes*. Negroes are the blacks of everywhere, the black blacks, the blackest blacks." For Gordon, blackness is the "prime racial signifier."[50] It is, he argues, the category of ultimate meaning to which modern thinking about race refers. Philosopher Tommie Shelby defines this notion of black identity as "thin blackness," which is "a vague and socially imposed category of 'racial' difference that serves to distinguish groups on the basis of their members having certain visible, inherited physical characteristics and a biological ancestry." Black people are those, according to this modern racial knowledge, who possess physical characteristics such as "dark skin, tightly curled or 'kinky' hair, a broad flat nose, and thick lips" and whose biological ancestry is said to be located in sub-Saharan Africa.[51] In other words, regardless of the cultural, phenotypical, historical, linguistic, sociological, and political differences among them, according to this thin notion of blackness, black people share certain physiological traits and are seen as having originated in a place known as Sudanic Africa, sub-Saharan Africa, or black Africa.

The global nature of these assumptions is further evidenced by the prejudices that many contemporary humans share about black and African-descended people in Europe, the Middle East, South Asia, and the Americas. Of course, there are exceptions to this generalization, the meaning of antiblack racism differs, and the impact of this racism is not the same everywhere. But, exceptions aside, no matter where African-descended Muslims practice Islam, from Mumbai, Amman, Paris, and London to Karachi, Chicago, and Rio de Janeiro, prejudices against people perceived to be of black African heritage mar their life opportunities. In all these places, as this book details, one hears these stereotypes about black people: they are good at dancing, sports, and sex; they excel at crime; and they are predisposed to violence, laziness, and ignorance. And these prejudices, combined with institutionalized and de facto discrimination, serve to limit black people's attempts to achieve economic success and social equality.[52]

This notion of blackness is related to narratives and systems of exploitation that have their roots in the African slave trade and its reverberations throughout the modern world, including Muslim lands dominated by colonial and imperial interests. Though slavery existed in Muslim and non-Muslim lands in premodern times, its meanings within modern economies, politics, and culture came to reflect not only local and regional considerations but also the Euro-American racism that legitimated modern chattel slavery. Those meanings are still powerful in the contemporary world. Black bodies, according to literary scholar Hershini Bhana Young, "remain embedded within the networks of violent identity formation that have characterized the African diaspora." There is an element of un-freedom in this definition of blackness; it is not something that black people get to choose. "To be black," Young continues, "is to have accrued a subjectivity haunted by spectral traces of social, political, and ideological history," a history tied, whether one likes it or not, to the African continent. "Blackness is a historically and culturally specific embodied discourse, constituted in and through a discursive tradition mobilized by the reconstituted figure of 'Africa' and brutal systems of oppression such as slavery and imperialism."[53] These are the ghosts, both creative and dangerous, of a black identity that was made *for* black people. It casts African-descended people as the victims of certain forces beyond their control—and who would deny that the African slave trade was something over which its victims had little control?

But that is only part of the story. From the very beginning, black people have challenged notions of thin blackness and its relationship to the trade in African human beings and other systems of oppression. In so doing, they have created what Tommie Shelby calls conceptions of "thick blackness." These are the identities that African-descended people themselves create, shape, and debate. Shelby argues that these black identities, contested just as much as ideas of thin blackness, include *kinship* blackness, the idea that blacks are part of the same family; *ethnic* blackness, "a matter of shared ancestry and common cultural heritage"; black *nationality*, an identification with a black nation-state or a territorial homeland; and *cultural* blackness, "an identifiable ensemble of beliefs, values, conventions, traditions, and practices (that is, a culture or subculture) that is distinctively black."[54] The point is that human beings perceived by others as "black" have also participated in creating, imagining, and interpreting the meaning of their own *peoplehood*.[55] Different meanings of this peoplehood are reflected in the lives of many African-descended Muslims in this book, though *The Call of Bilal* pays special attention to those black Muslims who emphasize notions of *religious* blackness, the idea that their identity as a people is tied together by their religious doctrines, ethics, material culture, and rituals.

Muslims of African descent respond, both religiously and otherwise, in diverse ways to the presence of stereotypes and institutional racism in their communities. Some of these Muslims appeal to an African identity as a form of political solidarity. There is a strong and perhaps growing population of African-descended Muslims who construct their Islamic identity through an African genealogy; that is, many Muslims of African descent in the diaspora profess forms of Islam that deliberately incorporate or allude to elements of a black and/or African heritage. Their imagined communities of Muslims are formed not only around appeals to the universal *umma,* or worldwide community of Muslims, but also around a shared sense of belonging to ethnic, racial, tribal, or national groups that are coded in some way as African. We will see where, how, and in what circumstances the Africanness of Islam, as socially constructed by Muslims themselves, is embraced, transformed, or eschewed in the modern world.

But the book will also examine the ways in which Muslim identity is constructed in a non-African key. Where there are Muslims of African descent who construct their social and cultural identities in ways that forgo any imagined connection to Africa, such persons do not tend to incorporate Islamic signifiers—that is, symbols, practices, narratives, rituals, and material cultures—that allude to their Africanness, whether that Africanness be defined ethnically, racially, or any other way. While it may seem odd to include those Muslims who do not consider themselves to be African in a study of Islam in the African diaspora, my argument is that these persons are important to set the limits of our understanding. They may be part of the historical scattering and dispersion of African people, but they themselves do not assign any meaning to that identity and do not attach themselves to that history. Their experiences point out where the African diaspora ends and something else begins.

For some scholars, especially those who have made the case that antiblack racism is essentially different in the Islamic world than in the Atlantic world, or that blackness is a vague and analytically useless category, this book's use of the terms "black" and "African-descended" will be, at the very least, unsatisfying. In fact, some scholars might reject the foundations of the entire project on the grounds that the African-descended people whom I am comparing have little to do with each other, that I am grouping together people who really shouldn't be grouped together. For these scholars, there are other, better stories to be told about the people and practices that I describe, stories that use different assumptions, characters, and settings. But my answer to those who challenge the approach in this book is that for at least some black and nonblack scholars and people of African descent themselves, this story is too obvious and too important to ignore. The call of Bilal is loud and clear. Both inside and outside Islamic religious institutions and among Muslim people, the phenomenon of antiblack racism and the contributions of African-descended Muslims demand an accounting. To deny the presence of people who see themselves as black or African-descended Muslims excludes the concerns of too many people and too many visions, interpretations, and embodied practices of Islam.

CHAPTER OUTLINE

This story about the heirs of Bilal starts inside Africa itself and traces the diaspora of West and Central African Muslims that was created as people from West, Central, and East Africa were sold into slavery and came to serve as soldiers, servants, concubines, and workers in North African cities such as Fez, Morocco, and Tunis, Tunisia. Chapter 2 first examines the historical origins of this internal African diaspora and then explores the Islamic practices that were developed among many of these enslaved Africans. This expression of Islam, sometimes called the Bori cult and other times categorized as a form of Sufism, incorporates music, dance, material culture, and various spiritual technologies to induce trance among some of its participants and to offer them spiritual and physical healing. It makes African diasporic meaning by linking Islam to African ancestors and, in many cases, to black saints. The second part of the chapter then crosses the border between Africa and Asia to examine the religious practices of Jordanian Ghawarna, people who live in the Jordan Valley. Thousands of them have African roots, though they do not call themselves African and do not practice any forms of Islam that they understand to be African. An exploration of Ghawarna practices surrounding Muslim weddings, the holy fast of Ramadan, and the healing of spiritual and physical illness through exorcism shows the limits of the African diaspora, marking an important boundary for this study. In examining both the Bori Islam of North Africa and the Islamic practices of the Ghawarna, this chapter pays as much attention to women as to men and thus presents a vision of the ways that Islam is actually practiced by African-descended people in the region.

Chapter 3 explores the Africana Muslim diaspora on the European landmass, examining the multiple origins of the African diaspora in Europe and focusing on the variety of ways in which the contemporary Islamic practices of black European Muslims establish transnational connections both to African homelands and to lateral transnational networks of fellow believers. The chapter begins with the African presence in Iberia during the Middle Ages but quickly moves to contemporary times. It first traces the transnational connections of the Murid Sufi order, examining the meaning and function of religious pilgrimages to

Touba, Senegal, among the devotees of the saint Ahmadu Bamba. The chapter then explores the religious practices and ethnic identities of Portuguese Mandinga who immigrated to Europe from Guinea-Bissau. This section pays particular attention to the ethical and ritual continuities and changes that occur in the Portuguese setting. Finally, the chapter compares and contrasts black British converts to Islam who were born in the United Kingdom or who emigrated from the Caribbean with Somali and Nigerian immigrants who have settled in London. While the return to Islam is also a form of pan-African unity and anticolonial consciousness for many converts, ideas of black liberation and Afro-Asian solidarity hold little allure for many of those Muslims who have arrived fairly recently from African nation-states.

Chapter 4 turns to the Indian Ocean world to examine the communities of African descent in Pakistan and India whose origins date from the Middle Ages. Recruited as soldiers and forced into both military and household slavery, people of African descent went on to establish at least one Indian dynasty and to serve as high-ranking officials in a few others. Today, however, their descendants—known variously as Siddis, Habshis, and Makranis, among other names—suffer from ethnic and racial prejudice in both India and Pakistan. After chronicling the history of these communities, this chapter looks at how some Siddis have created and sustained shrines, Sufi groups, and a culture of veneration focused on their African ancestor and the Muslim saint Bava Gor, also known as Gori Pir. Like the devotees of the black spirits and saints in North Africa, these Muslims create multidimensional experiences of diaspora by connecting with an African ancestor and in so doing transcending the normal realms of human consciousness. The second part of the chapter then examines how some Siddis in villages in the Indian state of Karnataka practice forms of Islam that incorporate Siddi practitioners of other religions in their celebrations of Muslim holidays such as Muharram, Ramadan, and ʿId al-Adha, the festival of sacrifice held at the end of the hajj. This ethnic solidarity is yet another way in which Islam helps to make African diasporic identity.

Chapter 5 ventures across the Atlantic Ocean to examine two instances of political revolt among Africana Muslims in South America and the Caribbean. Its goal is to probe the extent to which these revolts were inspired, informed, and/or sustained by the revolutionaries' understanding of Islamic religion. Put too simply, the chapter scrutinizes the use of what is sometimes called political Islam; that is, an Islam that expresses itself not only in personal pietistic terms but also in explicitly political ones. It will illustrate two different ways in which Muslims of African descent have looked to Islam as a resource in their political lives and struggles. The first section examines the Muslim-led revolt of African-born slaves and freedmen and freedwomen in Bahia, Brazil, in 1835. It asserts that rebels sought to protect their freedom to practice Islam and that Islam played a role in the revolt as a form of spiritual protection and social solidarity, but that other factors, including pan-Yoruban consciousness and protodiasporic racial resistance, are just as important in explaining this act of political violence. The second section interrogates the attempted coup d'état launched by black Muslim members of Jamaʿat al-Muslimeen in the Caribbean nation of Trinidad and Tobago in 1990. Called a jihad by the rebels themselves, the coup of 1990 was focused on the national politics of Trinidad and Tobago, not on a global struggle against infidels. The chapter shows how, in both cases of revolt, the diasporic imagination of African-descended Muslims was focused not on Africa or even on a shared notion of black or African diasporic identity but instead on justice within existing political orders.

The sixth and final chapter examines the practice of Islam among African Americans in the United States. It first recounts the practice of Islam among enslaved Muslims, emphasizing their dreams to return home to Africa. The extraordinary efforts of some African American Muslims to return to Africa are interpreted as an instance of diaspora consciousness. The second section of the chapter then explores the diasporic religion of the Nation of Islam, an Africana Muslim group that is neither Sunni nor Shiʿa and that has had an enormous influence not only on the history of Islam in the United States but on U.S. history as a whole. The transition for most members of the Nation of Islam from the unusual doctrines of Elijah Muhammad toward a Sunni form of Islam is included in this discussion in order to show the consistent concerns with a diasporic Africana Muslim identity. The final section of the chapter examines the contemporary meaning and functions of diasporic religious practices to both recent African immigrants and American-born black Muslims.

A conclusion summarizes the ways in which Muslims in the African diaspora practice Islam and examines Islam's relationship to their diasporic and African identities by tracing the many symbolic understandings of and embodied practices inspired by the figure of Bilal ibn Rabah.

Muslim women play central roles in the healing ceremonies of the Stambali in Tunisia. A male leader summons spirits that possess the bodies of female dancers by playing a stringed instrument called a *gumbri*, which is said to have been in the possession of Bilal ibn Rabah in heaven. Other men play iron castanets. Bizerte, Tunisia, 2008. Courtesy of Matthieu Hagene.

2

THE HEIRS OF BILAL IN NORTH AFRICA AND THE MIDDLE EAST

Healing, Spirit Possession, and Islam in the Village

In contemporary Essaouira, Morocco, Muslim members of the Gnawa, a spiritual and ethnic community associated in Moroccan history with Sudanic or black African culture, experience trance, healing, joy, and sadness in night ceremonies called *lila*. These rituals are conducted in a *zawiya*, or lodge, named after Bilal ibn Rabah.[1] Many Gnawa trace their Islamic identity to the very origins of Islam via their ancestor and patron saint, Bilal. Calling themselves the "children of Bilal," they claim that they converted to Islam even before the Quraysh did.[2] One Gnawa man told religious studies scholar Earle Waugh in 1995 that many Arabs had attempted to erase the deep influence of Bilal on the Prophet Muhammad; he said that collections of the Prophet's hadiths, reports of his sayings and deeds, did not frequently cite Bilal as a source despite the high regard in which the Prophet held Bilal. Emphasizing Bilal's role as a close companion of the Prophet became a way for black Moroccans to claim their rightful place in Islam and to challenge the racism that they faced in Moroccan society. In addition to singing about "Father Bilal man of God / The Prophet's servant, Bilal," some Gnawa have named an instrument made from the soles of shoes after Bilal. Used in the night ceremony, the instrument has cosmic significance: it symbolizes the fact that, according to the Prophet Muhammad, Bilal will wear shoes in paradise. It commemorates this belief and evokes the power of Bilal's children on the earth. Tracing one's origins to Bilal becomes a way to acknowledge the cruelty of slavery and racism, even perhaps as God's strange will, while also claiming the special role that God had in mind for Bilal and his heirs as religious exemplars.[3]

These stories and the rituals performed in Bilal's lodge and with his instrument weave the diasporic presence of black Moroccans into the narrative of Islam's earthly origins. They commemorate the role of their ancestor, Bilal, in the unfolding of Islamic history while also expanding the black diasporic imagination to include heaven, the cosmic abode of Bilal that exists outside of time and space. In so doing, the Gnawa carve out a particular sociological space within the country of Morocco for the heirs of Bilal. They embrace a redemptive reading of black diasporic suffering by claiming a special spiritual legacy.

But not all of Bilal's heirs in the Middle East or North Africa claim such a heritage. Some eschew any connection to a black African past. They may be black in that they suffer the kind of antiblack racism associated with their physical appearance and its relationship to the heritage of African slavery, but that does not mean that they turn automatically to racial consciousness and pride as a way to defend their humanity. Neither do they necessarily practice a form of Islam that is constructed as celebrating ethnic, cultural, or national forms of black identity. Their Islamic religion finds ways of coping with oppression and suffering without ever confronting antiblack prejudice and institutional racism.

This chapter will examine these two different streams of Islamic religious practice among black Muslims in North Africa and the Middle East: one that constructs diasporic meaning in both ethnic and religious terms and one that does not. Unlike other chapters in this book, this one begins its discussion of the Africana Muslim diaspora inside Africa itself. Africa is a huge landmass the size of China, Japan, India, Europe, and the continental United States combined. The life of Homo sapiens quite literally began in Africa, and the migration of human beings inside and outside of Africa is perhaps the most important event in human history. These dispersions and scatterings, or diasporas, have been given countless meanings by those who have participated in or identified with them. One of these diasporas was the forced migration of humans from one part of Africa to another, particularly from sub-Saharan Africa to North Africa.[4] Slavery in Islamic lands produced a diaspora that in certain instances defined its religious practices partly through conscious identification with sub-Saharan roots. The chapter will first describe the existence of Islamic practices that have been inspired by these traditions, which include spirit possession and ritual healing. This complex of black diasporic Muslim religion takes many different forms, and the chapter surveys the different kinds of music, dancing, and other Islamic rituals associated with what is often called Bori healing and spirit possession in Algeria, Tunisia, and Morocco. It will show how the metaphysical experience of diaspora is inscribed by these practices.

The chapter then turns to the religious practices of black Ghawarna in the rural Jordan Valley, religious traditions that have more to do with their rural, gendered, and largely local Jordanian and Palestinian roots than with any sub-Saharan African connection. I survey this "Islam of the village" for the sake of establishing the idea that black Muslims sometimes practice forms of Islam that they see as having nothing to do with their blackness. This section focuses on women's rituals of healing associated with the evil eye and the different components of rural Muslim weddings, including the all-important wedding *dabka*, or dance. It notes the absence of any claims of belonging among the Ghawarna to an African past, showing that while some Ghawarna may be part of the physical scattering of African human beings, they do not identify with that history and do not assign any personal or collective meaning to it. But this section also reveals the nagging persistence of racism and how it sometimes intersects with Ghawarna religious identities.

SLAVERY AND RACISM IN NORTH AFRICA AND THE MIDDLE EAST

As outlined in the introduction, African Muslims have been a part of Islamic history from the very first days of the Prophet Muhammad's mission. Islam did not simply come to Africa. Africans helped to bring it there. What has often marked Muslims of African descent as sociologically different is not any unique way of practicing Islam but rather physical characteristics that have been used to distinguish these human beings as a racial minority in what today is the Arabic-speaking world, Turkey, Iran, and Israel.[5] For more than a thousand years, the term *bilad as-Sudan*, literally meaning the "land of blacks," has been used in the Arabic language to refer to West, Central, and East African territories, stretching today from Mauritania and Guinea to Ethiopia and Somalia. As the enslavement of people from these regions increased, this geographical designation also came to have ethnic connotations; that is, black African origin came to be associated with certain cultural values and sometimes traits. Premodern debates about the relative intelligence and character of black African people were joined not only in Arabic but also in Turkish and Persian literature.[6] The legacy of this racialized geography and ethnic nomenclature remains potent. "Black" is both an ethnic and geographic label with continuing, if contested, relevance to people of sub-Saharan and East African descent in the Middle East and North Africa.[7]

Many of those who are referred to as "black," which remains an insult in many parts of North Africa and the Middle East, do not wished to be called so. Many do not want to be associated with Sudanic, or black, Africa, which is still often viewed in the Middle East as violent and uncivilized. This is one of the consequences of slavery becoming associated with people from sub-Saharan Africa. "By the seventeenth century," writes John Hunwick, "blackness of skin/African origin was virtually synonymous in the Arab world with both the notion and the word 'slave.'"[8] Still used by some people in the region though contested by others, "black" indicates the shared social stigma suffered by those who possess the physical characteristics associated in a large number of modern societies with black or Sudanic Africa. What "black" does not mean is a monolithic culture, including religion, shared by all people with Sudanic roots. The historiography of black Muslims in the Middle East and North Africa emphasizes that much of the culture of black Middle Easterners and North Africans represents an adaptation and humanizing response to suffering, trauma, and oppression. In short, the religious expressions of black Muslims are often seen as the "blues"—that is, a cultural form that at once expresses sorrow, injustice, and hardship while also affirming the essential value of that life.[9]

At least a million enslaved black Africans were forcibly transported from sub-Saharan Africa to the Ottoman Empire during the nineteenth century.[10] In 1856 the Ottoman government outlawed the slave trade, but slavery itself remained legal. By the end of the 1800s, perhaps 5 percent of all imperial subjects were enslaved. Most black Africans—and some Circassians, Georgians, and Slavs, too—were the domestic servants of the elite, while a minority of enslaved persons were military pages, concubines, eunuchs, miners, agricultural workers, and carpenters.[11] Conditions varied in Egypt and other Muslim lands that were part of the Ottoman Empire, but generally speaking, the social status of enslaved Africans was determined largely by the household of which they were members. Historian Ehud Toledano has described the relationship between the slaver and the enslaved as one of attachment and patronage. While the patronage of one's master did not mitigate the violence and other forms of cruelty suffered by enslaved people, slaves often became associated with the entire extended kinship network of the master. This was especially true when a concubine gave birth to the master's child, who was, by Islamic law, a free person entitled to inherit from his or her father. In addition, enslaved people developed other social attachments, perhaps to their town, their chosen Sufi order, a nuclear family of their own, and/or an association or club specifically for black people.[12]

From the sixteenth to the nineteenth century, as enslaved people were brought from East, West, and Central Africa, they were often forced by their masters to convert to Islam. Sometimes already familiar with basic Islamic teachings, these enslaved persons would have been taught about the nature of God, the Prophet Muhammad, and other elements of Islamic religion. If male, they would have been circumcised. All would then be given new Muslim names.[13] These slaves were made members of the community of Muslims in the many households where they served. Though unfree, they thus became entitled to certain rights, including, in theory, humane treatment and the ability to seek redress in court. Enslaved black people in the Middle East and North Africa became socialized as Muslims and participated in a Muslim polity. In the Ottoman Empire, which included much of North Africa, the Middle East, and southeast Europe, such slaves sued in Islamic courts through the 1840s and then increasingly afterward in the civil imperial courts established by the Ottoman Empire as part of the Tanzimat reforms. Sometimes asking to be freed, but even more frequently seeking redress for grievances, enslaved people sued their masters because of physical abuse, forced abortion, rape, or the threat of sale of oneself or one's family members. In the second half of the nineteenth century, the Ottoman government began increasingly to see itself as the patron of enslaved people, adopting a role that had been reserved for the male head of household.[14]

FROM THE BORI TO THE STAMBALI: THE BLACK MUSLIM DIASPORA IN NORTH AFRICA

Enslaved people from sub-Saharan Africa and their progeny came to practice Islam in a variety of ways, some of which bore the influence of sub-Saharan culture and some of which did not. Perhaps the most distinctive Muslim religious practice with sub-Saharan and specifically Hausa roots was spirit possession, sometimes called the Bori cult.[15] As the Bori came to reside in North Africa, different Muslims who regarded them as real and as potent interpreted their presence in a variety of ways. For some, the Bori were *jinn*, the spirit beings who, according to the classical

Islamic teachings, were created by God out of "smokeless fire" and who, like humans, perform good or evil deeds and will be judged by God accordingly. For others, the Bori were not jinn but another kind of spirit. Though the Bori were venerated at first by Muslims with sub-Saharan roots, they eventually became objects of ritual supplication for some nonblack North Africans. Even if the religious practices associated with the Bori had not been Islamic in Hausaland, where these spirits were associated with non-Muslim Hausa, the religion of the Bori was adapted to the new Muslim identities of their devotees in North Africa.[16] In Tunis, references to the Bori would eventually disappear; they would come to be understood there as black spirits in the Stambali pantheon.

Bori practices are similar to those religious rites that have been referred to as the Zar cult, and scholars often treat them as manifestations of the same phenomenon, dubbed the Zar-Bori complex.[17] Zar's origins are located in East Africa, especially Ethiopia and Sudan. Janice Boddy defines Zar as a word having several overlapping meanings; it is "a type of spirit, the illness it can cause, and the ritual by which the illness is assuaged; more generally, [it is] the 'cult' that surrounds such spirits."[18] Zar rituals involve a person who is possessed by a spirit; the leader of the ritual, who is usually a woman; the spirit, who is often understood as male; and a group of other participants. Drummers and in some places bands of musicians play as dancers achieve a state of trance. In addition, the blood of sacrificial animals might be ritually consumed or applied to the skin of the person seeking relief. Rather than attempting to exorcise the spirit of the seeker, the goal of the ritual is to propitiate or pacify the Zar; it is a "long-term, inconclusive, and open-ended healing of possession by '*adorcism*,'" that is, by pleasing, sometimes cajoling, and making sacrifices for the spirit.[19] While the religious practices surrounding the Bori follow this basic pattern, it is important to realize that the meanings and functions of healing rituals and spirit possessions change depending on the local circumstances in which they take place.[20]

As Zar, Bori, and other forms of Sudanic ritual healing spread throughout Ottoman domains and other parts of the Middle East in the nineteenth and twentieth centuries, they became an expression of Islamic religion. Old techniques, ideas, and aspects of trans-Saharan material culture were adapted to new circumstances. The spirits themselves were often transformed. Those who participated in such rites saw them as perfectly appropriate Islamic practice, contrary to the criticism of some who denied the Islamic legitimacy of the Zar-Bori ritual complex. For example, in her research on Zar practices in 1970s Egypt, anthropologist Fatima al-Misri discovered that practitioners considered themselves to be "good Muslims." Moreover, her study documented how the female ritual leaders of the group were pious Muslims known to have performed the pilgrimage to Mecca. They engaged in *wudu*, or Islamic ablution, before they danced and entered into a trance. The ritual leader would then lead the women in reciting the Fatiha, the opening chapter of the Qur'an, and, as the ceremony continued, prayers for the Prophet, his family, and many saints would be offered.[21]

The origins of Bori and Zar practices in the Middle East and North Africa date to the eighteenth century if not before; Zar and Bori sprits eventually appeared in Dubai, Kuwait, Anatolia, Crete, Iran, and other locales.[22] In Tunis and other parts of North Africa that were part of the Ottoman Empire in the eighteenth and nineteenth centuries, many people in the black Muslim diaspora were organized into clubs or households—also called lodges or brotherhoods—dedicated to self-help and the performance of Bori rituals. Not all black residents in the area participated. Native-born free blacks, who often lived in the southern part of Tunisia, organized themselves into clans headed by shaykhs, or leaders. Their religious practice was far more akin to that of nonblacks.[23] It was instead the slaves and ex-slaves—and some West African pilgrims and waylaid travelers—that by the early 1700s created fourteen separate households with shared religious rites. Such households were as much kinship networks as they were actual lodges; members of the household would often live in other locations.

This was a clear case in which a diasporic community was organized as a way of claiming political participation and religious meaning at the same time. As new migrants from Sudanic Africa continued to arrive, the social structures and religious practices of black communities became even more diverse. In the middle of the eighteenth century, for example, leader Ali Bey I recruited black slaves to form his palace guard. These slave soldiers established their own private clubs, and by 1807 one of these clubs, Dar Kofa, or the Kofa Household, became the ritual center of Bori ritual practices in Tunis.[24] According to the account of Ahmad ibn Abi Bakr ibn Yusuf al-Timbuktawi, a pilgrim from Timbuktu who was in Tunis in 1808 and 1813, Dar Kofa housed the principal spirit of the Bori pantheon. Called Sarkin Goda, this spirit was Sultan al-Jinn, the patron of the jinn. Dar Kofa, the patron's palace, became a pilgrimage site where, during the Islamic month of Shaʿban, black visitors from all of Tunis and beyond would congregate for both social and religious purposes.[25]

Many elements of sub-Saharan culture, including the important ceremonial roles played by women, were combined with elements of North African culture to produce this form of Islam in the African diaspora. In Dar Kofa and other lodges, a chief priestess called an *arifa*, or "one who knows," was responsible for overseeing the healing rituals conducted in the lodge temple. Ceremonies were held each Friday and during the celebration of the New Year. The chief priestess summoned the spirits, who were asked to enter the body of a community member inflicted with spiritual and/or physical maladies. Once the spirit became "attached" to the body of the seeker, he or she would then offer periodic sacrifices to it.[26] Music was essential to the rituals of spirit possession. The *gumbri*, a stringed instrument decorated with cowrie shells, coins, and beads, was itself considered a sacred object, and those who played or touched it were required to be in a state of ritual purity. It was said that the instrument had descended from heaven where it had been in the possession of Bilal ibn Rabah, the man who had used only his voice to call worshippers to prayer. This instrument and other paraphernalia used during the rites of spirit possession were kept in the temple's storage bin or granary, which would also be used for animal sacrifice.[27]

According to the nineteenth-century visitor al-Timbuktawi, the ritual slaughter of animals was believed to help cure the seeker's illness. Red, black, or white hens would be selected, depending on which spirit was being summoned. Often the animal would be provided by the person who had come to the temple to seek healing. The hen would be given coriander seeds and other grains, which, if consumed, would inspire ritual participants to ululate and "place their hands in a begging position behind them and prostrate to their gods." If the hen did not eat the offering, believers would cry out, "O masters, why is it you are angry with us? Why is it you do not accept our offering?" Once an animal that would consume the offering was found, it was then killed, and its blood was rubbed on the skin of the person in need of healing.[28]

Eventually, black Tunisians from Bambara, Songhay, Wadai, Dar Fur, Baghirmi, and Kawar ethnic groups established their own clubs or households, even if the Hausa remained the dominant group and provided the dominant political language of household organization. Such households remained vital long after the official end of slavery in Tunisia in 1846. Households became associated with the name of their chief priestesses;

they were called Household of the Dar Fur Priestess, Household of the Bornu Priestess, and so on.[29] Most households possessed complex governing structures, including a king, a female head of household, a female patron of household, and a chief priestess. Households cooperated with one another, sending their representatives to perform healing rites at someone's home or to help a newcomer find his or her respective ethnic group's household. They also coordinated their own public activities, seeking collective permission from the government to make religious pilgrimages, for example. The person in charge of negotiating with the government on behalf of the lodge was called the king's deputy; each group sent this emissary to meet with a public official called "the governor over black-skinned people [*hakim fi al-qishrat as-sawda*]." The governor himself was black; he was often a eunuch serving in the court of the bey, or provincial leader.[30]

Though some Muslim religious scholars such as al-Timbuktawi found the households to be positively heretical, the fact that the households held ceremonies in public and negotiated openly with the bey's government shows how Tunis's Husaynid rulers encouraged the practice of the Bori rites.[31] By regulating the lodges and negotiating with them, the Husaynids were incorporating these Muslims into their political order while also supporting the emergence of separate ethnic communities tied together by a common racialized identity.[32] Scholars would later label these groups "the Bori cult," but this was not how Tunisians themselves usually referred to them.

Known as households or clubs, the Bori cult eventually came to be associated most closely with a small, largely black religious brotherhood called the Stambali (also called Stambuli and Stambeli), perhaps because their patron saint, Sidi Saʿad, was said to have come from Istanbul. The Husaynid government maintained the zawiya, or Sufi lodge, of this saint as part of its own Ministry of Awqaf, or charitable endowments.[33] Such lodges are characteristic of organized Sufism around the world. They are the places in which *baraka*, or blessings and spiritual power, of an Islamic saint is understood to reside. It is often in the name of the saint, generally an Islamic teacher or other religious virtuoso, that rituals of physical and spiritual healing, miracles, and celebrations are performed. And it is often in the lodge where students (also called *talibs* or *murids*) become initiated into a *tariqa*, a spiritual order or path, that will lead them to greater knowledge of and a more intimate personal relationship with God. These orders, also known as religious brotherhoods, are often named in honor of the saint who resides spiritually in the lodge. Of course, there is great variety in the practices performed in Sufi lodges around the world, and the Stambali lodges are no exception. In the Stambali lodge supported by the Husaynid government in Tunis, for example, it seems that Bilal ibn Rabah, understood to be a saint, oversaw goings-on there from a distance while the spiritual presence of other beings was more immediate. The Bori lived on there as black spirits, conjured at the same time as the jinn.[34]

The lodges that organized around the rite of spirit possession introduced other Sudanic religious practices into North African Muslim life as well, often combining religious technologies into a new form of Islamic practice. M. G. Zawadowski, a former translator who worked for Tunisia's French occupiers, wrote in 1942 that many of the black households and clubs orchestrated an annual *ziyara*, or religious pilgrimage and visitation, to the shrine of local Muslim saint Sidi Sa'ad. This saint, who was venerated in a variety of ways, was a freed slave originally from Bornu thought to have settled in Tunis by way of Istanbul.[35] The annual pilgrimage to his shrine and lodge in Mornag often began on a Wednesday and finished on a Saturday; the most important rituals occurred on Friday.[36] Each household would participate in a colorful procession honoring the saint; members carried striking banners and brought along a female goat for sacrifice. The arifa, who was a central participant in the ziyara rituals, summoned the jinn and then divined and communicated the spirit's desires to the assembled mass. Other participants in the visit danced, fell into a trance, and became filled with and possessed by a spirit. Non-blacks, including some Jews, would also attend.[37] Closed in 1958, the shrine was reopened in the late 1960s.[38]

Another way these households and lodges of Tunis remembered their saint was through a masquerade that incorporated the material culture of sub-Saharan Africa into the annual pilgrimage to his shrine. Incorporating various elements of West and Central African sartorial culture into his outfit, a ritual leader of the masquerade, called the Bu Sa'adiyya, dressed in "multicolored rags on which are hung an extraordinary number of amulets, cowries, little bells, and small mirrors." He also wore a skirt "whose hem is decorated with a fringe of jackal and fox tails." He draped a leopard skin around his shoulders and donned a headdress of animal tails that "half covers his face." On the very top of the headdress were a pair of horns, pendants, glinting mirrors, and ostrich feathers. The Bu Sa'adiyya whirled around as he danced, also playing a one-string guitar with a bow.[39] He still appears today on the streets of Tunis, where he is known to have followed his daughter Sa'adiyya all the way to Tunis when she was captured by slave raiders.[40] The incorporation of dress elements seen as sub-Saharan in origin and the retelling of the story about the lost daughter shows how memories of sub-Saharan origins mattered to the making of black Muslim religion in Tunis. In commemorating Sidi Sa'ad and calling upon his spiritual power, participants in these rituals were creating an Africana Muslim diaspora that interpreted the physical migration of Sidi Sa'ad as a religious event. The spiritual power of the saint was made available only because he had moved from Bornu to Istanbul and eventually to Tunis. Rather than mourning the loss of his home in Bornu, his devotees found reason to be thankful for his arrival in Tunis.

By the late nineteenth century, if not before, black Muslims in the city of Algiers performed similar rituals. As in Tunis, such rites were conducted by households or clubs that were established by slaves or by those whose families were once enslaved. Their lodges, which were organized along ethnic lines, contained not only a room for the group's chief but also a niche for its patron saint, whose protection from the jinn was constantly sought. The jinn might appear by making a noise or even by invading the body of a group member. The lodge also housed ritual objects, including flags, clothes for the spirits, musical instruments, and incense burners. As in the case of Tunisian households, Algerian lodges had complex governing structures. Five men performed various leadership functions: one leader conducted animal sacrifices in the lodge, one man coordinated both ritual musical performance and animal sacrifice outside the lodge, one man beat the drum, one man was treasurer, and another was designated as the lodge servant. But it was a female who was "the only true chief" of the lodge, as eyewitness J. B. Andrews put it in 1903. This keeper of the sacrificial knife had special abilities to contact the spirits, to figure out the cause of human illness, and to divine the future. She was assisted by other females who burned incense, distributed sacred water, and received offerings for the lodge. As in Tunis, the lodges in Algiers also joined together to perform public ceremonies. Their most important corporate religious function was to conduct rituals at the "Fountain of the Jinn," located in the "Seven Springs" of Algiers. Seeking both health and wealth, ritual leaders from the lodges sacrificed chickens at this site and gathered springwater for ministering to the sick. Nonblack residents joined them in these ceremonies, as parts of sub-Saharan culture were blended with Berber, Arab, and other influences to create new Islamic rituals. Lodges also held jinn possession ceremonies timed to coincide with major Islamic holidays. The jinn of the house would appear, for example, during the Prophet Muhammad's birthday or Layla al-Qadr, the Night of Power or Destiny during which the Qurʾan was revealed.[41]

By the 1950s, however, the lodges devoted to such rites had changed. No longer associated only with black people, one Algerian lodge, the Dar Zouzou, was run by a white person. What continued was the ritual of spirit possession, still timed to occur during auspicious moments of the Islamic calendar. During the Islamic month of Shaʿban, known as a time when one's fate is determined for the rest of the year, various lodges conducted possession ceremonies in which women danced and were possessed by the jinn. In one such ceremony held in 1950, a male shaykh danced to the beat of drums and the clash of iron castanets as sick children clung to his back. Other participants in the incense-filled room put on the children's legs an ointment produced from roasted corn. The shaykh then sacrificed chickens, sheep, and goats, applying some of the animals' blood to the throats, chins, and foreheads of the babies in the room. Other practitioners professed their belief in God and offered prayers for the Prophet. In this and other ceremonies, practitioners also invoked the names of saints, calling on the protection especially of Sidi Bilal, or Bilal ibn Rabah.[42]

Today the Stambali of Tunis continue to perform ritual healings that simultaneously conjure and appease the spirits. Scholar Richard Jankowsky's contemporary account of Dar Barnu (Dar Bornu), one of the historic lodges in Tunis, shows both change and continuity in the functioning of one Stambali troupe. During Jankowsky's apprenticeship at Dar Barnu, for example, there was no designated arifa, or female healer, who could invoke the spirits and care for the bodies of the humans whom they inhabited. The master of the house and its rites, a gumbri player named Baba Majid, conducted the spirit possession rituals with the help of his wife, who lived with him and his family in the lodge.[43] The musicians' expert knowledge of the spirit pantheon, which varies from lodge to lodge, is essential to the ceremony; they are musicians with the spiritual knowledge needed to heal human body and soul. They know which spirit likes which particular lyrics, instruments, melodies, rhythms, and dynamics; applying such knowledge, they call the spirits to appear in the correct order.[44]

In Dar Barnu, and in other contemporary Tunisian Stambali lodges, participants in the ritual healing ceremonies distinguish between black spirits and white saints, labels that in this case have nothing to do with race. According to Jankowsky, both species are capable of hurting or healing people and both require some sort of sacrifice. But they are also very different: the white saints are historical figures, are venerated in their own lodges, have many legends associated with them, and prefer abstract dance movement; contrariwise, the black spirits (*salhin*) were never human, have no lodges, have no legends, and prefer distinct dance movements. The saints can make you fall into a trance, but only the spirits can truly possess your body. When you dance with the saints, you perform repetitive, simple acts like swaying at the waist; when you are inhabited by a spirit, you perform only his or her unique movement, perhaps writhing on the floor or shaking your head violently. At the top of the white pantheon are Prophet Muhammad and Bilal ibn Rabah, who are tied together through song. Referred to as Jerma, Bilal is seen as a member of an ethnic group in Bornu that links the Stambali to the very origins of Islam. Nearest to God, both Muhammad and Jerma are prayed for at the beginning of each ceremony. They are too distant, too high above humans to induce a trance, as do the rest of the saints. The pantheon of saints also includes local figures such as Sidi Frej, a black Tunisian Sufi master, and international scholars such as Abd al-Qadir al-Jilani, for whom the Qadiri Sufi order is named. The pantheon of spirits incorporates the Kuri spirits, water spirits, and *beyet* or royal spirits; some, like the Kuri, have clear sub-Saharan origins, while others, such as the beyet, come from Tunisia itself.[45] The identities of the saints and spirits in the pantheon reflect the multiple imagined communities of the ritual participants themselves: they are part of Tunisia, a sub-Saharan or Sudanic diaspora, and the worldwide community of Muslims all at once.

In one healing ceremony witnessed by Jankowsky, a woman complaining of chronic and medically incurable fatigue and dizziness arrived at Dar Barnu. To speak in general terms, identifying which spirit is responsible for affliction requires a divination ceremony. A verse from the Qur'an may be recited or prayers to the Prophet may be offered, and if the spirit does not believe in God and God's Prophet, the afflicted person might scream and run out of the house. An arifa lights certain kinds of incense and uses the blood of certain animals to determine the spirit's identity. In this case, it was determined that a water spirit had inhabited the afflicted woman's body. Accompanied by the sounds of drums and iron clappers, gumbri master and ceremonial leader Baba Majid slaughtered both black and white hens, letting their blood drain into a large container of water. The woman's daughter applied some of the bloody water on her legs and neck—it is noteworthy that the blood was not consumed internally, as in some other Bori-inspired ceremonies in North Africa. The woman then danced, letting the water spirit have its way with her. Only by doing so would she rid herself, temporarily, of the spirit. Now a full spirit-possession ceremony of music and dance could be performed. Such a ceremony generally takes place in the stricken person's home, and he or she bears the full cost for the musicians, the sacrificial animals, and the arifa. The ceremony includes a meal, made from the meat of the sacrificial animal. After the meal is consumed, a ritual of celebration takes place. Everyone recites the Fatiha, the first chapter of the Qurʾan; songs are performed for the saints; an experienced dancer will become possessed by a spirit and will tell people about their futures. Then a candlelit procession is followed by the ritual consumption of couscous and water, a ritual said to be auspicious for unmarried women. Finally, another animal sacrifice is offered to the spirits, everyone once again says the Fatiha, and sweets are distributed as people part.[46]

The ceremonial highlight of the annual ritual calendar for Dar Barnu may be a ziyara to the shrine of Sidi Frej, the local Sufi saint who comes from Bornu.[47] Taking place from a Wednesday to a Friday during July, this pilgrimage contains many of the same rituals once part of the visit to the shrine of Sidi Saʿad mentioned above. The Bu Saʿadiyya appears in a street procession, musicians play a large number of songs at the shrine itself, and specialist dancers are entranced by the saints and possessed by the spirits. This pilgrimage does not reenact the journey of black people from slavery to freedom or from sub-Saharan Africa to North Africa; instead, according to Jankowsky, it brings together the overlapping and ultimately complementary identities of the ritual participants. As with the possession ceremony held in the lodge or someone's home, the main point is to evoke all members of the Stambali pantheon, both saints and spirits. These saints and spirits are from multiple worlds. Bringing them together, in Jankowsky's words, shows the compatibility of the "local, pan-Islamic, and 'African' worlds" of the Stambali practitioners.[48] Thus, the possession of black spirits, some of whom have identifiably sub-Saharan origins, is felt and understood as a unifying and healing community ritual in which all parts of the group's identity are celebrated. In its elaboration of the meaning of human dispersion, the ritual, rather than attempting to create boundaries, embodies the attempt to build connections among the diverse and possibly conflicting elements of black Muslim identity in North Africa.

THE GNAWA IN MOROCCO

Another black religious group in the region that incorporates music, dance, trance, and spirit possession and shares strong family resemblances to the Stambali in Tunisia is the Gnawa of Morocco. The Berber word "Gnawa," whose linguistic origins remain disputed, emerged over time as a generic label for many but not all black Moroccans, most of whose ancestors were once enslaved. While people from western and central Sudan—from Chad to Senegal—have been present in Morocco since Roman times, enslaved black Africans began arriving in larger numbers around the eleventh century. These slaves and many who would follow in the coming centuries became conscripted soldiers who sometimes composed all-black regiments in the ruler's army. Black women were also captured and sold into slavery, and as was the case in the Ottoman Empire, they were forced to serve in their masters' households, sometimes as concubines. Over time, these women gave birth to free men and women, who, along with manumitted slaves, established free black communities.[49]

Many of these slaves and free people came to use the word "Gnawa" to refer to their "collective identity"; historian Chouki El Hamel writes that today "black Moroccans perceive themselves first and foremost as Muslim Moroccans, and only secondarily . . . as belonging to a specific ethnic or linguistic, real or imaginary, origin."[50] Moreover, while their black identity was developed partly through the collective performance of a set of Muslim religious practices with Sudanic influences, there are now nonblack participants in Gnawa religious rituals. These nonblack initiates to Gnawa practices have sometimes referred to themselves as slaves—but slaves of God and the jinn, not of people.[51]

The music making and dancing associated with rites of trance and spirit possession are well known in Morocco, partly because elements of them have been adapted as tourist attractions, especially in the cities of Marrakesh, Essaouira, and Fez.[52] In addition, Gnawa performers have toured France and the United States. They have collaborated with African American jazz artist Randy Weston, helping to make Gnawa performance a potent genre of world music and the contemporary African arts diaspora.[53] Gnawa songs have become commodities in the contemporary

African diaspora at least in part because they are now perceived to be part of the musical heritage of other African-descended people. Here we have an example of an Africana Muslim diaspora that is clearly commercialized.

Contemporary iterations of classic Gnawa music, like the spirituals of North American black slaves, often ask: Why would our God separate us from our native land and make us suffer so much? These songs sing the blues on both sides of the black Atlantic:

> The Sudan, oh! Sudan
> The Sudan, the land of my people
> I was enslaved, I was sold
> I was taken away from my loved ones.[54]

A similar song, "Oh, Aisha," details the forced sojourn of the Gnawa from the Sudan to the land of the "infidel Touraregs," "the sand carriers of Suafa," and the "wine-drinking people of Jerid":

> And as for me, I search for mabruka [grace, beneficence]
> My shoes are grass, my staff tamarind
> With overburdened back, dagger in my sash
> I seek mabruka and I never find it.
> O misfortune! Guide me, wherever I go
> I've not found it![55]

Such songs also record the discrimination and structural racism experienced by both enslaved and free blacks in Morocco:

> Oh! God our Lord,
> My uncle Mbara is a miserable man
> What a fate does he have?
> My uncle Mbara is a poor man
> Our lady eats meat
> Our master eats meat
> My uncle Mbara gnaws at the bone
> Our lady wears elegant shoes
> Our master wears beautiful shoes
> My uncle Mbara wears sandals
> Our master wears beautiful shoes
> Oh! God is our guide
> This is the predicament of the deprived
> Oh poor uncle Mbara.[56]

Like African American slave spirituals, these songs sometimes do more than lament. One song, for example, complains that the nobles of Morocco made the Gnawa bow and serve them but recognizes that God will offer recompense for black suffering: "They brought us / Oh there is no God but God / We believe in God's justice."[57]

Though such music is now part of the world music stage, its origins are located in the lila, or night ceremony. Scholar Deborah Kapchan, who began researching Gnawa practices in the 1990s, provides a detailed description of one such ceremony in the Moroccan capital of Rabat: After sunset, women, dressed in caftans colored gold, silver, blue, and orange, streamed into a house with a tall courtyard, waiting for a master musician to appear. The master musician, male leader of the ceremony, picked up his drums at 11:15 P.M. and went into the street outside. A woman led the procession, carrying a brass tray full of incense bowls. Each of the different scents—musk, amber, myrrh, benzoin, and sandalwood—was meant to invoke a different spirit. The procession leader had a bowl of milk, some fresh dates, henna paste, and candles. Neighborhood residents came out to observe the procession, and as the Gnawa participants began to dance and spin, one man who had come to see the procession was possessed by a spirit and fell to the ground. As his friends took care of him, the ritual participants returned to the house, ready to begin the next part of the ceremony. The drums were set aside as iron cymbals were played loudly. The master musician plucked a gumbri. He was known to be able to "work the spirits"; that is, he could call on the spirits at will and help younger practitioners learn how to control the experience of inhabitation. All of the musicians sang to the Bambara spirits that traveled with them across the Sahara, and one man danced for the spirits, pretending to hunt game with a gun. Finally they chanted the words that they would use several times throughout the night ceremony: "Prayers upon the Messenger of God. Prayers upon our Master, Muhammad."[58]

One of the Gnawa asked for an offering, demanding, "Who will open the door?" After a few women made donations, this man put some incense into a brazier. As smoke rose, the master musician played and invoked the spirit of various Muslim saints, including Abd al-Qadir al-Jilani, the same saint so important to the Stambali. Women swayed from side to side as the clashing of the cymbals accelerated and then went silent, leaving only the quiet sounds of the master musician's strumming. One woman cried, "Allah." Some female participants had fallen into a trance. Bodies fell "to the floor . . . writhing, twitching, rolling." As they did, they were gently held and kissed by other women who were not possessed. Trancers later described this experience as one of intoxication, pleasure, and addiction; they felt loved by God. A series of the jinn appeared, and these spirits required propitiation. The black spirits came first, and those in trance cut their arms and legs and tongues with knives. Their blood dripped on their clothes and onto the blue-tiled floor. This self-inflicted injury was a sign of grace and blessing; the body of the possessed had undergone an "alchemical transformation," and it was the spirit, not the afflicted, that painlessly suffered the wound.[59]

Next came the blue spirits, those of the sea; one woman fell to the floor and started to swim-dance. Then the sky spirits arrived. Some women lifted their arms above their heads, "beating the air like desperate wings." The music quieted again and the musicians took a short break. Afterward it was time for the red spirits. One woman became possessed, contorting her body as the female procession leader gently guided her to the incense burner, helping her inhale some sacred smoke. As her head twisted from left to right, she tied a red scarf on her waist and a red veil over her head. She placed the flame of lit candles directly under her open mouth. Then the music stopped. Finally Aisha Qandisha, the most powerful female jinn, was invoked and one woman fell to the floor in a trance. This woman had often spoken with Aisha before. For a long time, the musicians sang to Aisha. And then Aisha and the other spirits departed as the morning light filled the room.[60]

This particular night ceremony contains several aspects common to all such ceremonies: there is an invocation to God and prayers for the Prophet and the saints; the use of candles, incense, and food; the playing and singing of songs; dancing; and the use of different colors for different jinn. As with Bori ceremonies, a sheep or goat might also be sacrificed. Such elements can change depending on the historical circumstances. For example, some songs might emphasize different themes or seek to propitiate different spirits. Different saints might be invoked and long genealogies of the Gnawa might be eulogized in song.[61]

Many scholars of Islamic religion and history have struggled to categorize the practices of the Gnawa. Some intellectuals in Morocco, expressing a prejudice against the sub-Saharan origins of Gnawa practices, have criticized the Gnawa as "a cult influenced by pagan black traditions and embraced mostly by lower-class people with little literacy or learning."[62] Many non-Moroccan scholars writing in English argue that there is a difference between Gnawa practice and Sufism, the mystical branch of Islam.[63] They point to the facts that Gnawa worship is not organized around the shrine of a saint, there is no master-disciple relationship in Gnawa practice, and the trance of the Gnawa is different from the spiritual intimacy or union with God achieved by Sufi practitioners.[64] In addition, many Gnawa, when asked, make an explicit distinction between themselves and Sufis. At the same time, it is clear that a cultural exchange among these various groups has occurred. The ways in which the Gnawa honor their ancestors has been affected by various Moroccan Sufi orders.[65] Moroccans, whether Berber or Arab, have welcomed Gnawa ceremonies in their homes or joined a Sufi order whose practices are similar to those of the Gnawa. Some scholars also suggest that Gnawa practice has changed elements of Moroccan Sufism, especially in the ways that the Isawa and Hamdushi Sufi orders have incorporated Gnawa beliefs about spirit possession.[66] Whatever the precise nature of exchange and mutual influence, the retention and adaptation of sub-Saharan symbols and practices speaks to the vitality of the Africana Muslim diaspora and its responsiveness to a social context of racism and oppression.

Knowing about the adaptations and appropriations of sub-Saharan African religious culture is necessary for understanding the practice of Islam among black Muslims in North Africa and the Middle East. But limiting the discussion of black Muslim religiosity to such practices may send the signal, however unintentionally, that the only authentically African Islam is that Islam that expresses some element of sub-Saharan African culture. It may make it seem as if those people of African descent who do not practice parts of their West, Central, or East African heritage have lost or abandoned their authentic culture. This patronizing attitude ignores the way that many tens of thousands, perhaps hundreds of thousands, of Muslims in the Middle East and North Africa with a connection to a sub-Saharan origin have fashioned their understandings of Islam. Put simply, Bori, Zar, Stambali, and Gnawa practices of Islam are not the only forms of Islamic religion practiced by black Muslims in the region. The next section of this chapter explores the Islamic practices of some African-descended people who have not retained major elements of their Sudanic heritage, and, in so doing, it shows where the limits of the Muslim African diaspora can be found.

THE GHAWARNA IN JORDAN

The Jordanian Ghawarna make up a rural population who have lived in the Jordan Valley for hundreds of years. Thousands of them have African roots, though it is impossible to determine, both practically and theoretically, what percentage of the population is African.[67] For contemporary Jordanians, their origins are shrouded in mystery. Though some consider the Ghawarna to be the original inhabitants of the Jordan Valley, the available historical evidence reveals that they have intermarried with African populations arriving in the Ghor at various points in the past millennium. The demand for labor on sugar plantations in the southern Jordan Valley during both the Ayyubid (1187–1260 C.E.) and Mamluk (1250–1517 C.E.) eras led to the introduction of slaves there, though whether such slaves were African is not clear.[68] Since approximately 1500 C.E., African slaves have arrived in or passed through southern Syria, including the regions now occupied by the Hashemite kingdom of Jordan, via three main routes: enslaved Somalis were purchased by Syrian and other Muslim pilgrims in the Hijaz, enslaved Abyssinians arrived in Palestine via Cyprus and sometimes Istanbul, and slaves purchased in Egypt passed through Palestine, perhaps on their way to Syria, Iraq, or Anatolia.[69] In the nineteenth and twentieth centuries, African slaves to Bedouin tribes such as the Adwan served as pages, bodyguards, and poets to tribal leaders.[70] Though the Ottomans attempted to suppress the slave trade, their power to effect change in places such as Jordan was apparently nonexistent.[71] Officially speaking, slavery was banned in Transjordan in 1929, though the institution apparently continued after World War II.[72]

As slaves were freed both before and after legal emancipation, they intermarried with the Ghawarna. Ironically, perhaps, as slaves left the houses of their masters and claimed belonging to a Ghawarna tribe, they may have lost some of their social status; in some cases, Ghawarna were treated more poorly than slaves.[73] This fact indicates that social status in the Jordan Valley has been dynamic, never *solely* determined by those physical characteristics considered to signify black racial identity. Through the 1970s, for example, some Ghawarna made social distinctions among themselves in relation to their former status as slaves. During this period, according to one account, they still referred to themselves as *ahrar*, or free people; *abid*, or slaves; and Ghawarna, meaning the original people of the valley. At the same time, all Ghawarna, whether connected to a slave past or not, possessed higher social status than Egyptian farmworkers and Palestinian refugees, who were viewed as foreigners—a practice that continues today.[74]

As in southern Tunisia, social differences in the Jordan Valley have been constructed in large part through tribal, village, and clan affiliations. For example, many members of the relatively powerful Abbadi tribe considered the Mashalkha tribe, some of whom exhibit African traits, to be of a higher social status than other Ghawarna. The Mashalkha may not have performed agricultural labor for other tribes as did those Ghawarna living in the southern end of the Dead Sea. The Mashalkha differed from the southern Ghawarna in that they were perceived as authentic Bedouin and thus were able to play roles in national politics and to achieve relative economic prosperity.[75] The Ghawarna in the southern region of the Dead Sea claim such tribal lineages but with little effect on how others treat them. In addition to seeing themselves as Muslims, Arabs, and Jordanians, they trace their genealogy to one Bedouin tribe or another.[76] Unlike some of the Mashalkha, however, Ghawarna in the southern Dead Sea region were and largely are unable to translate what is a relatively weak tribal status into increased political power or wealth.

In addition to the progeny of enslaved Africans, other contemporary black residents of the Jordan Valley include Afro-Palestinian refugees from both the 1948 and 1967 Arab-Israeli wars. These persons of African descent trace their origins in Palestine to multiple sources. Their ancestors include black defectors from Muhammad Ali's army in nineteenth-century Egypt, black Bedouin from the Negev who became refugees in Gaza in 1948, and nineteenth- and twentieth-century African Muslim pilgrims from Chad, Nigeria, Senegal, and Sudan who settled in Jerusalem, one of Islam's holiest cities.[77]

Like other subjects in this book, many Ghawarna suffer from antiblack racism, which includes personal prejudice and institutional discrimination. The degree of personal prejudice that Ghawarna people experience is often a function of the extent to which they possess physical characteristics tagged in Jordan as black and African. The "blacker" the person— often determined by their skin color and hair texture—the more prejudice they face. As illustrated by one woman's comments in the southern Jordan Valley, where I interviewed several women as part of a research project on race and religion among the Ghawarna, prejudice against dark individuals can have a particularly detrimental effect on girls and women. "A lot of guys make fun of, find fault with dark girls," explained this woman. "They develop low self-esteem." In order to mitigate the effects of such discrimination, women use whitening creams "so that they become more attractive," as another woman put it. Consumer culture in Jordan and other parts of the Middle East constantly remind women of color that they can become "fair and lovely" if they purchase the right skin care product. "If the guy is dark and even ugly," one woman said, "that's OK. The focus [of the prejudice] is on women." Another explained that her husband wanted a second wife because he desired a lighter-skinned woman: "But the family refused him, because he was too dark himself." This refusal is typical in Jordan, where the only light-skinned persons willing to marry a black person are often those of low status. As the middle-class father of a light-skinned woman put it, "I would never let my daughter marry a black man."[78]

Jordanians generally use the terms *asmar*, meaning dark or black or brown, and *abiad*, meaning light or white, to describe skin color. This typology represents a semantic shift in Jordanian society. The word that was formerly used in both Jordan and Palestine to describe someone who exhibits phenotypes typically associated with black Africa was the same word for slave, ʿ*abd*.[79] Nowadays, "slave" is not uttered in polite company, although it is still in use among some Jordanians. As in other former slave societies, being associated with a slave past remains a source of shame. Stereotypes of blacks as lazy, adept at sports, sexually permissive, funny, musical, and poetic—stereotypes maintained across a variety of societies that have held slaves from or colonized Africa—continue to inform Jordanian and much of Middle Eastern popular culture.[80] Many of these stereotypes remain discursively tied to memories of slavery, as elements of Jordanian consumer culture show. Peanuts, which are associated with Africa, are still called "slave nuts" in some quarters. A chocolate-covered marshmallow-like confection, popular in both Europe and the Middle East, is called *ra's al-ʿabid*, or "slave/nigger's head." Recognizing the racism inherent in the product's name, one Lebanese company rebranded the product Tarboush, or "fez."[81]

The consequential nature of skin color for one's life opportunities and social relationships in Jordan derives not only from overt prejudice but also from institutional or structural racism, a covert form of social, political, and economic inequality embedded in a lack of access to resources and the perpetuation of past social injustice. The contemporary poverty of the Ghawarna is a product, in part, of the systematic dispossession of their lands in the twentieth century. As irrigation improved and other factors led to better agricultural production in the Jordan Valley, members of more powerful tribes and merchants from Jordanian cities sought to acquire the Ghawarna's lands through various means, including exploitative ones. In some cases, the Ghawarna sold their lands because they needed money for a marriage or a death settlement. But in other cases, merchants loaned farmers the money to purchase tools and seeds, charged exorbitant interest—as much as 100 percent annually—and then seized the land when the farmer could not repay the loans. In addition, shopkeepers in the Jordan Valley sometimes cheated farmers, selling tools, groceries, and supplies at high prices. This resulted in a system of debt peonage. Finally, some members of more powerful tribes such as the Adwan and the Majaly simply stole the land by threatening the Ghawarna.[82]

Do the Islamic practices of black Ghawarna refer or respond to this institutional racism, the personal prejudice suffered by individuals, or the distant memory of African roots? Unlike black Muslims who propitiate the Bori or seek to become possessed by spirits or guided by black saints, the Ghawarna do not seem to embody or interpret any form of black or African diasporic identity in their practice of Islam. They do not refer to Bilal as their ancestor, and they do not celebrate any African saints. Their Islamic practices are largely indistinguishable from those of the nonblack Muslims with whom they live and work in the rural setting of the southern Jordan Valley. The absence of any Islamic practice that constructs black diasporic meaning does not mean, however, that the issue of race is insignificant to the Islamic identity of the Ghawarna. The remainder of this section will first give readers a sense of the rural practices of Islam performed by both black and nonblack Muslims in the Jordan Valley. These practices include rituals of healing, the celebration of the Islamic holiday of Ramadan, and the traditions associated with weddings. It is in the discussion of weddings where race can be seen as a concern that sometimes intersects with the religious identities of African-descended Ghawarna.

Like many Muslims and other religionists throughout the world, many Ghawarna believe that at least some of life's maladies are caused by the evil eye. People's envy of good fortune, such as a marriage or graduation, can lead to divorce, unemployment, or something worse. Children are thought to be particularly vulnerable to the evil eye, which is drawn to a child when someone looking upon the child or his or her picture either fails to utter formulaic Arabic sayings or draws undue attention to the child by complimenting his or her good looks. The idea of the evil eye's existence is based, at least for some, on the Qurʾan, various hadiths, or, in the case of the Shiʿa, the words of the imams. Several regional techniques exist to counter the effect of the evil eye. Despite the relatively recent criticisms of traditional Islamic practices to defend against or cure problems caused by the evil eye, Muslims in the Middle East have traditionally believed that the use of material objects such as amulets, in combination with the recitation or writing of the Qurʾan, is a practice sanctioned by Islam. A volume of the Qurʾan itself can help to ward off the evil eye, and many drivers in both urban and rural areas still put a copy on their dashboards to prevent any harm while on the road. Various people also own amulets meant to ward off the eye, though some who do explain that it is a harmless superstition. Middle Easterners also keep such amulets on their key chains or in their houses.[83]

Other techniques for defending against the evil eye include the use of incense, alum, and salt.[84] In Ghor al-Mazraʿa, a village in the southern Jordan Valley, the Dead Sea provides unique rocks of salt for the performance of such rituals. Some women who fear that their children have been the object of envy turn to relatives or friends who know how to conduct a healing ritual with Dead Sea salt. The child is taken to the house of the ritual specialist where his or her head is first covered with some form of heavy, protective cloth. A pan is held over the child's head. Salt rocks are then heated until they burn red. Finally water is added to the pan, and as the salt rocks fizzle and steam is released, the evil is believed to dissipate. Some women in Ghor al-Mazraʿa, like other Middle Eastern peoples, also use alum to confront various maladies and problems such as infertility or a cheating spouse. In this case, women visit the home of a *shaykha*, a female Muslim religious specialist capable of conducting healing and fortune telling. The shaykha places the alum into a fire. She reads verses from the Qurʾan over the head of the seeker and gives a reading from the alum as it changes shapes. Someone then buries the alum in the ground.[85]

Finally, women use a folded piece of paper called a hijab—the same word used for the head scarf—for the purpose of both healing and harming. A shaykha writes down various Qurʾanic verses and perhaps other words, folds the piece of paper over and over, and then instructs the supplicant to sew it into her clothing, hide it under her bed, or put it in some other secret place. In some instances a hijab can be used to heal oneself. But the hijab can also be used to harm others; such a curse could be meant, for example, to prevent one's husband from taking another wife or to bring misfortune to one's meddlesome mother-in-law. This form of Islamic practice is private. It cannot be discussed publicly in a self-proclaimed modern Muslim country like Jordan, where it is seen as anti-Islamic to most Islamic leaders and as backward and irrational to urban, middle-class Muslims who are also believers in Enlightenment rationality.[86]

This aspect of religious life is also associated more closely with women than with men.[87] The mosque in the southern Jordan Valley is a male space, and women seldom pray there. The domestic spaces in which healing and sometimes harming take place seem to be largely female. It is perhaps because these practices take place in private, domestic, and female spaces that they have endured the criticism of modern Muslim reformers. Some venerable Islamic traditions associated with women's religious practice may have withered under the intense public heat of Islamic reform. For example, in the 1970s women from across the Jordan Valley still lit candles at the tombs of the Prophet Muhammad's companions and Muslim saints.[88] There is no evidence of the visitation rituals today.

Healing and harming rituals are only one aspect of religious life in Ghor al-Mazra'a and other villages in the Jordan Valley. Other Islamic practices, more typically used to represent Islam in world religions textbooks, also give meaning and perform important social functions in the lives of the Ghawarna. Take, for example, Ramadan, the holy month of dawn-to-sunset fasting. Ramadan encourages—or forces, depending on one's point of view—families and friends to spend more time together. At the end of the first day of fasting, nuclear families enjoy *iftar*, the evening meal in which the fast is broken, in their own homes. But in the days following, nuclear families visit one another. Grown children visit their parents, cousins come calling, and food is often brought to the houses of the elderly and the sick. In some homes the culinary emphasis during Ramadan is on the sweets. A family might consume *qata'if*, cream-stuffed pancakes; *muhallabiyya*, rice pudding; and *kunafa*, a syrupy-sweet pastry with cheese. Those who cannot afford expensive treats may eat inexpensive cookies such as sesame biscuits. Some eat the special soups of the season that include carrots, squash, potatoes, and tomatoes. But Ramadan is about more than food and family, at least for some. Pious Muslims, of various colors and racial backgrounds, read a *juz'*, or one-thirtieth of the Qur'an, each day, trying to finish the entire text by the end of the month. Some men and women also perform *dhikr*, in this case meaning that they recite litanies or meditative formulas meant to bring them closer to God. Religious men go to mosques more frequently during Ramadan; some women might visit during Layla al-Qadr, the Night of Power or Destiny, although they are just as likely to commemorate this sacred occasion at home.[89]

In some areas of life in Ghor al-Mazraʿa and Ghor el-Safi, as everywhere else, Islamic religious practices are deeply intertwined with what many people there regard as customs. Though various physical, temporal, and doctrinal boundaries attempt to distinguish cultural customs from religious practices, even then the sacred and the profane are interrelated. For example, dress can be a form of religious expression, especially for women in the Jordan Valley, though its meanings are constantly shifting as women change styles, test the boundaries of cultural taste, and subvert the religious and cultural expectations in the Jordan Valley that all women cover their hair in public. As in the rest of Jordan and much of the Middle East, women's wearing of shirts and pants, especially if they are tight, is controversial, with some men and women insisting that the only proper form of dress for women is a loose-fitting gown.[90]

The line between religious and nonreligious culture is also blurred in the celebration of marriage. Historically speaking, fiqh, or Islamic jurisprudence, casts marriage as a contractual relationship of obligation between a husband and a wife.[91] Weddings, however, tend to be governed primarily not by fiqh but by local customs. In the Jordan Valley, as in many other rural Muslim communities, weddings are far more elaborate affairs than the actual signing of the marriage contract. A wedding can take place over an entire week, but it generally lasts at least two to three days. The rhythm of the event varies from neighborhood to neighborhood and house to house. On Sunday, the family of the groom may begin to decorate their house, hanging strings of small flags and sometimes distributing formal cards or simply spreading the word among neighbors that a wedding is going to take place. On Monday, chairs may be brought to the house, and perhaps an Egyptian-style tent will be erected. Perhaps a few musicians begin to play music for the family on Monday, and women may dance among themselves. Arabic coffee may also be served. On Tuesday, family and friends might participate in a large dabka, or dance, hosted by the groom's family. Sometimes the men and women dance together, violating both Western stereotypes about Muslims and socially conservative interpretations of Islam. Dance parties can also take place on Wednesday or Thursday, depending on the traditions popular in the village or neighborhood and the wishes of the family. Wednesday or Thursday is henna night at the bride's house, a practice that is seen as *sunna*, or a prophetically sanctioned tradition. The bride's hands and sometimes the groom's are elaborately decorated with henna. During this party, the groom may give the bride a gift of gold jewelry, still a significant source of wealth for many women. The bride may also receive money or other gifts from her female friends. On Friday or sometimes Saturday, the bride and the groom go to different salons to prepare for the wedding lunch. The bride's family may also bring breakfast to the house of the groom's family. If it is Friday, those who wish to attend communal prayers do so, and then the friends and family of the couple are served a large meal generally featuring rice and lamb. Hundreds of people may attend the wedding lunch. Because many people in the Jordan Valley are poor, neighbors often offer monetary gifts to cover the costs of the meal.[92]

Weddings in Jordan are expensive, sometimes prohibitively so for the average Jordanian. In poor neighborhoods, a complicated exchange of gifts makes it possible for the newly married couple to begin their lives together. The bride's family might provide the new couple with a television, a satellite receiver, a refrigerator, furniture for the living room, clothes, and kitchenware. As mentioned, it is the responsibility of the groom's family to supply the *mahr*, a contractually obligated wedding gift, sometimes translated as "dowry," that is often given to the bride in the form of jewelry. The groom also arranges for the new couple's housing, buys furniture for the couple's bedroom, and gives money to the bride's family. Sometimes the groom's family cannot afford a separate home, so they rent an apartment or offer the couple a room in their own house. In a simple wedding, the mother of the bride might receive 300 Jordanian dinars (or $420) while the father of the bride might get 200 Jordanian dinars ($280). If the woman is marrying a Pakistani or Egyptian worker, her family asks for more, reflecting the lower social status of these guest workers and the need for the bride's family to save money on her behalf in case of a divorce; since they are guest workers, Pakistanis and Egyptians are also more likely to be forced by various circumstances to return home.[93]

In the Jordan Valley, it is practically impossible to have a wedding without also having a dance party, or *hafla*. The dabka, a line dance featuring swift and complicated footwork, is the dominant style of dance performed during these parties.[94] Though the dabka has become a symbol of Palestinian national and cultural identity, especially since the 1967 war created a second wave of Palestinian refugees in Jordan, the dabka has overlapping and contested meanings and functions, as seen by its more local iterations in the Jordan Valley. The best dance leaders (*lawih*) are often said to be black, specifically "members of black communities, usually of slave origin (*'abid*) coming from Palestine."[95] In some places it is *expected* that blacks will perform this role.[96] According to researcher Mauro Van Aken, "Most of the famous *lawih* and animators of parties are black (*samr*) young men, a status publicly recognized in ritual performance that contrasts to their stigmatization in daily life and to their perceived low social status."[97]

Such dance leaders create a space where a black man is in charge, as he simultaneously imposes order, creates excitement, encourages appropriate behavior, and leads by example. This style of leadership is seen by many of the dance-goers as masculine, and the dance thus becomes a space in which racial hierarchies are inverted as a dark-skinned man becomes a strong and powerful leader. But this leadership may come with a social cost, since many dabkas are religiously liminal spaces where Islamic taboos are broken or challenged. In some villages and some dance sites, for example, men and women dance together. This is one of the attractions for men—and presumably for women, too—of such dances. However, this breaking of more socially conservative notions of proper behavior also then produces a social stigma outside of the dance, a stigma that attaches to the Ghawarna and reaffirms stereotypes about the questionable moral character of all Ghawarna people and especially black Ghawarna. In addition, such dances become especially dangerous, quite literally, when they "become hot"—that is, when feelings of "ceremonial intensity" are multiplied by the consumption of liquor by young men. For some men, mixing more freely with women while also drinking liquor is exactly what makes the dance fun. But this environment, fertile for social boundary crossing, also leads to serious fights among people from different towns and sometimes from differing ethnic and national groups. This fighting is also seen by Jordan Valley inhabitants as another immoral outcome of a "hot" dance.[98]

Those dancers who are or become religiously observant generally eschew hot dancing. One black dance leader told Van Aken that before he got serious about Islam, "I was the best dancer. . . . All the girls were looking at me!" But after he began to pray on a regular basis, he altered the way that he danced. No longer leading the dance, he kept a "low profile" and avoided any sexually provocative moves.[99] It is important to note that he did not stop dancing. This fact indicates that the dabka itself is not necessarily seen by people in the Jordan Valley and Jordanians more generally as religiously impermissible. It is the way one dances that separates religiously permissible dancing from impermissible dancing.

This moral calculation reveals another element of Islam at play in the lives of Ghawarna. A commitment to Islamic piety in the Jordan Valley, as in much of the world where Islam is practiced, often means paying attention not only to the Qur'an and the hadith but also to the interpretations of these sacred sources by the great scholars of Sunni or Shi'a tradition. The whole package is what Muslims generally refer to as the *shari'a*, God's path to salvation. Contrary to images portrayed in mainstream European and American media, shari'a has more to do with personal religious obligations than with criminal penalties.[100] Ethical contemplation is at the heart of many Muslims' religious practice, no matter what their race or ethnicity. Shari'a is literally embodied by the black dancer in the Jordan Valley. Choosing to regulate the ways in which he dances—his gestures, his moves, and the words he shouts and sings—is a form of religious devotion to the will of God. For him, shari'a is an essential element of Islamic religious practice. Not following the shari'a has both personal and social consequences. In addition to showing a lack of seriousness about his personal commitment to Islam, sexually provocative dancing has the social cost of reifying negative stereotypes about all black people. In this instance at least, it seems as if antiblack racism is reinforced by an ethical system that punishes black men for performing the very thing, the dance, for which they are admired and sought out.

CONCLUSION

The discussion above has established a boundary marking what does or does not constitute a meaningful form of black diasporic Islam. There is a dividing line between those Muslims who identify in some way with an African heritage, identity, or culture and those who do not. Some residents of the Jordan Valley may indeed be of African descent, and their racial identity does matter to their life opportunities and social interactions. But there is no evidence at this point that any Ghawarna self-identify as African-descended or define their religious or other cultural practices as having been influenced by aspects of a black African heritage.

Another boundary that gives meaning to this book's description of the African Muslim diaspora is that which crosses the line between the heavens and the earth, the material and the spiritual, the transcendent and the immanent. As the introduction suggested, for the category of diaspora to be useful in understanding human religious activity, it must be able to incorporate meanings of human dispersion and scattering that recognize but also go beyond this-worldly limits. Diaspora must be flexible enough to incorporate human beings' own insistence that their dispersion includes travel to, residing within, and return from the spirit world, the heavens, the unseen realm, and other places that do not appear in an atlas. In the case of both Gnawa and Bori practices of Islam, this chapter has shown that African diasporic communities of Muslims construct rituals of celebration, healing, and commemoration in which the boundaries of the natural and supernatural are transgressed. The Gnawa and the Stambali combine various local traditions with cultural elements that they themselves identify as having a sub-Saharan connection or origin—things such as an ancestor, a piece of clothing, a name, a mode of authority, or a song—to produce meaningful and efficacious Islamic religious practices. They use these Islamic practices to access the unseen spiritual power of a saint, to become inhabited by a spirit (sometimes also seen as having a sub-Saharan origin), to divine the future, or to become healed of spiritual and physical illness. For them, the African diaspora has both this-worldly and otherworldly meanings and consequences. In their dancing, their wearing of special clothing, and their playing of special instruments that are inspired, created, or given to them by black African saints or spirits, entities that cross the boundary between the heavens and the earth, these Muslims quite literally embody black African and Islamic identities that link their physical diaspora to metaphysical wholeness. It is not possible to understand their practice of Islam outside that holistic framework, a claim that is useful in analyzing the African Muslim diaspora in other settings as well.

Finally, this examination of Islam among various groups with black African roots reveals the religious diversity of Muslims in the African diaspora and in Islam more generally. It is important to point out that all of these Muslims are Sunnis, or more formally, those who follow the Sunna, or tradition of the Prophet Muhammad, and the consensus of his community. In general terms, they recognize the theological, doctrinal, and ethical traditions of Sunni Islam as articulated in the Qur'an, the Sunna, and authoritative interpretations of them in fiqh, or Islamic jurisprudence.

They observe, to a greater or lesser degree, the five pillars of Islamic practice. This chapter illustrates that to understand how Islam is actually lived by Muslims in the African diaspora, or in any other setting for that matter, one must go beyond such "textbook" approaches to Islam. Even if all of the Muslims discussed here are Sunni, there is great variety in the ways that they obey God's commands and cultivate their spirituality. The practices of spirit possession, physical and spiritual healing, and masquerading in peacock feathers are not usually associated in textbooks as part and parcel of Sunni Islam. Generally speaking, the more widespread rural practices of warding off the evil eye through the use of salt, alum, or another material are similarly excluded from authoritative lists of acceptable Sunni Islamic practices found in media accounts and introductory college lectures, despite their widespread use in the Islamic world.[101] In the continued focus on the "high culture" tradition of the texts and in an effort to make Islam intelligible to large non-Muslim audiences, U.S. and European media often make a distinction between these sorts of practices and "orthodox Islam."[102] Most Sunni Muslims in these places may agree with this distinction. But that does not change the fact that the Muslims described above consider themselves to be followers of the Prophet's Sunna. Studying Islam in the African diaspora means taking into account ways of being a Sunni beyond what is immediately available to many media consumers in the West.

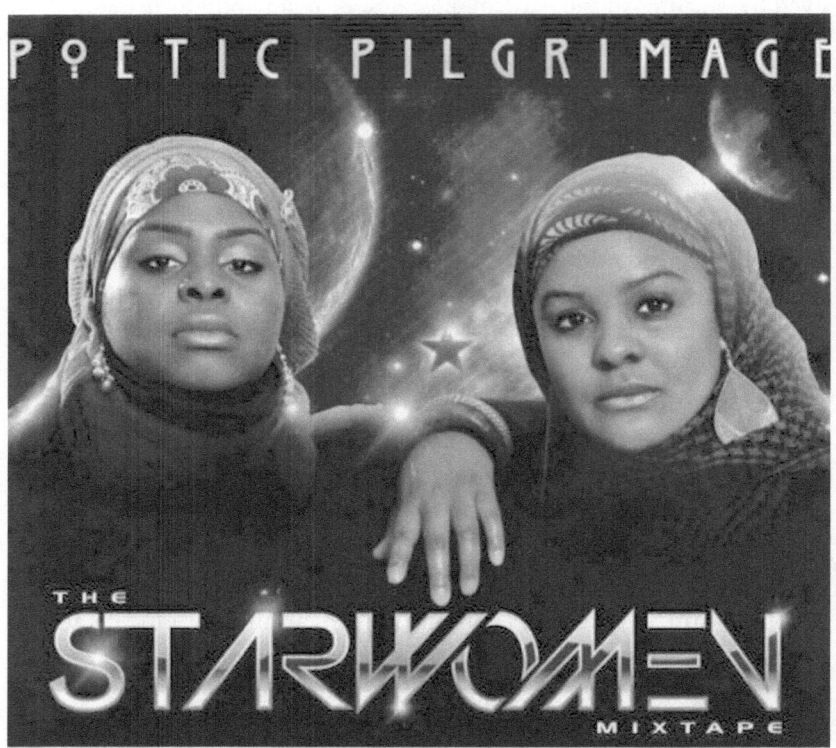

Cover of Poetic Pilgrimage's CD *The Starwomen Mixtape* (2010). The British hip-hop duo Muneera Rashida and Sukina Abdul Noor of Poetic Pilgrimage converted to Islam in 2005 after studying the thought of Malcolm X. Rashida is a DJ and Sukina sings. Both are emcees. Courtesy of Muneera Rashida and Sukina Abdul Noor.

3

AFRICAN MUSLIMS IN EUROPE

Mandinga, Murids, and British Black Muslims

We're the descendants of Bilal . . .
And even today
The descendants of Bilal bring the message of Islam to the West and far away
Dropping science and books
And in hip-hop
Cheikh Anta Diop
Brought the knowledge nonstop
Shaykh Uthman dan Fodio
Brought the . . . to Kano
The Mahdi of Sudan was the man with the plan
Shaykh Abdul Hakim Quick brings the . . . real quick
Imam Siraj Wahhaj is large and in charge
Shaykh Babikir is the master of *dhikr*
And Imam Zaid Shakir makes the *din* real clear.

We're descendants of Bilal
To Allah we pray and bow
Forbidding the *haram*
Calling all to the *halal*
We call to the *din*
The *sirat al-mustaqim*
We fear no man
Only He who is Supreme
You can find us in Sudan,
Somalia, Nigeria, Gambia, Senegal,
Mali, Chad, and Ghana
And Morocco,
Trinidad and Tobago,
All over the States
New York, Chicago.
—Mecca2Medina, "Descendants of Bilal"[1]

Toward the end of the first decade of the twenty-first century, London-based hip-hop group Mecca2Medina, founded by British rappers Rakin and Ismael, recorded a song about Bilal ibn Rabah. "Descendants of Bilal" draws from the traditions of both Afrocentric historiography and Islamic piety to proclaim pride in both Muslim and African diasporic identities. One section of the song features African and African-descended Muslim leaders: Cheikh Anta Diop, the mid-twentieth-century Senegalese historian and politician who argued, among other things, that black history, including that of ancient Egypt, can inspire black political self-determination; Uthman dan Fodio, the Sufi master and *shariʿa* scholar who established the Sokoto caliphate in West Africa in the early nineteenth century; Abdul Hakim Quick, a prominent Canadian Muslim religious leader, educator, and historian; Siraj Wahhaj, the popular Brooklyn-based imam, community activist, and U.S. Muslim leader, the first Muslim to offer an invocation in Congress; Babikir Ahmed Babikir, a British religious leader and educator of Sudanese origin who leads Ulfa Aid, a London-based philanthropic organization; and Zaid Shakir, the African American Islamic scholar with an advanced Islamic studies degree from Syria's Abu Nur University. All of these Muslims of African descent, living in different times and places, have shared a commitment to both learning and public activism.

The idea that Islam could be a vehicle of political self-determination is one deeply rooted in the modern black Atlantic experience and especially in the travel, pilgrimage, and migration of English-speaking black people in West Africa, the Middle East, the Caribbean, North America, and Great Britain during the nineteenth and twentieth centuries. Its most important proponent was Edward Wilmot Blyden, the nineteenth-century Liberian nationalist who argued forcefully that Islam was already and would become an even more powerful moral and political force among Sudanic peoples, or those he called the "Negro race."[2] Like Blyden and the many English-speaking Muslims of African descent who came to articulate his arguments for the efficacious nature of Islam, Mecca2Medina links black political power—sometimes at the national level and sometimes at the local level—to following the *din*, the religion of Islam; *sirat al-mustaqim*, or the straight path; and the Islamic ethical injunctions that separate *haram*, or prohibited human behavior, from *halal*, or permitted human behavior.

This rap signifies the promise and attraction of Islam to many black Londoners, generally born in Great Britain or more often in the Caribbean. But not all Muslims of African descent in the United Kingdom identify with this transatlantic, English-speaking tradition of what might be called black liberation Islam. African-descended Muslim immigrants from Somalia, Nigeria, and other African countries are a growing presence in the United Kingdom. Though united by a commitment to following ethical guidelines outlined in *fiqh*, or Islamic jurisprudence, and to practicing the ritual requirements of prayer and fasting, these Muslims often hold understandings of their racial, ethnic, and national identities that are different from those of Anglophone black Muslims.

Such diversity in just one nation begins to suggest the rich variety of Islamic practice and African diasporic identities among Muslims of African descent in Europe. This chapter first outlines a history of the African Muslim presence in Europe, a history that dates from the Islamic conquest of Spain in 711 C.E. Then it presents three case studies that illuminate local inflections of Islam and transnational connections among Muslims of African descent, not merely in Europe but also with African-descended people across Africa and the Americas—in short, across the black Atlantic world and beyond.

The first case study is that of Mandinga migrants from Guinea-Bissau who have migrated to Lisbon, Portugal. Before departing for Europe, many Mandinga saw their ethnic and religious identities as one and the same; there was little separation between practicing Islamic religion and claiming Mandinga identity. But this situation has changed in Portugal as Mandinga persons have encountered Muslims from other parts of the world. In response, some migrants have sought to reinforce their ethnic identity while others have reinterpreted their religious identity as part of the global *umma*. Two factors, gender identity and mosque participation, have been particularly important in shaping the choices that people have made, as accounts of the "writing-on-the-hand" ritual and funerary practices recounted below will show.

The second case study explores the transnational world of the Murids, a Sufi order founded in Senegal whose members have migrated to cities around the world. In Europe, the largest populations of Murids can be found in Italy and France. For most of them, migration has often deepened connections to their country of origin and to Touba, their holy city, the city of saint Ahmadu Bamba, in Senegal. Through a number of mechanisms, including visits from religious leaders and the use of videos and other forms of media, Murid migrants are able to recreate the experience of Senegal while living in Europe.

The final case study examines African-descended Muslims in the United Kingdom, focusing particularly on Somali migrants, Afro-Caribbean converts, and the phenomenon of Muslim hip-hop. While there are multiple communities of African-descended Muslims in England, many have in common an emphasis on the core principles of Islamic practice, including the five pillars and various aspects of fiqh. Some of them, particularly those born in Great Britain and/or those with Caribbean roots, emphasize the connection to Africa as a mechanism for anticolonial struggle, while others, especially Somali migrants, do not imagine themselves to be connected to an African diaspora.

HISTORY OF AFRICAN MUSLIMS IN EUROPE

The first African Muslims to arrive on the European landmass came as conquerors from Morocco. In 711 the Arab warrior Tariq ibn Ziyad defeated Roderic, king of the Visigoths, at the Barbate River in Spain. African Berbers composed a large part of his army. Rewarded with less productive land in the mountainous regions of Galicia and Cantabria, these transplanted Africans rebelled against the Umayyad leaders of Islamic Spain. The rebellion was put down, but Berbers developed into a powerful community by becoming a professional class of Muslim soldiers. Muslims from North Africa came to play important roles in the creation of a unique European Islamic culture associated with glorious architecture, poetry, philosophy, and science. Supporting Abd al-Rahman I, a relative of one of the Umayyad caliphs from Damascus, Berbers were essential to the Umayyad consolidation of power in what would become known as Andalusia, the civilization that one Christian would call "the ornament of the world." And Berbers were also at the center of the breakdown of centralized political structures in Iberia. Over the next two centuries, as political power devolved to the local level in Islamic Spain, Berbers came to dominate the towns of Toledo and Badajoz, and in Granada they allied with a Jewish clan, the Banu Naghrila, to rule one of Andalusia's most fabled cities. In the eleventh century, military alliances across religious lines became the norm, not the exception. In the north Muslim power generally receded, but in the south there were twenty-odd ministates, supported by alliances among Jews, Christians, and Muslims who were constantly at war with one another. During this period, Christians and Muslims in the south were as likely to be on the same side of a battle as to battle one another.[3]

African Muslims of Berber heritage once again altered the political map of Spain when in 1086 C.E. the Almoravid dynasty, having arrived from Africa only recently, defeated Christian king Alphonso at Zallaqa, also known as Sagrajas. The Almoravids emerged as a major power under the leadership of Yusuf ibn Tashifun. It was Yusuf who crossed the Mediterranean and extended his authority to Spain. Almoravid political suzerainty in Iberia was supported not only by Berber, Arab, and

Iberian troops but also by enslaved soldiers from West Africa. Moreover, the Almoravid presence in Iberia ensured the presence of West African women, who were forced to serve their masters as housemaids and concubines. The Almoravid conquest of southern Iberia was an important turning point in the history of relations between Muslims and Christians in Spain and Portugal. In its aftermath, battle lines were increasingly drawn in religious terms. Armies created by and for Christians sought to eliminate Muslim political power. By 1492 the last Muslim ruler of Iberia was conquered, and Muslims and Jews were officially expelled from the peninsula.[4]

Even though the rise of Christian hegemony in Iberia would mean the marginalization of Africans' contribution to both Portuguese and Spanish culture, Europe was never really sealed off from African Muslim influence. After the Reconquista, African Muslims arrived in Europe, in part because of the expansion of European seafaring power in the fifteenth and sixteenth centuries. The creation of an "Oceanic world" that tied Africa, Europe, the Americas, and Asia together inevitably resulted in some African Muslims arriving on European shores. European domination of this world not only led to increased profits for European merchants and the conquest of the Americas but also to the enslavement of millions of sub-Saharan Africans. More than a million of these Africans were Muslims. Most were sent to the Americas, but some made their way to Europe.[5]

Examining the historical experience of African Muslims in Europe during the Middle Ages and the Renaissance is made more difficult because of the imprecise language used by Europeans of the time to describe Africans. The label "Moor," for example, was employed to refer to a variety of people, sometimes emphasizing their Muslim religious affiliation and sometimes emphasizing their skin color and ethnic origin. While originally used to denote people from the western parts of North Africa (ancient Mauritania), later—based on both ideology and flawed etymology—the term conflated racial identity and religion.[6] According to historian David Northrup, "The imprecision was a product of the fact that in European minds the symbolism of the terms was more important than the reality of individual pigmentation."[7] Likewise, the term *maurus*, meaning "black" in Latin, was tied to the word "Moor," thus equating Moor with black.[8] The result was that, in common parlance, "Moor" could be used to refer to Africans of any sort, both Muslim and non-Muslim, from North Africa and from sub-Saharan Africa. Further, the Castilian word *negro* could also be used to categorize a wide array of people with dark skin, including sub-Saharan people from a wide array of language and ethnic groups; people with sub-Saharan ancestors, whether their immediate origin was Spain, North Africa, or the Americas; and people from India.[9] Enslaved Africans were often given the same name as the slaveholder, making it possible to infer their past religious identities from their European names.[10] Similarly, while Europeans were often categorized according to their religious affiliation, the modes of differentiation for sub-Saharan Africans ignored religion, revolving instead around their slave status and their nature as "barbarian" in contrast to European "civilization."[11]

No matter what religion they were, however, it is clear that Africans were an important part of the European Renaissance and that at least some of them were Muslim.[12] Africans in Renaissance Italy included a man identified only as Thomas who refused for many years to convert to Christianity because of his Muslim faith.[13] "Most blacks in Europe before the fifteenth century may not have been born below the Sahara," Northrup argues, "but came from slave populations born in North Africa whose ancestors had been brought across the desert."[14] Later, from the mid-seventeenth century through the mid-nineteenth century, most Africans in Europe had originally been enslaved in the Americas before being brought to Europe.[15]

Perhaps the best known of these persons in the eighteenth-century Atlantic world was Job Ben Solomon. His memoir, among the earliest English-language slave narratives, provides a glimpse into the life of this renowned figure.[16] Ayuba (or Hyuba), Boon Salumen Jallo (Job, son of Solomon, of the Fulbe tribe; sometimes rendered in English as Ayuba Suleiman Diallo), was born in eastern Senegal around 1701 into an aristocratic and religious family, where he was educated in Arabic and the Qur'an. Like many in the region, he was involved in the slave trade and was himself abducted, enslaved, and transported to North America in 1730.[17] As a slave in Maryland, Job worked on a tobacco plantation. He escaped from slavery, then later was captured, imprisoned, and returned to the plantation, where he wrote a letter to his father in Senegal, asking for his assistance. James Oglethorpe, founder of the colony of Georgia, somehow obtained the letter—probably with the assistance of Thomas Bluett, Job's later biographer—and had it translated into English; Oglethorpe was so impressed by Job's erudition that he purchased his freedom and brought him to England. It appears that Job spent much of the voyage to England learning English, and when he arrived he was sufficiently proficient to hold conversations. Once in England he met King George II, Queen Caroline, and members of the royal family. He impressed the British aristocracy with his prodigious recollection, writing copies of the Qur'an from memory.[18]

Job's religious commitment was admired by those he met in England. He continued his devotions and fasting, and he butchered his own meat so that it would meet halal requirements. Similarly, he refused alcohol when it was offered to him. While he was eager to participate in conversations about religion and read the New Testament in Arabic, he was not interested in converting to Christianity. He argued that the concept of the Trinity was an instance of *shirk*, or associating something with the one God; God was not three, he explained, but only one. Similarly, he argued against the divinity of Jesus, noting that although Jesus was born of a virgin and performed miracles, he was not God. The next year, in 1734, the Royal African Company took Job back to Senegal, where he lived for the next four decades until his death around 1773. His return to Africa seems to have been linked to a desire to build trade networks between England and West Africa rather than because of an opposition to slavery itself.[19]

The trade networks that various European countries had developed with Africa eventually gave way to full-scale colonization in the latter days of the nineteenth century, as England, France, Portugal, Germany, and others engaged in the "scramble for Africa." Ongoing interaction between Europe and Africa began as early as the fifteenth century, with Portuguese exploration of West Africa and later the Atlantic slave trade. While there were some limited European colonies, such as the French colony of Senegal, that began in the seventeenth century, there was not widespread imperialism until 1870.[20] Then, over a few short decades, the whole of Africa was brought under European control.[21]

Industrialization in Europe meant increased demand for raw materials that Africa could provide, and colonial control meant access to both agricultural products, such as palm oil, coffee, and cotton, and mineral resources, including copper, bauxite, iron ore, and more.[22] In addition to economic interests, a number of factors, including "burgeoning scientific interest in the continent; the struggle against the slave trade and consequent discourse regarding the economic and thus political 'modernization' of Africa; the evangelical drive and the interventionism made possible by 'Christian conscience'; and increasingly racially charged interpretations of the nature of African policy, society, and culture," set the context for the rapid colonizing efforts, according to historian Richard J. Reid.[23] By 1887 Portugal, Britain, France, and Germany had colonized some coastal areas of Africa. By 1896 these efforts had extended substantially into the interior of Africa, and Spain and Italy had begun their own colonies. By 1912 the European annexation of Africa was more or less complete, with Belgium joining the other countries.[24] During the two world wars, African colonies provided people and resources to support the European war efforts. Following World War II, Africans began concerted efforts to throw off the colonial powers, and by the late 1960s nearly all African countries had achieved independence, with the few remaining countries not far behind.[25]

Today most black Muslims in Europe either have ties to Europe through past colonial relationships or are refugees seeking asylum from conflict in their home countries. In the sections that follow, I describe several different groups of the European black Muslims, noting both significant differences and similarities in their practice of Islam. I first turn to Mandinga Muslims from Guinea-Bissau who migrated to Portugal, which had colonial control over Guinea-Bissau for much of the nineteenth and twentieth centuries.

MANDINGA MUSLIMS FROM GUINEA-BISSAU IN PORTUGAL

Portuguese ships were traversing the west coast of Africa by the mid-fifteenth century, bringing Africans back to Portugal to work in hospitals, homes, and the court system. As a result, perhaps 10 percent of the Portuguese population in the mid-1500s was from Africa. The conditions of enslaved Africans in Portugal during this period were harsh, leading to the development of Afro-Portuguese religious mutual aid societies and fraternities. Over the following centuries, Portugal laid claim to parts of the African continent as its colonies. For instance, what is now the Republic of Guinea-Bissau became a Portuguese colony, Portuguese Guinea, in the nineteenth century, though parts of the region had been under Portuguese control since the sixteenth century. It achieved independence from Portugal only in 1974. The colonial relationships that Portugal had with Guinea-Bissau, Mozambique, and Angola shape the population of Portugal today. Though today Portugal has relatively few immigrants—only about 1 percent of its overall population of twelve million people—most of the immigrants are from its former colonies in

Africa. The largest number of immigrants, and immigrant Muslims, live in Portugal's capital, Lisbon.[26]

Relatively little scholarship has attended to the experience of African Muslims in Portugal. One notable exception is the work of anthropologist Michelle Johnson, who has written on Mandinga Muslims in Guinea-Bissau and Portugal. As Johnson notes, "Since the introduction of Islam in the Sengambian region centuries ago, Mandinga have conflated ethnicity and Islam, such that to be Mandinga is to be Muslim."[27] That conflation of culture and religion, in which life-course rituals are seen as inevitable and natural—necessary to be Muslim and necessary to be Mandinga—is called into question as migrants encounter Muslims from other parts of the world with their own sets of ritual practices. Suddenly the taken-for-granted is raised to conscious awareness, requiring a response.

While emigrants from Mozambique, most of Indian origin, began arriving in Portugal in the 1950s, the Guinea-Bissauans, who include both those of Indian origin and those with African ancestry, are more recent, most arriving since 1990, with additional migratory pressure caused by the 1998 civil war in Guinea-Bissau. At present there are more than twenty thousand Guinea-Bissauan migrants in Portugal, some portion of whom are Mandinga, who make up 13 percent of the population in Guinea-Bissau. While many of the Muslim emigrants from Guinea-Bissau arrived in Portugal as students and have spent time in the city, the Mandinga often come to Portugal directly from rural areas.[28]

The Mandinga occupy a working-class niche in Lisbon, the men employed, Johnson notes, as "construction workers, musicians, shopkeepers, street merchants, and Muslim healers," known as *mooroo*, while the women do cleaning, run restaurants, or assist with their husbands' healing businesses. Many Mandinga immigrants live in *barracas*, a term that denotes either the dwellings in shantytowns or abandoned apartment complexes in which immigrants sometimes squat. The social life of the Mandinga community revolves around clubs and other organizations, such as Badim Clubo, the Maternal Kin Club, which provides a range of resources for recent migrants, such as providing funds as a rotating credit association, supporting life-cycle rituals, celebrating Muslim holidays, and sponsoring social events. Among the various religious rituals, including ceremonies marking the return of pilgrims from Mecca and initiation ceremonies, are three obligatory rituals through which Mandinga identity is conferred: infant name-taking, circumcision, and the writing-on-the-hand ceremony.[29]

As Mandinga Muslims migrated from Guinea-Bissau to Portugal, they brought their life-cycle rituals with them. The migration process often reinforces religious identity as migrants seek to create a sense of meaning and to define themselves in a new environment in which their religious practices and beliefs are not taken for granted by the surrounding population. While somewhat altered, the rituals performed in Portugal maintain continuity with practices in Guinea-Bissau, and the transnational circulation of migrants means that material culture is accessible in Portugal, as migrants bring with them food and other resources to sell in the marketplace. This is apparent, for example, in the writing-on-the-hand ritual, a practice in which ink is used to write Qur'anic verses on the hands of seven-year-old children as "a permanent stamp of identity as a Mandinga person and of dedication to the global religion of Islam."

After writing *bismillah*, "in the name of God," on the palm of the child, a religious specialist puts a pinch of salt on the palm and directs the initiate to use his or her tongue to imbibe the word of God. The religious specialist then asks the child and all present at the ceremony to repeat each letter of the Arabic alphabet as he or she gazes at the traditional wooden slate on which they are written. Those in attendance give the child money and kola nuts, and the family of the child reciprocates by giving the attendees *munkoo*, rice flour sweetened with honey. Johnson notes that while the ritual is clearly linked to Islam, drawing on Qur'anic verses, it is not a common Muslim practice, limited to the Mandinga and the nearby Jakhanke group. It functions as preparation for Qur'anic study; it "purifies the child by 'opening' the head, 'cooling' the heart and 'steadying' the spirit," as well as by providing pardon for "the child's social transgressions" and connecting the child to his or her angels. Both the salt and the sweetened rice flour serve as potent symbols and are necessary ingredients in the ritual process. The flour is distributed to family and friends at the completion of the ceremony and is understood to "possess magical healing properties." Johnson has noted that the writing-on-the-hand rituals conducted in Portugal are more extravagant than those in Guinea-Bissau, "with 'normative' aspects of the ritual—such as dress, food and capturing the moment through film or photography—taking on exaggerated importance." This may highlight the need among the Mandinga to reinforce their religious and cultural identity in a new context.[30]

The Mandinga also perform a series of funerary rituals following a person's death. In Guinea-Bissau, according to Johnson, female relatives are the first to mourn the departed by engaging in ritual wailing. Then they make munkoo, which will be given to those who attend the gathering after the burial. This transition from wailing to making munkoo is important since it "marks the end of the 'shock' and the beginning of the 'work' (i.e., ritual obligations) associated with death. Indeed, relatives of the deceased may not carry out their daily work routines, engage in friendly conversation, or even offer routine greetings to passersby until they have made the funerary rice flour." The deceased's body is washed by members of the same gender and then dressed in white cloths. A "rite of pardon," in which the person's transgressions are pardoned, "render[s] the heart of the deceased 'light'" and makes it possible for the person to enter paradise. Prayers are offered and the person's body is buried, with the head pointing toward Mecca. Following the burial, an animal is slaughtered and a meal is prepared for all mourners, who are also given meat, munkoo, and kola nuts before leaving. The ritual in Portugal follows a similar format, although the ritual process has undergone some change. For instance, it is difficult to transport large mortars and pestles from Guinea-Bissau to Portugal. The mortars and pestles used in Portugal are much smaller, making the production of large quantities of flour more difficult. Because of this, Maria biscuits, a kind of tea cookie, are substituted for flour. In addition to the shift from rice flour to Maria biscuits, funeral rituals often take place indoors, rather than in the open-air compounds of the deceased person, as in Guinea-Bissau. In Portugal, conducting the ritual indoors puts it beyond the eyes of non-Muslim Portuguese neighbors and adjusts for the cold weather and lack of open courtyards in Portuguese apartment buildings.[31]

If writing-on-the-hand and funeral rites continue in Portugal with relatively few changes, however, the automatic association of Mandinga ethnic identity with Islamic religious identity is challenged more profoundly in the Portuguese context. As Mandinga migrants interact with Muslims from around the world, they negotiate their identities in a new community, one that is sometimes hostile to their presence and often does not see them as part of the broader Muslim community. According to Johnson, "Non-African Muslims and the Portuguese alike categorize Mandinga immigrants in Lisbon as *pretos*, or 'blacks,' rather than as 'Muslims.'"[32] Thus Mandinga migrants in Portugal experience multiple forms of dislocation, both in the mosque and in the marketplace. Their responses to this external racialization of their identities—what I referred to in the introduction as a "thin" notion of blackness—fall along a continuum, with a turn toward strengthening Mandinga traditions on one end and an emphasis on participation in a modern, scripturalist reform Islam on the other. This "modern" Islam questions all tradition based on its reading of the Qur'an and the Sunna as believers seek to discover whether their practice of Islam is sanctioned and authorized by the holy scriptures of Islam.

Responses to this question and the place of Mandinga identity within Islam often shake out along gendered lines, in great part because men dominate the public space of the mosques, just as they do in the southern Jordan Valley and many other Muslim-majority settings. The mosque becomes a site where reformist models of Islam based on original readings of the Qur'an and the hadith flourish under the leadership of a central authority. In addition, gender also plays a role in the refashioning of Muslim Mandinga identity because women appear to face more discrimination in the broader Portuguese Muslim community. For instance, one of Johnson's informants, a Mandinga woman, described her experience at the local mosque: "The Indians think they own the mosque, but the mosque is for all of us, not just for them. They stand at the entrance and ask African women for I.D. One day an Indian asked me to show him [documented] proof of my conversion to Islam. I told him that my ancestors converted to Islam centuries ago and that they didn't keep records back then." As a result, many Mandinga women choose to live out their lives as Muslims not primarily in the context of the local mosque but instead through participation in local community events, informal instruction of their children, and domestic Islamic rituals.[33]

Gendered differences are also visible in the response of men and women to various Mandinga traditions, such as funeral wailing and the use of healers. For instance, the ritual wailing of women following a death is seen, particularly by men, as contrary to "proper" Muslim practice, in which all deaths are understood to be the will of God. Yet even those women who see it as contrary to standard Muslim practice "confessed openly that they regularly wailed at funerals, and they even considered it a social obligation to do so." Similarly, although Mandinga men and women both visit spiritual healers in the Portuguese and Guinea-Bissauan contexts, Johnson found that women visit healers—both Muslim and non-Muslim—more often, while "in general men are more inclined to be critical or skeptical of their powers, asserting their preferences in times of need for 'God and the Qur'an' over intermediaries."[34]

But even those men—and some women—who choose to follow the path of modern, reform Islam must face the question of whether their specifically Mandinga Islamic traditions are to be abandoned altogether. Two of Johnson's informants, Ibrahim and Bacar, both Muslim healers, have differing strategies for addressing the tension that can arise between a reformist Islam and Mandinga life-cycle rituals, particularly the writing-on-the-hand ritual. While both healers participated in Lisbon's central mosque and in Mandinga organizations, Bacar believed that spending time at the mosque was more important, while Ibrahim spent much of his time with Badim Clubo, which is indicative of their differing positions. Ibrahim's experience in Portugal has "only intensified his belief that 'traditional' Mandinga life-course rituals confer simultaneously ethnic and religious identity." He argues that the writing-on-the-hand ritual can be found in the Qur'an and is obligatory (so he too draws on the scripturalist tradition of reform Islam, though to different ends). Johnson notes that Bacar, on the other hand, is in favor of reinterpreting the ritual, explaining it in such a way as to make clear its meaning and significance within the doctrinal boundaries of his more standardized, modern Islam. Bacar notes that the ritual is not mentioned in the Qur'an or the Sunna of the Prophet, so it is not a religious obligation for all Muslims. But Bacar also sees the ritual as valuable for promoting one aspect of Islamic ethics—alcohol avoidance: "It is nearly impossible for people who have had their hands written on to develop an alcohol problem during their lifetime. . . . If you see that someone develops a drinking problem, you will know that this person never had his or her hand written on."[35] For Bacar, this old ritual is too valuable to do away with completely, and so it is reconfigured to serve as a means not to create a particular Mandinga or African identity but as a way to encourage adherence to the alcohol taboo incumbent on all Muslims.

While other groups of Muslims in Europe respond to the experience of migration with a community-wide debate over the place of culture and ethnic difference in their practice of Islam, not all Muslim immigrants and visitors do so. In contrast to many of the Mandinga voices above, most Senegalese Murids seem to embrace a more full-throated marriage between their ethnic and religious identity. They, too, may suffer from antiblack and anti-immigrant sentiment and prejudice, but their response is to use such outsider status and the economic opportunities afforded by residence in Europe to buoy their national and religious commitments. Going to Europe becomes a way to come home to the sacred land of Senegal.

MURIDS: MAKING SENEGALESE HOMELANDS IN EUROPE

While there have been Muslims in Europe for more than a millennium, immigration patterns have shifted dramatically since the second half of the twentieth century, with substantially more migration from sub-Saharan Africa to Europe from the 1950s to the present. Among these migrants have been large numbers from Senegal; for instance, more than fifty thousand Senegalese live in France, and Senegal continues to send more migrants to France than does any other sub-Saharan country. The numbers in Italy are similar, with more than eighty thousand Senegalese migrants now living there.[36] Most people from Senegal are members of one or another Sufi brotherhood, and many of those who have migrated to Europe are members of the Muridiyya, or the Murid Sufi order. While this Sufi group, with more than three million members worldwide, is not the only order with a substantial presence in Europe (there are substantial Tijani communities in Italy and elsewhere, for instance), its members are by far the most widely studied.[37] Most of the research has centered on cities in Italy and France, although there are Murid communities in Belgium and other places on the European landmass.

The migration of Murids from Senegal to Europe is linked to substantial changes in the Senegalese economy over the past century. While groundnut production had provided two-thirds of the crop export total in the 1960s, it had declined to only one-fifth by 1990, in great part a result of severe droughts.[38] Accompanying this decline was a rapid increase in foreign debt—fifteen times higher in 1984 than in 1970 and ending the 1980s at a level much higher than that of other sub-Saharan countries—which in turn resulted in a structural adjustment program imposed by the International Monetary Fund.[39] The accompanying reduction in spending and decreased social services has made life more difficult for many in Senegal. Since the groundnut economy collapsed, many families send one of their male members to Europe to work and provide support for the family back home in Senegal.[40] After a few years, that person generally returns to Senegal and is replaced by another younger male in the family.[41]

The organization of the Murid Sufi order had been linked to the groundnut economy, so it has been undergoing a parallel set of changes. The Murid group was founded in Africa by a sub-Saharan African Muslim, Cheikh (Shaykh) Ahmadu Bamba.[42] The Murid community, like many Sufi orders, is organized around the central relationship between the marabout, or teacher (also known as the shaykh or pir), and the *talibs*, meaning students or disciples, also known as *murids*. The relationship between the two is mutual, although not equal. In the Murid order, the talib's obligation is to provide both physical and spiritual work on behalf of the marabout, originally in the peanut fields and now in cities around the world. In exchange, the marabout provides *baraka* (blessings, or spiritual power) as well as practical assistance on a range of problems, both personal and economic.

Historically speaking, the students participated in *daaras*, religious communities that included weekly meetings in which the talibs would provide physical labor, cultivating the marabout's groundnut fields, as well as spiritual labor, praying and reciting Bamba's *qasa'ids*, or poems. As the agricultural economy declined, Murids moved first from their rural villages to Dakar and other cities in Senegal, then, over time, to Turin, Paris, and beyond.[43] As the community moved, some of its religious institutions changed as well. The rural *daaras* were replaced in the cities by *dahira*, or religious circles, where people come together to pray, converse, and recite qasa'ids.[44] Among their various activities, the dahiras, which are often centered on a particular marabout to whom the participants are attached, collect donations from the members, using those funds for gatherings and feasts (and for supporting the needs of group members), as well as for the marabout and for development projects in Senegal, particularly in Touba, the Murids' holy city. As the structural adjustment program led to decreased social services, the Murids and other philanthropic organizations began to address those needs.[45] For example, Murid migrants provided the funding to build the largest hospital in Senegal, provided electrical service to a number of villages, and built and renovated schools, among other projects.[46]

In addition to meeting some of the material needs of their families and communities, Senegalese Murids also experience their migration as a religious pilgrimage. After clashing with the French colonial government through peaceful resistance to colonialism, Ahmadu Bamba, the founder of the Murids, was forced into exile, first in Gabon and later in Mauritania. This exile has become an important part of the Murid imaginary, shaping the self-understanding of Murid migrants in Europe and elsewhere as they emulate the experience of their spiritual leader. Just as Bamba was exiled by the French authorities, so they too suffer their own economic exile, traveling to Europe to provide support for their families and their community. As Sylviane Diouf puts it, "The *talibs* (disciples) must relive the pain of the Shaykh by going through their own exile."⁴⁷ Murids take pride in Bamba not just as a Muslim but as an African Muslim, and through the ongoing conversations about Bamba and his sufferings in exile, Mayke Kaag argues, "their feelings of pride and dignity are continuously nourished."⁴⁸

As Senegalese Murids no longer engaged in peanut cultivation but rather sought out entrepreneurial opportunities in cities around the world, they have retained close ties to their African homeland, often much closer than other migrants; compared to other groups, more expect to return permanently to their home country.⁴⁹ Rebecca Sheff notes that "all the Mouride transmigrants I interviewed, without exception, expressed aspirations to return permanently to Senegal. Several were in the process of constructing houses in Touba in anticipation of their retirement."⁵⁰

Yet Senegal exists not only in a hoped-for future; it is recreated and made present in the lives of migrants every day. The religious and cultural lives of Senegalese migrants in Europe parallel their experience in Senegal. Bruno Riccio describes a campsite frequented by Senegalese migrants near Rimini, Italy, noting the way that the "memory of Senegal" is suffused through the community: "Minor marabouts come around to visit and gain some economic support in exchange for blessings and suggestions. Old griots, once very famous in Senegal, come for a week to perform their show and to sing about other people's lives in exchange for money. The culture of exchange (with its rights and duties) overlaps with the outside culture of the market exactly as in Senegal."⁵¹ Donald Carter, in turn, describes the use of material culture in the dahiras: "The spaces of Touba are re-created in the Da'ira, which are held in the rooms of the Senegalese in Turin: through the placement of photographs of the *Serin* [the Shaykh, Ahmadu Bamba] in the houses and on the pins that are worn daily (an innovation resembling the pins of Italian political parties); in the drinking of the tea and the turning of the tea cup three times before handing it to the consumer of the tea; in eating Senegalese foods ('We eat in the African way all together from the same pan'); and extending hospitality to others."⁵² The ritual practices and material culture of the Murids enable them to experience Senegal in their everyday lives.

The relationship between marabouts and talibs is central to the Murid tradition. In response to the material offerings of the talibs, the marabouts assist their students with a range of life problems. In Europe, marabouts often provide assistance with the myriad day-to-day struggles of surviving in a new culture, whether that involves finding a place to live, obtaining a job, or negotiating a new relationship.⁵³ While there are marabouts in European cities, Murid migrants often remain connected to marabouts in Senegal, and these men travel to meet with their followers.⁵⁴ Visits from the more noted marabouts, such as descendants of Ahmadu Bamba, can be celebrated events. Vendors sell clothes, cassette tapes, and pictures of Ahmadu Bamba, both before and after such events. When the marabout arrives, there can be hushed silence. Bruno Riccio describes one such event, when Shaykh Murtada, the son of Ahmadu Bamba, visited Italy, observing that as silence filled the hall where the marabout was visiting, "everyone knelt down at the sides." Greetings and offerings were made to the Sufi master, who in turn gave his blessings to the congregation. "There were moments of silent prayer at the end of which every believer lifted his hands to his face. These were the times when everyone was receiving baraka [blessings]."⁵⁵

The marabouts' presence is not the only way that they provide a connection to Senegal. Various religious items—photos, leatherwork, amulets, and so on—have become increasingly important as the direct physical experience of Senegal must be mediated for migrants. Among the religious items are gris-gris, or amulets, that provide protection for the wearer. They are often made by the marabouts in Senegal to protect migrants in Europe.⁵⁶ In addition, images of Bamba or of the Khalifa General, the leader who governs in his stead, often adorn cars and homes.⁵⁷

More than many other diasporic African Muslims, then, the Senegalese Murids have an interconnected network of relationships and practices that pull them back toward a national homeland, Senegal, and particularly to Touba, their spiritual center. DVDs available for sale in communities worldwide recall the annual pilgrimage to Touba. Books, pictures, and music serve as devotional material to be discussed in the dahira. Online radio stations broadcast news and religious content available to all with Internet access. Marabouts travel to visit their talibs wherever they might live. Migrants travel back and forth, circulating both material goods and religious culture. And remittances from migrants travel back to Touba to rebuild the city and maintain connections to migrant communities.⁵⁸

The holy city of Touba plays a central role in the life of the Murids. Riccio quotes Bara Lo, a blacksmith who has lived in Touba his whole life: "Touba is a peculiar place, it is above all a holy city and must be an example for the rest of the world. It is the Mecca of West Africa, all good things must converge on Touba."⁵⁹ While Murid migrants live their lives far from Touba, they remain deeply connected to it through religious material culture and through the annual pilgrimage to Touba, which, according to Carter, has among the Murids "eclipse[d]" the Meccan pilgrimage.⁶⁰ Whether or not that is true, Touba is constructed, both physically and spiritually, as the earthly center of their particular Africana Muslim diaspora.

Various forms of religious media provide a connection to Senegal and to the holy city of Touba. For instance, Radio Lamp Fall FM, named after Shaykh Ibrahima Fall, broadcasts from Senegal, but Murid communities worldwide listen to it, particularly to *Pinthie des émigrés*, a call-in show specifically aimed at migrants.⁶¹ Most important, however, among the religious devotional media are videotapes and DVDs of the Maggal, the annual pilgrimage to Touba. The use of this media parallels the ubiquitous broadcast of the pilgrimage to Mecca on satellite television stations around the world. The video presentations of the Maggal often follow a stylized format, as Beth Buggenhagen notes. The videos often begin with images of Bamba near the mosque in Touba, followed by an image of the Khalifa General. Near Touba's main mosque, believers are "dressed in new, stiffly starched Muslim boubous made of locally dyed brocade cloth known as bazin riche." *Dhikr*, the religious litanies recited by all Sufi practitioners but which differ in form from group to group, are sung "by accomplished Murid griots." Males and females, in gender-segregated groups, approach the tomb of the saint and throw "offerings over the railing surrounding it." Images of the pilgrimage on TV also feature "the prayerful masses filling the streets, and long lines of dignitaries greeting the shaykhs . . . [and] aerial shots of Tuba [Touba], most likely taken from one of the minarets of the mosque, in which one can see the radial plan of the streets of Tuba emanating from the mosque and view the crowd below."⁶² In addition to showing the pilgrimage itself, the videos also demonstrate the effect of the talibs' remittances on the city of Touba, as viewers see the hospital, electricity and water systems, and offerings of food, all made possible by the migrants' monetary commitment to the holy city.

These video presentations are more than educational; they are part of a religious discipline. Moreover, the videos are not simply "watched"; they are experienced as part of religious practice. Buggenhagen explains, "When watching or listening to these programs, disciples often sit on prayer mats, work prayer beads, sway their bodies to and fro, and add commentary in Wolof and Arabic such as bisimilahi (thanks to God), bilay (truthfully), and wow wow (yes)." The videotapes, experienced as a religious practice, are a mechanism for making Touba present to migrants thousands of miles away: "Disciples viewing Maggal videocassettes describe them as transporting; they take the viewer back to Tuba within the realm of the Sufi masters and ultimately the divine."[63] The videos, along with the amulets, religious images, and other elements of religious material culture, pull the migrants back to Africa, reinforcing and rebuilding a deep spiritual connection.

While the Senegalese Murids reconnect with Africa by experiencing the Maggal on DVD, they continue to live in Europe and interact with European society. The relationship between the Murids and the European host communities is complicated by the hosts' deployment of racist stereotypes. Black African Muslims are often perceived through the lens of "African" or "migrant" stereotypes rather than through the lens of "Muslim" stereotypes.[64] As one Senegalese migrant in Milan noted, "As I am black, it's extremely difficult to get work in a bar. I have gone along to so many interviews. Sometimes they have told me that if I were a little fairer then I would have been suitable."[65] They are also marginalized, Diouf argues, by the rest of the French Muslim community; as noted earlier, that experience of marginalization among other Muslims is shared by the Guinea-Bissauan migrants in Lisbon.[66]

Members of the Senegalese Murid migrant community have differing approaches to their host community and differing life strategies for addressing their experience in a new culture and locale. The community itself is diverse, including traders and street sellers, students and intellectuals, and marabouts. Kaag, Riccio, and Giulia Sinatti all note a tension among these groups, particularly between formerly rural street sellers and urban intellectuals, as they have different visions of Islam. Sinatti divides the Senegalese community between what she calls "locals" and "cosmopolitans." While the first wave of immigration was of Murid rural folk, more recent immigration has included "younger urban elites," often from other Sufi brotherhoods. The locals are "trying to reproduce the time-space of origin in the country of immigration out of a spirit of self-conservation." In contrast, the cosmopolitans "prefer recognition in a shared nomadic condition as their distinctive feature."[67]

Riccio notes a similar tension. He argues that the rural group, known as *modou modou*, is less open to the host society, while the urban group is more interested in "outward movement." He notes that "among street peddlers or workers from a rural background, there is a widespread mistrust of the 'intellectuals.'" Importantly, Riccio notes that these divisions are not without exception and that the two groups often work together toward a mediating position.⁶⁸ Using different means, both groups attempt to maintain a connection to Senegal. Shaykh Murtada's son, on a recent visit to Italy, highlighted the importance of both approaches, as Kaag points out: "In his sermon he encouraged the Mourides gathered not to isolate themselves from Italian society, but to work together and to give a good example of how to behave. In addition, he stressed that one should not forget one's own group, because unity is power."⁶⁹

The ongoing circulation of people, resources, and information within the Murid community ensures a deep connection with Africa, and with Touba in particular. Sinatti argues, in fact, that migration deepens the connection many Senegalese have to their African identity: "In the absence of opportunities at home, they have discovered migration as a way of ensuring they can remain Senegalese." She continues, "During numerous informal conversations, for instance, I observed how people 'travel' to their homeland revitalising and reconstructing their memory of places through the accounts of who has last been there."⁷⁰ Other scholars echo this point, arguing that the visits of the marabouts, the recollection of the Maggal, and the practices of the dahira serve to make the diasporic experience one not only of moving away but also of coming home. As Buggenhagen writes, "For Murid men and women, travel may take them further from their life in Senegal, but it brings them closer to their spiritual master, not only Bamba, but also their present-day shaykhs in Tuba, and thus, closer to God."⁷¹

For the Senegalese Murids, Senegal, and particularly Touba, remains their spiritual home. Moving to cities in Europe, North America, and other locales has been an essential element in forming that connection to their homeland and to their specific religious practices and culture. While associating with and claiming membership in the umma, the global community of Muslims, the Murids follow a path toward God through the teachings of their saint. Like most Sufi followers all over the world, no matter what their particular Sufi brotherhood or order, it is only through the knowledge and experience of their shaykhs, in this case called marabouts, that the meaning and significance of the Qur'an and the Sunna can be realized. Murids imagine their diaspora to be tied not to Africa in general but to Senegal and the transnational Murid community in particular. Generally speaking, their diaspora does not seem to be a tortured separation from their origins or their true selves but rather a necessary journey, both spiritual and economic, toward home. Racism and its ties to African slavery may shape how Murids are perceived in Europe and beyond, and they may experience the sting of discrimination, but racism does not seem to force a wholesale questioning of their mission or a reconfiguration of their faith, which sees Africa, the place of origin, not as a deficit but as a blessing.

In order to meet a group of black European Muslims who embrace an African diasporic identity while also regarding the experience of slavery and forced dispersion as central to their Muslim identities, the final section of the chapter travels across the English Channel to the United Kingdom. But there, along with African-descended Muslims who link their practice of Islam explicitly to an African diasporic identity and an antiracist agenda, one can also find Muslims from the African continent who do not consider themselves black or African at all.

MUSLIMS IN THE UNITED KINGDOM

African-descended British Muslims are highly diverse. Some are recent migrants from West Africa; others are recent migrants from East Africa; still others were born and raised as Muslims in England; and some grew up Christian and are recent converts (or "reverts," as new Muslims in Britain often put it). Most black British Muslims are Sunni, though there are some Shiʻa Muslims. Some are also members of Sufi orders; for instance, some West African migrants are members of the Tijani brotherhood.[72]

Muslims have been present in Great Britain since at least the seventeenth century, though encounters likely began much earlier. Similarly, there were African-descended people in Britain from at least the mid-seventeenth century, as Britain participated in the Atlantic slave trade: "Slaves landed in Britain, escaped in Britain, were bought and sold in Britain, were advertised, auctioned and examined in Britain."[73] Membership in these two communities—Muslims and black enslaved people—certainly overlapped in England, as it did in the Americas. By the end of the eighteenth century, there were likely between five thousand and twenty thousand African-descended people in London, many of them Muslim.[74] In the centuries since then, various groups of African-descended Muslims, particularly those from British colonies, though also from other parts of the world, have taken up residence in the British Isles. More recently a number of black Britons have converted to

Islam, further enlarging the black Muslim community. By 2010 there were nearly three million Muslims in the UK, served by more than six hundred mosques.[75] More than two-thirds of Muslims in the UK are from the Indian subcontinent, with most others from North Africa and the Middle East. Thus, those from sub-Saharan Africa and those with African-Caribbean ancestors make up a relatively small portion of the overall population.[76]

Among the significant groups in the highly diverse British community of African-descended Muslims are Nigerians, Somalis, and those from the Caribbean, particularly Jamaica. Great Britain has a colonial history with both Nigeria and Somalia; Nigeria was a British Protectorate during much of the twentieth century, and a portion of Somalia was under British control from the late nineteenth century into the twentieth. Similarly, England controlled Jamaica for several centuries. African-Caribbean people began arriving in England in sizable numbers since the late 1940s.[77] While most members of that community are Christian, more recently there have been an increasing number of converts.[78]

Since the 1980s there have also been increasing numbers of Nigerians migrating to the UK. Data from the 2001 census suggests that in the UK there are perhaps fourteen thousand Nigerian Muslims, just less than 10 percent of the total Nigerian population in England.[79] The Somali community, in contrast, is much larger and has a long history, beginning with Somali sailors, part of the British Merchant Navy, who settled in England at the end of the nineteenth century.[80] Since the late 1980s their numbers have swelled as refugees have arrived, fleeing the ongoing conflict in Somalia. Currently there are perhaps one hundred thousand Somalis in Great Britain. Nearly 90 percent of Somali migrants in the UK are Muslim, primarily Sunni; the Nigerian Muslim migrants are also mostly Sunni.[81] There have also been a growing number of conversions among black prisoners in England. Over the past fifteen years, the number of Muslim prisoners has increased substantially, and there are proportionally more black Muslim prisoners than their numbers in the broader British population.[82] More than 80 percent of Somali and Nigerian Muslims, as well as most African-Caribbean and other black converts, live in the greater London metropolitan area.[83]

Muslim groups popular among African Americans in the United States have also made some inroads among black Britons. The Nation of Islam has a small presence in the United Kingdom, numbering in the thousands, though its influence, particularly through the figure of Malcolm

X, is larger than its numbers. Malcolm X visited England during the last few weeks of his life, giving speeches and interviews and stirring some interest in Islam, particularly among African-Caribbean Britons. The Nation also sent representatives to the UK, though Minister Louis Farrakhan has been prohibited by the British government from visiting, a ban that remains in place today. More recently the release of Spike Lee's film *Malcolm X* reinvigorated a new generation of black British Muslims. There have also been efforts in England by W. D. Mohammed, who took over the original Nation of Islam following the death of his father, Elijah Muhammad. In the 1990s he sent a representative to engage in prison ministries, particularly among African-Caribbean inmates. Mohammed's efforts led to the first *masjid*, or mosque, in the British prison system, which opened in 1998 at Holloway Prison.[84]

Despite such diversity, there are some shared religious characteristics among these communities: the practice of Islam more often than not includes an acknowledgment of the universality of the five pillars and of basic ethical guidelines—seeking to follow the straight path, the *sirat al-mustaqim*. For instance, many black converts whom author Richard Reddie interviewed, most of whom are African-Caribbean, see their Muslim identity and practice revolving around the five pillars, changes in dress (such as wearing a *kufi* and *thobe*), halal food requirements (particularly not eating pork or drinking alcohol), changing one's name, and engaging in forms of piety such as reading the Qur'an and listening to Muslim clerics. Reddie notes that after his conversion a man named Jamal wore "simple Islamic clothing," no longer smoked marijuana, and stopped eating pork. Hakim, in turn, stopped eating pork, grew a beard without a mustache, began carrying a Qur'an, and, instead of going to church with his parents, "prefer[red] to spend his time watching DVDs of Islamic clerics." Maryam stopped wearing clothes that are "short and tight" and was "saving herself for a 'good Muslim husband.'" Abdul stopped going to dances, instead spending his time praying and reading the Qur'an.[85]

Idris, a Tanzanian migrant Muslim convert, also emphasized the ethical impulse that was central to his understanding of Islam: "Islam is about how you lead your life, how to live. Islam shows you there is a meaning to life, only to worship Allah. We pray five times a day. Islam gives you time to focus on the divine and not just on your own pleasure. It helps you understand that it is not all about you. One thing is that people who have just come to the religion recently need to learn about it, they need to read and study."[86] In the opening lyrics of "Like a Soldier,"

Muslim Belal, a convert to Islam and noted British Muslim hip-hop artist, emphasizes the five pillars:

> Like a soldier, Imma stand up and pray to my Lord.
> Like a soldier, Imma fast my thirty days for my Lord.
> Like a solider, calculate zakat and pay for my Lord.[87]

A 2010 report by the chief inspector of prisons noted a set of concerns among Muslim prisoners that echoed this emphasis: "Muslim prisoners were extremely consistent in the factors they felt were most important to them as Muslims. Halal food, facilities to pray and access to the mosque for Friday prayers, and ablution facilities were named by most interviewees."[88]

For Somali migrants, arriving in England often provides the opportunity to reflect on one's religious practice and requires deciding how to live out one's Muslim identity, according to scholar and activist Rima Berns-McGown. For example, one informant named Ali told Berns-McGown that he understood Islam to focus on a specific set of moral precepts, such as avoiding alcohol and adhering to strict gender segregation, with a prohibition on men touching women: "The hand-shaking is actually a big thing, because it is a test to many people, something that keeps coming back. . . . Sometimes it feels like you're the only person in the world not doing those things." Similarly, Abdurahman's religious practice revolves around the five pillars and specific moral behaviors: "He prays, fasts, and attends the Tottenham Court mosque once a week and sometimes on Sundays. He is careful not to consume pork products and chews *qat*—a plant that has long been used as a stimulant in the Arabian Peninsula and the Horn of Africa—once a week or so with friends, 'but not everyday like some people do.'"[89]

The women that Berns-McGown spoke with were actively constructing a set of Muslim practices by drawing on the Qur'an and hadith and applying them in their own cultural context. For instance, she notes that once arriving in the UK, many Somali women choose to wear the hijab or *jilbab* as "a sign of their Muslim identity and of their increased adherence to their religion," often because they feel they have an "increased understanding of the Qur'an and hadiths, which gives women the sense they can make decisions about their lives based in part on their own understanding of religious teachings." Other women face pressure from within the Somali community to wear the hijab. For many migrants there is renewed interest in studying the Qur'an. Islam becomes the centerpiece of many Somali migrants' identity in the British context. Yet these decisions occur in a place where Muslims are the minority, which also has an effect on people's religious behavior. For instance, Hibaq, one of Berns-McGown's informants, "always takes off her hijab off when she goes for job interviews, because, she said, she knows that if she wears it people will see nothing but the scarf. Once she has the job, she will work for a week or so and then begin to wear the scarf. . . . 'Sometimes you have to compromise,' she said, adding that, for the same reason, she and her husband have taken a mortgage, something that some Muslims will not do. 'Otherwise I would not have my own house.'"[90]

For young people, the question of religious practice is even more pointed, as they are facing multiple socializing forces—the British public school system, their peers, their families, mass media, Qur'an schools, and so on. Berns-McGown found that young Somalis in the UK were not abandoning Islam, but they were practicing Islam in ways that made sense to them, not necessarily following the dictates of their parents. For instance, Layla no longer prays or wears a hijab, unlike in her childhood when her mother required it. On the other hand, she explains, "I should wear it when I mean it, when I'm up to it, when I'm ready. I want to go back to it one day, but I'm not ready now." Berns-McGown says that Layla "still fasts on Ramadan and eats halal meat when she can. She will eat chicken sandwiches at McDonald's, but 'I don't eat and I never will eat pork stuff!'" The way that "being Muslim" is defined as "moral practice" is also visible in Mubarak's comments: "'I don't go to parties except birthday parties or weddings. It's against my religion.'"[91]

Black British Muslim parents, like parents everywhere, seek to inculcate in their children their own values in the face of multiple socializing forces. In this case, participation in the five pillars and behavioral mandates is supported by both formal religious communities and material culture. In order to provide an adequate religious education for their children, many Somali parents seek out Qur'anic schooling. Because Qur'anic education is not integrated into the British public school system, other strategies for addressing this need must be found through education, whether provided at mosques, in private homes, or with a tutor.[92] In addition, there are a number of shops in London that cater to the spiritual needs of new Muslims, providing videos, CDs, books, and so on. Members of the Nation of Islam in England, like the Senegalese Murids, also depend on tapes and web transmissions to support their religious practice, which often includes listening to the weekly broadcasts of Minister Louis Farrakhan.[93]

Mosques play an important role in the lives of many black British Muslims. While there are many multiethnic mosques in the greater London area, there are also many that tend to attract particular groups. There are several mosques, such as Old Kent Road Mosque and the mosque at Kennington Road in London, that are predominantly Nigerian, but many Nigerian Muslims pray at whichever mosque is most geographically convenient. Similarly, many Somali migrants pray at mosques whose membership is predominantly South Asian, but there are several mosques, such as the Al-Huda Mosque in Tower Hamlets, that were started to meet the needs of the Somali community in particular.[94] For recent converts, mosques serve as much more than simply a place to pray, providing religious education and support for those facing substance abuse or psychological problems and addressing other social needs.[95] Mosques also function in a variety of ways in the lives of Somali migrants, "playing an important role as information-sharing networks and receiving news about 'home'" as well as providing an opportunity for community socializing.[96]

The question about whether to become more fully part of the broader culture or to retreat into one's ethnic or religious enclave is a question that emerges in most migration contexts. A number of African migrants indicate that the British reserve they have experienced since their arrival makes it easier to keep themselves separate. The Change Institute, which examined the experience of a number of minority Muslim communities in England, describes a phenomenon that parallels the experience of the Mandinga in Portugal: "The increased hostility and negative representations of Muslims following [9/11] has led some to recoil into the shell of Muslim identity as one person put it, or it has led others to more positively identify themselves as part of the global ummah."[97] The same two choices emerge here as elsewhere: reinforce ethnic identity, on the one hand, or reinforce a generalized religious identity, on the other.

One Somali respondent in the Change Institute study noted, "People generally feel less warmth and more formality in their social relationships in the UK. The culture is so much different from what they experienced at home. This makes the community inward looking and closed in on itself."[98] One of Berns-McGown's informants made a similar point: "The conservatism of this country is probably good because it helps us keep our culture. If the neighbours and other people were friendly, there would be more cultural interaction, so the unfriendliness is good for our culture." Some black Muslims seek to remain separate, which "might include defining what jobs may or may not be taken, what restaurants may be eaten in, and where food may be bought. It would include being vigilant about each and every activity of the day. A taxi driver would need to learn how to explain to an obviously liquor-toting client that he cannot transport him or her."[99] Others, such as Hibaq, who chooses to remove her hijab for job interviews, seek to negotiate with British culture, though not at the expense of their Muslim identity.

Thus, to retain one's Muslim identity for Somali Muslims in England is often—though certainly not always—to avoid the corrupting influence of the surrounding culture. For African-Caribbean converts and for Somali migrants alike, then, to be Muslim is also to live a certain kind of countercultural life. But Somali Muslims in London have not seen themselves as sharing the same culture, interests, or origins of other African-descended Britons. The case of Somali migrants is shaped by their understanding of their own identity in relationship to the continent of Africa. Most Somalis, for instance, do not view themselves as "African." Instead they trace their ancestry to the Arab world, which they do not see as part of Africa, even though more Arabs live in North Africa than in the Middle East. Somalis, as Berns-McGown explains, "are black but do not identify themselves with sub-Saharan Africans or their Caribbean or North American descendants." In light of this, they do not turn back to Africa as they reconstitute their identity in a new European context. Instead they connect themselves to Islam conceptualized, as described earlier, as a universal set of defined rituals and behaviors.[100]

In contrast, many African-Caribbean Muslims feel connected to Africa, though not because of their immediate migratory context. Instead they see themselves connected through the long history of Atlantic slavery to Africa by way of the Caribbean. This can be seen in the description that Muneera Rashida, one of the members of the British Muslim hip-hop group Poetic Pilgrimage, provides in an interview: "I'm British; I'm also Jamaican. I find strength in my Caribbean roots, especially looking back historically at the people who were taken to the Caribbean, one in three of them were Muslim."[101] For her, both her religious and ethnic identity are linked back to the Caribbean. Sukina Abdul Noor, her partner in Poetic Pilgrimage, completes the circuit, explaining, "The spirit of resistance that you hear in our music is born out of the legacy of the African enslaved people in the Americas and our fight for freedom

African Muslims in Europe 79

through music."[102] Here the connection to Africa by way of enslavement in the Americas becomes visible. Aisha Joseph, one of Reddie's informants and a black Muslim convert, connects her own conversion to her African roots: "All we are doing is going back to our roots. You read African history . . . and you'll see that centuries ago our women were dressed like this," she said, motioning to her attire.[103]

As the comments from the members of Poetic Pilgrimage make clear, the question of African diasporic identity is visible in the burgeoning black Muslim hip-hop community in the UK. The influence of this community is growing within the broader Muslim community, despite differing understandings of the acceptability of music, from complete prohibition of "musical singing" to "those who allow for all the array of musical expressions."[104] For instance, every year the Muslim Council of Britain holds a public event to celebrate the Muslim holiday of 'Id al-Fitr. This gathering generally features hip-hop artists.[105] These artists frequently allude to Africa as the "motherland" and to black identity and black consciousness in a racist society. Mecca2Medina, whose members are converts to Islam, speak explicitly about the role of Africa in the song "Descendants of Bilal," whose lyrics serve as the epigraph for this chapter. Rakin Niass, Mecca2Medina's founding member, explains the way that he was influenced by KRS-One. Hip-hop, he says, "was about empowering black people, about exploring African history and the true story of slavery—stuff that wasn't being taught in schools."[106] Mohammed Yahya, a Mozambican migrant and member of Blind Alphabetz, has described being influenced by both U.S. hip-hop and African music. As he told an interviewer, "To see rappers like Public Enemy, who were not only black but celebrating their blackness by wearing African colours and pendants, that was very affecting and empowering for me."[107] The group's song "African Rhythms" discusses Africa as the motherland.[108] Muslim Belal, a Jamaican convert in the UK, also speaks of Africa as the motherland in "I Can See Clearly."[109]

In addition to harking back to Africa, the lyrics of British Muslim hip-hop crews often emphasize a critique of both racism in the British context and the long history of European colonialism and neocolonialism. Interestingly, it appears that among Muslim youth, markers of black identity are serving as an overarching identity through the production and consumption of hip-hop culture. This claiming of blackness among Muslim hip-hop artists is often accompanied by a claiming of Africa. Again and again, among black Muslim hip-hop artists, Africa serves as a touch-point, both as a site of sustenance and as a site of European exploitation. That emphasis on Africa extends even beyond African-descended artists to other UK hip-hop groups.[110] For instance, Fun-Da-Mental is one of the earliest Muslim hip-hop groups in the UK, and most of its members are South Asian (they have been called the "Asian Public Enemy"). The title of their song "Mother Africa Feeding Sista India" highlights Africa as a rich resource. Their song "English Breakfast," on the other hand, is a scathing critique of British imperialism, in Africa and elsewhere, ending with these biting lines:

> Out of Europe whence they came
> Demons and devils in a land of gods
> Hunting the prize like hungry dogs
> In the British museum is where you can see 'em
> The bones of African human beings.[111]

Hip-hop serves, as these lyrics make clear, not only to provide a sense of cultural identity but also as a vehicle for and part of political liberation and postcolonial justice. This platform is attractive both to African-descended and South Asian Muslim youth, as it enables them to engage in a struggle for a better social position in London, even though they may have no Africa to go back to. Instead they have a campaign against local racism that can be waged by reference to an African past and by tying the local struggles to the global anticolonial struggle.

CONCLUSION

This analysis of African-descended Muslims in Europe makes visible the diversity of Islamic practice in the African diaspora. Within that diversity, there are communities of people seeking to practice Islam in places where they are surrounded by people who often differ from them in religion, culture, and ethnicity. In many cases, the migration or conversion process reinforces religious identity, as migrants or new converts seek to define themselves in a context in which their religious practices and beliefs are in the minority. This is the case with recent Mandinga migrants as they reflect on their ritual practices in Lisbon and with African-Caribbean converts as they interact with their Christian families in London. Some seek to reinforce their Islamic particularity, separating themselves from both the broader culture and from other Muslims. They continue to engage in the practices with which they were socialized in their homelands, seeing them as the authentic version of their Islamic commitments. Others seek to distance themselves from ethnic-specific practices, moving toward participation in what they understand to be a more standard, universal, and often reform-minded Islam. There are a number of factors that shape their choices. Women and men often see their participation differently, as in the case of the Mandinga in Portugal. First-generation migrants and their children often understand their identity differently, as in the case of Somalis in London. Rural migrants and highly educated urban migrants often relate to their host societies in differing ways, as in the case of the Murid community. And those who grow up in a Muslim context often differ from those who convert to Islam as adults, as we see with African-Caribbeans in England.

Black Muslims in Europe also map their African diasporic identities in a variety of ways. In the case studies discussed above, there is little exploration of religious interpretations of the diaspora—that is, of diasporic identities and practices that cast the dispersion or fracturing of black people in metaphysical and spiritual terms. While future research may reveal a stronger role for the metaphysical experience, much of the scholarly literature now available on black Muslims in Europe nevertheless provides a rich portrait of African diasporic identities. For some Muslims of Somali descent, Africa holds little meaning. Reminiscent of African-descended Muslims in the Jordan Valley, Africa does not say anything to these Muslims about their religion, which is Islam, nor about their ethnic identity, which is Arab. Their Islam seems to grant no special meaning to the African continent, black suffering, or black saints, and their diaspora, one caused partly by the trauma of a long-running civil war, seems focused for many on what is going on "at home," that is, in Somalia. Other black Muslims, like the Senegalese Murids, remain closely tied to their ancestral homeland but also see it as a religious and spiritual home that they remember through embodied Islamic practices. Their version of Sunni Islam includes a special role for their Senegalese saint and the transnational networks of Murid followers devoted to his memory and teachings. Their diaspora is national and religious, not racial. Contrariwise, African-descended Muslim Europeans, like African-Caribbean hip-hop artists in London, see all of Africa as a symbol of global black identity and of the anticolonial struggle, a struggle that is of the same cloth as their own local battle against racism. For them Islam is a religion of justice and liberation tied inextricably to liberation from slavery and neocolonialism in Africa in particular and in the postcolonial world in general. The diaspora of these black Muslims stakes out territory not in a particular African nation or even in the continent itself but instead in the global dispersion of black African people. This is a lateral, racial diaspora linked by a shared experience of suffering and the will to overcome the pernicious consequences of racism.

Sidi Malang Mohamad holds a *malunga*, or African bow, as he utters a prayer and blesses a woman with the *orhni*, or veil, of Saint Mai Mishra during his *basti*, or mendicant rounds. Kapalsadi village, Bharuch district, Gujarat, India, February 2004. Production still © 2004 Amy Catlin-Jairazbhoy from the *Sidi Malunga Project* DVD (Apsara Media, 2004).

4

SIDDIS AND HABSHIS IN SOUTH ASIA

Shrines of the African Saints and Life-Cycle Rituals in the Village

> Bava took from the ocean, from the sea,
> And gave to the wise men and friends of Allah
> It is joy/waves from the ocean
> A gift of waves/ecstasy.
> —Gujarati *dhikr*[1]

Sufi Muslims of African descent in Gujarat, a state in western India, are known for their abilities to perform *dhikr* (*jikr* in Gujarati). Literally meaning "remembrance," an Islamic dhikr is spoken or sung to meditate on the presence of God, to praise the Prophet Muhammad, and, for some Muslims, to evoke the blessings of Muslim saints or the family of the Prophet. In the Qur'an, God directs human beings to remember the one who created and has sustained them. As we have already seen, Muslims around the world—both Sunni and Shi'a—have a variety of methods for remembering God. For some, dhikr means the sober recitation of God's many names such as Merciful and Compassionate or even the recitation of Qur'anic passages as they apply to an everyday situation. For others, dhikr can mean sacred dancing, the playing or singing of religious music, or the recitation of poetry in Arabic, Urdu, Persian, Turkish, or another language. In the state of Gujarat, India, like in other places in the country, those who become professional performers of dhikr are patronized not only by Muslims but also by non-Muslims, since they are seen to have a talent for traversing the gulf between the profane world and the sacred world. Despite media headlines that make it seem as if Hindus, Muslims, Sikhs, and other religious groups in South Asia are constantly in conflict, the world of South Asian religions is one in which people of many different faiths often share the same holy places, borrow from one another's religious traditions, and patronize one another's religious festivals and religious experts.[2] Gujarati Hindus, for example, sometimes hire South Asian Muslims of African descent to perform dhikrs at religious celebrations such as an 'urs, the death anniversary of a saint, the day on which the saint left his or her earthly coil and found spiritual union with God. Performers choose from dozens of songs that have been passed on from generation to generation, songs that preserve distinctly East African time signatures or rhythms and that are sometimes accompanied by an African bow. They begin by invoking the name of God, extolling God's many qualities such as compassion and forgiveness, and asking for prayers on the Prophet, who is seen as master of remembrance. Then they call out to their patron saints such as the female Mai Mishra and remember their Muslim ancestor, Bilal ibn Rabah. Line after line is sung to Bava Gor, also known as Gori Pir, the saint in whose name their spiritual authority is practiced. They remember him crossing the Indian Ocean to establish the community of African-descended followers. Tracing their lineage to his journey, these South Asian Sufis of African descent employ words with double meanings to compare the ocean's waves and Gori Pir's travel over them to spiritual ecstasy and divine joy.[3]

Perhaps as many as one hundred thousand South Asians in the modern nation-states of India and Pakistan trace their origins, at least in part, to East Africa. Half of them may live in Sindh, the Pakistani province that borders the Indian Ocean. Crossing the eastern border, tens of thousands live in villages and cities located in the western and southwestern Indian states of Gujarat, Maharashtra, and Karnataka and to a lesser extent in the southeastern state of Andhra Pradesh. They often refer to themselves as Siddis, and sometimes Shidis, Siddhis, Sidis, Makranis, and Habshis, meaning Abyssinian or Ethiopian.[4] Comparatively little has been written about African-descended Indians and Pakistanis and other African diasporic populations in Asia, and there are still basic questions about their history and culture that remain unanswered or to which only tentative responses can be given.[5] Not all South Asians of African descent are Siddi: the term is generally not used for very recent immigrants or visitors from Africa. In addition, not all Siddis are Muslim. In Uttara Kannada, a district of Karnataka state, the Siddi Development Society estimated in 1999 that of twelve thousand or so Siddis in the district, 45 percent were Roman Catholic, 25 percent were Hindu, and 30 percent were Muslim.[6] In other locales, especially in Pakistan, the proportion of Muslim to non-Muslim Siddis is much higher. But such sectarian distinctions do not always matter to Siddis, many of whom often traverse religious boundaries with ease.

Like other communities in South Asia, Siddis see themselves as both biologically and spiritually linked. In India they sometimes use the word *jamat*, or group, to refer to their identities as members, simultaneously, of a certain class or "caste" and a religious brotherhood.[7] These are some of the "thick" notions of blackness to which they ascribe; these are the identifications that they themselves create. But the very label that unites them, Siddi, does not always mean the same thing in the cities or villages where they live. Like all social identities, its meaning is contextual and dynamic. In some places Siddi is linked explicitly to a Muslim religious identity and even more narrowly to a set of religious practices that venerate African saints, while in other places Siddi refers more generically to anyone who identifies with the history of African-descended people in the Indian Ocean world. In addition, not all South Asians of black African descent refer to themselves as Siddis, and it will be important to keep in mind that the observations made here do not apply to all African-descended South Asian Muslims.

This chapter examines some of the shared religious characteristics of Muslim Siddi communities, but future research will likely show more religious diversity among Muslim South Asians of African descent than can be described presently. That is, the composite picture that I present is likely to be complicated in the future as more ethnography and historical research is conducted among Siddi people. The first section of the chapter explores the medieval and modern history of the Siddi communities in South Asia; it documents the role of warfare, slavery, and trade in the development of these communities during the Islamic and European colonial periods of South Asian history and goes on to present a sociological portrait of Siddis in contemporary India. The second section reveals the meanings and functions of Muslim saints Gori Pir, his sister Mai Mishra ("Mishra" meaning "Egypt"), and their brother Bava Habash ("Habash" meaning "Ethiopian") within Siddi religious cultures, both among Muslims and non-Muslims. Muslim Siddis devoted to the power and authority of these saints maintain shrines for their African ancestors and offer religious healing and performances for South Asians from a variety of religious backgrounds. Their devotion is a form of diasporic identity construction that celebrates their own sense of ethnic and religious particularity, or peoplehood, amid the many other ethnic-linguistic groups and classes that are part of both the Indian and Pakistani nation-states.

Even as they incorporate religious ideas, traditions, and practices that are shared across a wide variety of religious and ethnic groups in South Asia, they consciously embody and imagine themselves as both apart from and part of the larger world of non-Siddis.

In addition, it will be shown how devotion to these African saints and to the many rituals performed in their name is nurtured in part through a formal relationship between Sufi masters (shaykhs or pirs) and their students (*talibs* or *murids*). It should be recalled that Sufism is a label used by scholars and among Muslims themselves to refer to a variety of pietistic and mystical practices. These practices can include the individual acts of devotion performed at the shrine of a Sufi saint in order to access his or her *baraka*, or spiritual power, or gain his or her intercession with God on mundane or spiritual matters. Sufism also refers to the history of religious orders established in the name of an Islamic saint such as Ahmadu Bamba or Sidi Sa'ad who is seen to be the putative founder of a formal religious order. In the case of Siddi Muslim religious practice, as we will see, both men and women can become spiritual masters by following Bava Gor or Mai Mishra.

The final section of the chapter looks beyond the religious practices surrounding the African saints to examine other forms of Islamic religious life popular among rural Siddi Muslims in the Indian state of Karnataka. In addition to venerating African saints, Siddi Muslims adopt and adapt South Asian religious traditions, both Islamic and non-Islamic, to the needs of everyday life and life-cycle events. For example, Siddi Muslims marry their children and bury their dead according to local Islamic traditions that use Hindu and other religious rituals and traditions, and they celebrate festival days such as 'Id al-Fitr, which marks the end of fasting during the month of Ramadan, and commemorations such as Muharram with their non-Muslim neighbors. These embodied rituals and traditions both reflect powerful cultural assumptions shared across South Asian cultures and function to strengthen the Siddis' sense of ethnic and religious solidarity.

THE HISTORY OF SIDDIS

African and Asians have been migrating to each other's continents for thousands of years.[8] While overland routes have likely been used the longest, by the third century B.C.E. the trade winds across the Indian Ocean made it possible for dhows to sail from the east coast of Africa to India from April to September and then to go from India to Africa between November and February.⁹ Trade across the Indian Ocean, including trade in human beings, shaped the economies and societies of both Africa and Asia. Asian slaves in Africa and African slaves in Asia performed important economic, political, and cultural functions, and their legacies are part of both continents today. From 800 C.E. to 1900, millions of Africans may have been transported to sites in the Indian Ocean world, including East Africa, the Persian Gulf, South Asia, Southeast Asia, and East Asia.¹⁰ A relatively small number of enslaved Africans settled in what today are Pakistan, India, and Bangladesh, three contemporary nation-states that were once occupied by Great Britain. Historian Ralph Austen estimates that during the nineteenth century perhaps three hundred thousand Africans from the Swahili coast were transported to destinations in the Middle East and South Asia, but most of those slaves went to the Persian Gulf, Yemen, and the Hijaz and eventually to Egypt, Syria, and Anatolia.¹¹ During the eighteenth and nineteenth centuries, perhaps fewer than one thousand African slaves per annum arrived on the Indian subcontinent.¹²

No matter the number of Africans brought to Asia, it is important to keep in mind that, unlike in the Americas, African slaves did not compose the majority of slaves in most parts of Asia. In South and Southeast Asia, most slaves were not Africans but other Asians. Slavery in the Indian Ocean world was different from the "peculiar institution" in the Americas in other ways as well. Although American-style plantations in places such as Mauritius and Réunion were made possible by hundreds of thousands of African laborers, most African slaves in Asia were not farmers. As in the Middle East, many enslaved men and women of African descent in South Asia were servants, sailors, warriors, and concubines, and their relationships to masters need to be understood partly through the lens of patronage—slaves were no doubt abused, but slaves and masters in Muslim contexts were generally tied to one another in relationships of mutual rights and obligations.¹³

By the second millennium C.E., African slave elites and free Africans had become powerful political and military actors in South Asia.¹⁴ As with the Mamluks, the warrior slaves of Egypt, African slaves in South Asia rose to the highest rungs of power in Indian society. In the 1200s, Queen Raziya of the Delhi sultanate named Jalal ad-Din Yaqut, a Habshi slave, as master of the royal stables. It was only a harbinger of things to come. As he sailed along the west coast of India, the fourteenth-century world traveler Ibn Battuta of Morocco noted the "Abyssinian Lords of this sea . . . whenever one of them is on a ship, the Hindu pirates and infidels avoid attacking it." In 1490 Sidi Badr, a royal guard, staged a coup and ruled the region of Bengal for three years; he became known as Shams ad-Din Abu Nasr Muzaffar Shah. Even though he was eventually killed and African soldiers were expelled from Bengal, the era of African leadership in India was not over. During this same period, two of four governors of the Bahmani kingdom, located in the south of India, were African.[15] Then, from 1600 to 1626, Malik Ambar, an African-born slave, emerged as the real power behind the throne in the Ahmadnagar sultanate. In 1601 Ambar defeated an invasion force sent by the Mughal Empire. He also founded a new capital, which came to be known as Aurangabad, oversaw the construction of a complicated water supply system, and restructured the tax system.[16]

In the next century more Africans migrated or arrived against their will as military slaves; their expertise in naval warfare allowed them to extend control over much of the Gujarati and Maharashtra coasts. In 1618 Malik Ambar appointed Sidi Surur to command the island fort of Janjira, located off the coast of Maharashtra. Janjira's link with Malik Ambar and the Ahmadnagar sultanate was severed by Janjira leader Sidi Ambar the Little, who became the first effective monarch of Janjira state. While the fortunes of the Siddi elites of Janjira would rise and fall, by 1689 they controlled a navy of forty thousand sailors. A group of Siddi *sardars*, or nobles, established endogamous marriage patterns that kept a Muslim of African descent on the throne of Janjira until 1948, though they recognized the British as their overlords in 1870. Members of this remarkable African diasporic community were all Muslims. Coming from various places in Africa, they cohered into an Indian ethnic group and consciously referred to their African past by calling themselves Habshis, or Abyssinians/Ethiopians. Their everyday language was Urdu, though some Siddis in Janjira also spoke Marathi and Konkani, the languages of their subjects. Offering protection to passing ships, the Siddis of Janjira gained the respect of European powers such as the Portuguese and later the British while also making important alliances with the Mughal Empire and other regional powers. The British would continue to support Siddi leadership of Janjira during the imperial era. By 1941 the *nawab*, or ruler, of Janjira was titular head of a state with a population of more than one hundred thousand and a total area of 326 square miles.[17]

During the same historical period in which Siddis were leading their own Indian kingdoms, European businesses and governments were importing African slaves to work in their new colonies and commercial endeavors in South Asia. In the Portuguese colony in Goa, for example, some enslaved African men worked in Catholic monasteries as housekeepers and cooks. Enslaved African men served in the military while women became the concubines of Portuguese traders. The Portuguese were followed to India by the Dutch and the British, who also imported slaves from East Africa.[18] During the colonial period, even as Janjira was prospering, African leadership declined or disappeared in other parts of India. By the 1700s, for example, the powerful African military elites of the Deccan (in central India) were no longer a separate community. According to historian Richard Eaton, the nineteenth-century halt of the slave trade in India, along with, and just as important, intermarriage with non-Africans and property ownership, led to the integration of African elites into other communities in this region.[19]

The African Cavalry Guards in Hyderabad were, along with the nobles of Janjira, one of the last vestiges of African military power in South Asia. In 1948, when Hyderabad's leaders agreed to join the newly independent state of India, this unit was dissolved. Its members, who understood themselves to be a separate community of Siddis, then increasingly integrated with other social groups and communities. Some retained a historically constructed and deliberately distinct identity as Siddis, though they began to separate along religious lines as Christian Siddis and Muslim Siddis. Others dropped reference to a Siddi identity altogether, calling themselves Arab, Anglo-Indian, or something else, but still often seeking to marry someone of their same religious background.[20]

As the era of slavery ended, many Siddis were denied the patronage of their masters. Many left these relatively powerful households and formed small rural communities in both southern and western India.[21] What has never been satisfactorily documented is the historical link between the long-gone communities of slaves and today's Siddis, though it is assumed that contemporary Siddi populations are descended at least in part from elements of the once-powerful slave sailors, soldiers, concubines, and servants who formed the Siddi community of the eighteenth and nineteenth centuries.[22] In the district of Uttara Kannada, for example, it has been conjectured that Muslim Siddis may be the descendants of migrants from the Deccan and the kingdom of Janjira, whereas Hindus and Christians are more likely to have descended from the slaves who were brought by the Portuguese to Goa.²³ It is also possible that today's Siddis may trace their African roots to traders, warriors, and slaves who came from Africa during the first millennium or even before.²⁴

Today South Asian Siddis live in cities, towns, and the countryside. In Uttara Kannada, Siddis settled both on slopes and plateaus: those who live in the hills often occupy homesteads with a small plot of land, perhaps one to three acres, while villagers live together in a more centralized fashion on plateaus. A village may be composed of twenty-five to seventy-five houses, dirt roads, gardens, and cattle sheds. Siddis themselves make distinctions between the two types of habitation, and some associate living in remote and disconnected homesteads in the hills with cultural backwardness. While Siddis continue to live in villages and in the countryside, they have also moved to cities. In Goa, men work construction while women serve upper-caste Hindus and Christians as domestic servants.²⁵

Many Siddis have faced discrimination as a result of social and economic inequality and the kinds of antiblack racism that are present throughout the black African Muslim diaspora. In India, for example, some of their fellow citizens think of them as inferior and untrustworthy, while others label them as "good athletes, singers, and dancers."²⁶ They are often compared to Dalits, the so-called untouchables, in that they are seen as socially impure, or at the very least as persons who exist at the lowest point of Indian social hierarchies. Some Siddis receive negative comments about their curly hair, which is seen as an African trait, while some other Indians refuse to eat with them in professional situations. A 1990 article about the Siddis in a Karnataka newspaper described Siddis as having an "ugly countenance" and said that "to raise them from darkness we have to wait several years" but concluded that Siddis are "well-built people . . . hardworking and heroic."²⁷ These prejudicial attitudes have resulted in unequal access to social resources, unfair treatment, and abuse. One of scholar Charles Camara's informants told him, for example, that Siddis experienced discrimination when police officers refused to accept their complaints against landlords, when shopkeepers intentionally cheated them when weighing purchases of sugar and rice, and when bus drivers insisted that they give up seats for other passengers. Another middle-aged Muslim Siddi named Hussein told Camara about his experiences growing up:

> We Siddis were not allowed inside the house of other castes or to dine with them or marry them. When we worked for the landlord food

was given to us on a plantain leaf and not on a plate. After the meal we had to clean the place with cow dung [which is considered a purifying agent in India]. In some restaurants we were not given entry. The owner chased us away. In teashops we were given a separate cup which we had to wash and keep separately in the corner. No one but Siddis used this cup. All this was very humiliating for us, so we avoided interacting with other people unless necessary.[28]

Landless, disenfranchised Siddis often moved around in search of employment, engaging in hunting, gathering, and farming land that was not their own.[29]

In the 1980s Siddis and their advocates began to lobby the government for targeted aid. By 1990 Siddis had taken to the streets in towns such as Yellapur to claim what they called "their right to be treated as human beings." Forming the Siddi Development Society, activists demanded equal treatment on buses, fair pay, and formal ownership of the lands that they had occupied for as long as anyone could remember.[30] Scholars such as Kiran Prasad, formerly known as Cyprian Lobo, argued that the Siddis deserved to be recognized as a scheduled tribe under Indian law; this designation recognizes a group as a formal community and one that is deserving of government benefits. That recognition came in 2002 and 2003, granting financial aid and incentives to Siddis who attend and complete school, university, computer training, or other forms of job preparation. Additional benefits include protection against and compensation for hate crimes, personal insults, and sexual harassment, as well as support for people who are ill or disabled.[31] Siddi activism also resulted in the formation of several communal institutions and initiatives such as women's associations, children's hostels, professional cooperatives, youth clubs, and dance troupes.[32]

Nearly every contemporary scholar who has studied Siddi culture has located the struggle for Siddi empowerment not only in the formal political activities aimed at improving the life opportunities available to contemporary Siddis but also in Siddis' traditional cultural survival strategies. Siddis have responded to discrimination not only through economic self-reliance and subsistence farming but also through religious, cultural, and social affirmations of their own humanity. Siddi religious cultures play a vital role in creating opportunities for physical and psychological healing, shared joy and fun, spiritual transcendence, and social solidarity. The following two sections explore these religious meanings and functions among Muslim Siddis, beginning with a discussion of their most beloved saints and continuing with an examination of other Muslim practices such as life-cycle rituals.

ISLAM OF THE AFRICAN SAINTS: GORI PIR, MAI MISHRA, AND BAVA HABASH

For many Siddis, membership in the African diaspora is the product of what they understand to be shared history, blood, and spiritual power. Like the Stambali in Tunis, many Muslim Siddis trace their Islamic genealogy to Bilal ibn Rabah. According to many Siddis, proof that they descend from Bilal can be found in physical attributes such as their self-described curly or kinky hair as well as in their moral, spiritual, and ritual powers—like the abilities to invoke the saints and to call others to prayer in an artful manner.[33] Endogamous marriage patterns are sometimes explained in terms of the desire to preserve the spiritual power inherited from Bilal and the African saints to whom they trace their historical origins.[34] Bilal's name is generally uttered at the start of a dhikr, or religious litany, regularly performed as part of Siddi rituals at a local shrine. But if Bilal authorizes a connection to both Islamic origins and an African past, it is from afar. As in the case of the Stambali, it is through another agency that many Siddis seek healing, experience joy, and find God's love. One of those spiritual agencies is Gori Pir, also known as Bava Gor and Sidi Mubarak Nobi (that is, Mubarak from Nubia), who is believed to be the spiritual kin of Bilal. This ancestor and his family represent deeply felt links to an African identity.

Many Siddi songs, now performed on the international music stage as well as in their traditional village and shrine settings, praise Gori Pir and ask for his assistance: "Gori Shah Bava [Gori Pir], you are a man of God / Bava, fix my wretchedness," begins one recited poem dedicated to the saint. Siddi *faqirs*, or mendicants, still roam the streets of some Muslim villages in places such as Bharuch, Gujarat, invoking Gori Pir's name as they sing Islamic poetry and ask for alms, often on Thursday nights and especially during Ramadan. These faqirs offer their blessings and ask for healing upon the ill. Sometimes accompanied by the *malunga*, a musical bow originating in Africa, a faqir might profess that there is no god but God and weave verses of the Qurʾan and praise for Gori Pir into a story about Medina, the city of the Prophet Muhammad. Performers might ask for Gori Pir's help in songs performed near the tomb of the saint:

> No matter who comes to Gori Shah
> Their prayers will be answered.
> Come once with any distress
> It will be solved.[35]

Gori Pir is as much a mythological figure as a historical one, and the many stories about his origins illuminate his different meanings to Muslims—as well as to some Hindus, Christians, and Parsis—who believe in his saintly powers.[36] Scholar Helene Basu, who has researched the shrines of Gori Pir for two decades, points out that many Siddis tell an origins story different from that of historical scholarship. This is a hagiography that establishes the sacred origins and purpose of the saint; it reveals the meanings of the saint to his followers: Gori Pir was a Habshi, or Abyssinian, but lived in Mecca. He was sent to India by the Prophet Muhammad himself, meaning that the patron saint of the Siddis derived his charge from God's Messenger, even if he was not of his bloodline. His followers thus trace their own authority back to the Prophet Muhammad. On his way to India, according to one version of the myth, Gori Pir stopped in Baghdad or Basra, where he became the student of the great twelfth-century Sufi master Ahmad Rifa'i. This is significant, for it links Bava Gor to one of the most popular and revered Sufi masters and saints in the history of Islam. After Rifa'i appointed him vice-regent of Hindustan, thus clothing him with the authority of the great teacher, Gori Pir continued on his way to South Asia. His mission was to defeat the Makhan Devi, a powerful female demon who had a taste for human flesh, destruction, and general chaos. Gori Pir was a "cool customer," having conquered his own desires through discipline and meditation. This use of "cool" reveals a usage common to Hindus and other South Asian religious practitioners. Bava Gor brought an army of Africans with him, leaving groups of them behind as he rested in various South Asian locales; this explains why Siddis live across the Indian Ocean world. Finally Gori Pir met Makhan Devi, by one account in southern Gujarat. Because Makhan Devi was a woman, however, Gori Pir was not allowed to be violent with her. So he sat down to play chess instead. In the meantime, Gori Pir's younger brother, Bava Habash, who was a bit of a hothead, appeared, but he too was not permitted to harm the demoness. Finally Mai Mishra, the sister of Gori Pir, arrived on a ship full of other African women. Unlike Makhan Devi, Mai Mishra was a woman of both hot and cold qualities, able to give life, nurture it, *and* take it away. Being allowed to mix it up with the female demon, she easily dispatched Makhan Devi by using a wooden sandal to pound her into the earth.[37]

These narratives of origins describe the ways in which Siddis imagine their genealogy, and they also inform many of the rituals performed at the shrines of Gori Pir, Mai Mishra, and Bava Habash. Shrines to this family of saints exist throughout the Indian and Pakistani regions of Sindh, Gujarat, Maharashtra, and Karnataka. While future research may reveal variations at each of these shrines, a composite picture based on the current state of scholarship indicates that these shrines are generally staffed by ritual specialists who sometimes call themselves faqirs or *murshids* (spiritual masters); they include shrine leaders, shrine keepers, and honorary guards.[38]

It is remarkable that, in contrast to many other Sufi orders in South Asia, these specialists derive their authority through both male *and* female saints. While male and female followers of other religious brotherhoods, such as the Chishti order and Qadiri order, trace their spiritual lineage back to the male saint, in this case female Siddi faqirs claim their pedigree not from Gori Pir but from Mai Mishra, a female.[39] For many Siddis, Mai Mishra embodies the qualities of the virtuous woman: she helps her brother, obeys rules of modesty, heals the infertile, and exorcises evil spirits.[40] Moreover, it is through this female saint that certain female powers, unavailable to men, are practiced. Emphasizing "complementary male and female domains," Siddi rituals do not place women in auxiliary positions; instead, their ritual functions mirror the cosmic role played by Mai Mishra, whose shrine "occupies a central, designated symbolic space associated with values of femininity," as Basu notes.[41]

Both Siddi and non-Siddi Indians and Pakistanis come to these shrines to celebrate life, to mark important holidays, and to seek both individual and communal healing. These rituals clearly use techniques, materials, and other cultural elements that are present in other South Asian shrine activities, but they do so in a way that constructs and invokes the special spiritual authority of Siddis to perform them. Faqirs, like other Sufi masters, are known to be able to "work" the saints, meaning that they can call upon their presence to divine the truth or heal the body. Since Gori Pir is seen as cool, self-controlled, and truthful, he is invoked during a ritual in which the shine is turned into a court of law. "Divination through ordeal" involves bringing a person accused of a crime, often someone suspected of engaging in adultery, witchcraft, or workplace theft, to the shrine for a trial. The accused is bathed, made pure for the judgment that is to come. A male on trial then ties a wet loincloth around his waist; a female wears a wet sari. Iron rings are placed around the accused's ankles, incense is burned, and the accused rushes toward the saint's tomb accompanied by a ritual specialist. If the iron rings open during the run, the accused is deemed innocent. If not, he or she is guilty, and the accuser decides on appropriate punishment for the accused's transgression of social norms.[42]

The shrine also plays host to rituals performed to heal both female and male infertility. Since Bava Habash is associated with heat, his powers are called upon to transform an infertile man's blood into semen. At least seven Siddi men consume a hot drink of milk, ginger, and spices. What is left is shared with the man for whom the rite is performed and other devotees. Finally some drumming and dancing is performed.[43] In the case of women who suspect that they are unable to conceive a child, Mai Mishra is called upon to do the work of the saints. The infertile woman or one of her relatives comes to the shrine looking for assistance from a female faqir, one who knows the rituals necessary to access the healing power of the saint. Perhaps the supplicant will donate sacks of sugar, rice, or lentils to the saint. Then seven Siddi women prepare a dish of lentils, rice, sugar, and ghee, or clarified butter, and ritually consume the dish on behalf of the saint. The women do so in private, eating out of the same dish. They share what is left from the sacred dish with the female for whom the ritual is being performed and with other devotees of the saint. After sharing the meal, women sing dhikrs, invoking Mai Mishra and the special hair that distinguishes those who can access the power of Mai Mishra on behalf of others:

> Come playing, O Mai!
> On the hill of Mai Mishra we will have fun
> Frizzy hair
> O, hair, frizzy hair.[44]

Such lyrics evoking the playfulness of Mai Mishra and the type of hair associated with black people weave the powers of the saint above to the earthly origins of her followers in Africa. One of the seven women is then possessed by the saint's spirit, and others follow. They move their hips and dance, and after they are done, the supplicant is thought to be cured.[45]

Another ritual performed at the shrine is the exorcism of evil spirits. Though the possession of one's body by the spirit of a saint can be joyous and healing, possession by demonic forces is an illness that must be treated. Faqirs first determine the nature of the possession and, if they decide that they can help, ask the person to make a pilgrimage to the shrine of Gori Pir five times. It is at the sacred space of the shrine—the place where the charisma of the saints is present—where one can be healed. First, however, the possessed person may deny the sacred water or ashes offered to him or her. The spirit may spit on the saint or curse him. But if the evil spirit begins to yield to the power of the saints, then he is eventually exorcised and banished to a tree near a shrine of Mai Mishra.[46]

While the rituals above are a kind of service performed for members of the general public, the staff of shrines devoted to Gori Pir also celebrate various holidays. The most important event of the ritual calendar is the 'urs, or death anniversary, of Gori Pir held at his shrine in Bharuch, Gujarat. The word "'urs" means "wedding" in Arabic, but it is also used to label the death anniversary of a Muslim saint. The two meanings of the word are related since some Muslims believe that the earthly death of the saint's body leads to the spiritual union—or wedding—of his or her soul with God. This event is celebrated annually for six days during the Islamic month of Rajjab. Thousands of South Asians of African descent, mainly from India but also sometimes from Pakistan, arrive for the ritual dancing that occurs during the celebration.[47]

Traditionally the 'urs has begun with a ritual washing of the tombs of Gori Pir, Bava Habash, and Mai Mishra—a process called *ghusl*, the same word used to describe the complete bath sometimes performed before making *salat*, the prescribed prayers in which believers prostrate their bodies in the direction of the Ka'ba, or sacred house, in Mecca.[48] The night before the ritual bathing of the saints, the keepers of the shrine and other religious specialists share a simple meal of rice and lentils. Men beat drums while women shake rattles. Attendees also sing dhikrs and burn incense to invoke the presence of the saints. It is common for the person who represents Gori Pir to become possessed and enter into a trance. All partake of shared drinks—one black and hot, the other cold and white—and then the washing commences. Men wash the shrine of Gori Pir while women clean that of Mai Mishra. At the same time, other attendees listen to *qawwali*, the ecstatic music associated most closely with the Chishti Sufi order but also played by Siddis. Like a bride and groom, the shrines of the saints are perfumed and dressed in new clothes. The tomb of Mai Mishra is decorated with the same red cloth that Gujarati brides wear. Bava Habash, the hotheaded brother, also wears red. But Gori Pir dons the cool color of green. The presence of both hot and cold dress, as well as hot and cold drinks, is desirable; both hot and cold qualities are required for physical and spiritual health.[49]

After the ritual cleansing is performed, the celebrations can begin in earnest. For several nights, men and women perform *dammal*, a type of dancing also called *goma*, the Bantu word for drum, dancing, and spirit possession. Accompanied by the sounds of drums, dancers move in a counterclockwise direction.[50] The climax of the celebrations occurs the night before the death anniversary. In the late afternoon, devotees of Gori Pir perform a procession from the village to the shrine. Gori Pir's flag is hoisted, and a plate of flowers, clothes, food, and sandalwood is carried to the tomb. Seven men—an auspicious number in South Asia, as elsewhere—grind the sandalwood into a paste that will be applied to the tombs of the saints. Dhikrs are performed and dancing begins in front of Gori Pir's shrine. During this night, men and women of all backgrounds are often possessed by the saints, entering a state of trance as they move to the beat of large drums. The singing and dancing continue for hours. Then some dancers start clowning around. These performers stand on their hands, perform acrobatic stunts, and may dance in a vulgar fashion as audience members throw coins at them. Possessed by the spirits of saints, they cross the boundaries of normal behavior; such boundary crossing is acceptable and even embraced at this special time and in this space. Finally, very late at night, unmarried boys and girls dance with one another, which represents another suspension of a social norm.[51]

As central as Gori Pir's 'urs is to the life of the shrine, however, his is not the only death anniversary celebrated there. The 'urs of Mai Mishra, his sister, also plays a vital role in Siddi Muslim religious practice. In Karachi, Pakistan, for example, Siddis, who call themselves Shidis, celebrate Mai Mishra's 'urs by performing a rite called "the Weight of the Mother." In Karachi the ritual takes place in a shrine dedicated to the memory of Baba Farid, a saint from the Chishti Sufi order. Mai Mishra's 'urs is thus associated with a popular saint of a popular Sufi order. Underneath a large tree in the section of the shrine dedicated to Mai Mishra, Shidi male and female practitioners stage a drama that celebrates the making of family ties, both physical and spiritual, among fellow Pakistanis of African descent. After invoking the name of God, Muhammad, and many saints, drummers beat special rhythms for each of the seven sisters of

Bava Gor. They dance and sing about Mai Mishra. Then they reenact the initiation first of sisters and then of brothers into the family of Bava Gor, the family of Siddis. Seven initiates, playing the role of seven sisters, put clay pots full of food, representing the mother's womb, on their heads. They carry this "weight of the mother" into the streets around the shrine as others play drums, dance, and sing. After returning to the shrine some dancers experience trance, and then, a couple of hours later, the food in the pots will be distributed and the ritual will conclude.[52]

Mai Mishra's death anniversary and the other rituals associated with the saints continue to be celebrated today, although their religious legitimacy has been challenged by the current trustees of Gori Pir's shrine complex in Gori Pir Hill in India. In the past several decades, Siddi practices performed at the shrine have not escaped the larger trends toward reforming the practices associated with the shrines of saints. For example, the daily ritual schedule of the shrine complex has been organized primarily around the practice of salat, the daily prayers. The movement of women around the tomb of Gori Pir has been restricted, reflecting the increased emphasis on the practice of limiting female contact with the tomb of the saint. At the annual death anniversary of Gori Pir the trustees of the mosque also put pressure on the faqirs to reduce the amount of dancing and to increase the volume of Qur'an recitation performed. Many of the non-Muslims who used to come to the shrine have disappeared, and non-Siddi, urban, middle-class Muslims from Surat, Bharuch, and Ahmadabad have become a major presence. According to Helene Basu, the character of the shrine complex in Rijpala has begun to reflect the growing sectarianism of Indian society. That is, rather than being a place that encourages religious pluralism, the shrine is increasingly a place where religious boundaries between Muslims and non-Muslims are produced and reaffirmed.[53]

While that may be the case with this Gujarati shrine, however, it does not characterize the religious pluralism that continues to define relationships among Siddis themselves in small towns across the Indian state of Karnataka. Like many Indians both past and present, these Siddis maintain distinct religious identities as Muslims, Hindus, and Christians *and simultaneously* participate in each other's rituals, visit each other's sacred places, and celebrate each other's holidays. Understanding how these Siddis construct and maintain their Muslim identities while also practicing elements of other religions reveals yet another way in which the African Muslim diaspora is negotiated along both religious and social boundaries.

SIDDI MUSLIM RELIGIOUS LIFE IN KARNATAKA

Religious studies scholar Pashington Obeng's ethnographic research in rural Karnataka state conducted from 1998 to 2006 reveals that many poor and rural Siddis define themselves in terms of their religious identity and of their racial, ethnic, and tribal status as African Indians. While Siddis in Karnataka do build and maintain shrines for Gori Pir and his siblings, Siddi Muslim religious life in this state of over sixty million people includes the veneration of other saints besides Gori Pir, the celebration of Islamic holidays such as Muharram, and the observance of Islamic marriage and funeral rites. This section begins with a discussion of Islamic holidays in Siddi villages throughout Karnataka.

Muharram, the annual commemoration of the 680 C.E. martyrdom of Husayn, the son of Ali and Fatima and grandson of the Prophet Muhammad, is generally known in the mainstream English-language press as a specifically Shi'a holiday. In Iran, Iraq, and Lebanon, nation-states with large Shi'a populations, Muharram is a major event on the Islamic calendar as followers mourn Husayn's suffering at the hands of fellow Muslims and await the return of the Twelfth Imam, who will restore peace and justice on the earth. But this holiday, so central to Shi'a identity, has also been celebrated at various times by Sunnis who identify strongly with the family of the Prophet Muhammad, and this is especially true in various part of South Asia.[54]

In the villages of Karnataka, Muslims often organize Muharram rituals, but both Hindus and Christians participate in the rites. Muslim faqirs or other religious specialists lead processions through the towns' streets as Muslims and non-Muslims call out the name of Husayn and his brother, Hasan. The rite varies from village to village and from year to year. In many places, the leader of the procession recites the Fatiha, the first chapter of the Qur'an, as practitioners hoist the *doli*, which is a replica of Husayn's tomb or coffin. The doli might rest on a platform that rotates automatically or on one that is hand-rotated by its bearers. Flowers, glittery paper, and photographs of the Ka'ba or the tomb of the Prophet might adorn the doli. Flags featuring the names of the Prophet's family, including Muhammad, Ali, Fatima, Hasan, and Husayn, may be attached to the doli or carried alongside it by those in the procession. As the doli is paraded through the streets in the village of Kendelgeri, people play drums and sing. The procession sometimes stops near a body of water where the doli can be bathed. In Kendelgeri, Gunjavatti, and

Kirvatti, the feet of the doli bearers are sprinkled with water, and attendees might sprinkle the heads of the carriers with flowers. In Mainalli, it is specifically women who have the job of bathing the feet of the doli carriers. These doli bearers might enter into a trance. "We believe that when we carry the doli," Abubakarsab Siddi told Obeng, "Allah's spirit comes into us. Suppose a man carries a doli, and he's possessed by evil, it has to leave him as he carries a doli, otherwise he may fall down as a sign that Allah's spirit has struck him down." In Manchikeri, as the procession ends, participants cry and call out remembrances of Husayn's sacrifice at Karbala. Fatima Siddi, one of Obeng's informants in Kendelgeri, told him that when she hears the story of Husayn, "it makes me cry. Since he died for our religion, he also can understand our struggle." In Tategeri, however, people do not cry visibly over the death of Husayn.[55]

Whether or not participants in the procession lament Husayn's death by crying, many of them celebrate his sacrifice by sharing charity with the doli bearers and others. In Kendelgeri, a group of twelve men who also act as doli carriers collect money and then serve the entire community a feast marking the occasion. A Muslim imam is tasked with sacrificing both goats and chickens, which will be shared with all present. In Tategeri, participants in the procession meet outside of the shrine that houses the doli during the rest of the year. An imam offers prayers and later ritually slaughters the goats that have been donated for the feast. He distributes the meat, designating some of it for the communal feast, some for the poor, and some for the carriers of the doli. Later this same imam enters a trance, repeating the phrase, "God is great!" He chastises the audience for not obeying God's commandments. Other men, now in a trance as well, run to and fro, invoking the name of God. Finally the evening ends with much drumming, dancing, and singing.[56]

For many of those who participate in the rites, Muharram is a time during which God will hear one's pleas. Some go to the shrine where the doli is stored to ask for a successful marriage, a good job, or a child. "If you ask for help, hoping that you'll receive," promises Fatima Siddi, "you surely will get it." Others participate in this sacred holiday by purifying themselves, hoping to exhibit some of the baraka, or blessings, that are evoked in the commemoration of Husayn's death. For example, some Siddis walk across hot coals, a practice known to be associated with the Rifa'i and some other Sufi orders and other religious communities in South Asia. If these fire-walkers are ritually impure, it is believed, their feet will burn. In order to achieve a state of purity, the practitioners, whether Muslim or not, abide by Islamic prohibitions against the use of alcohol, fornication, and immodest clothing. Some wear a wristband, a physical reminder of their obligation to tell the truth and to abide by ethical standards.[57]

In sum, during Muharram, Siddis in Karnataka ritually mourn the passing of Husayn, access his baraka, receive and distribute charity, perform communal rituals and sometimes amazing feats, and experience a trancelike state in which God's presence feels particularly close. Despite the fact that Siddis in Karnataka generally understand themselves to be Sunnis, they commemorate the death of Husayn during Muharram as if they were Shi'a. The Sunni commemoration of Husayn's martyrdom is not unusual for Sunni Muslims in South Asia, where many Sunnis venerate the *ahl al-bayt,* the family of the Prophet Muhammad. It does not seem to be a ritual that marks Muslim Siddis in India as black or African-descended but instead associates them with a larger religious practice on the Indian subcontinent. But even as this ritual seems to link Siddi Muslims to non-Siddi Muslims, it simultaneously functions to create multifaith, pan-Siddi social unity. Many Muslim Siddis share charity with non-Muslim Siddis, and non-Muslim Siddis visit a shrine and remember the sacrifice of the martyr by dancing and singing late into the night. Thus, this holiday plays an important role in creating Muslim identity while extending the boundaries of Siddi Muslim community to include non-Muslims.

Muharram is not the only Islamic holiday that Muslim Siddis share with their non-Muslim neighbors. The two main *'ids,* or festivals, of the Islamic calendar are also holidays during which Muslim and non-Muslim community is created among the Siddis of Karnataka. The lesser 'id, 'Id al-Fitr, marks the end of Ramadan, the Islamic month of daytime fasting. While many Siddi Muslims who work among other Siddis in villages are able to observe the fast, those laborers who spend long days on construction sites and in other difficult workplaces are not able to go without water the entire day. During Ramadan, Siddi women play leading roles in organizing the *iftars,* the daily meals consumed after sunset. They invite guests, cook, and arrange the seating in their homes. For many, this is the definition of piety since it involves sharing one's often-precious resources with guests and even strangers. During these iftars, goat and chicken are often served along with roti, or fried bread. Puffed rice is sometimes offered for dessert. Whether Siddi Muslims fast or not throughout the month, they all celebrate the 'id. New clothes are obtained for the occasion, especially for children. While men are generally assigned the ritual slaughter of the animal whose meat will be consumed in the large feast, women sometimes perform this task, saying prayers in Urdu, which is perceived as a sacred language.[58]

The greater 'id, 'Id al-Adha, is also celebrated. This festival of the sacrifice occurs at the end of the annual hajj, or pilgrimage to Mecca, and marks the occasion during which, according to Islamic tradition, God commanded Abraham (Ibrahim) to sacrifice his son Ishmael (Isma'il) but replaced the boy with a goat at the last minute (Qur'an 37:99–113). In the village of Kendelgeri, 'Id al-Adha is celebrated for two days. Men and boys, all wearing *kufis*, gather publicly to perform salat. They proceed together from the village mosque to a special patch of earth designated for the prayer. Someone lights incense, and those at the rear of the procession carry water for *wudu*, or ablution. An imam leads the prayers and reads from the Qur'an, after which the men return home. Women also pray together on this day, but they do so at home. When prayers are finished, a lamb or other animal is sacrificed, and the meat is shared with other family members and those in need. Sharing the meat, according to one of Obeng's informants, is a necessary part of *zakat*, or alms, one of the five pillars of Islamic practice. "The fullness of the sacrifice," Hydersab Siddi of Kendelgeri said, "is in how the meat is distributed among people, including non-Muslims and the poor."[59]

In addition to celebrating Islamic holidays, a second manifestation of lived Islamic religion in the villages of Karnataka is one that we have already examined above—namely, the veneration of Muslim saints. Siddi Muslims in Karnataka venerate Gori Pir in some of the same ways outlined earlier, but they are also devoted to saints other than the mythic founder of their community. In villages and people's homes, some Siddis build shrines to Abd al-Qadir al-Jilani, who is called Mahbub Subhani. In historical terms, Mahbub Subhani was a tenth- and eleventh-century Muslim scholar of *fiqh*, or Islamic jurisprudence, in whose name the popular Qadiri Sufi order was later founded. But across much of the Muslim world, al-Jilani is also known as a saint. This is the same saint who some Stambali and other North Africans of sub-Saharan descent venerate. Mahbub Subhani is, quite literally, a miracle worker. Those who specialize in his veneration relate stories of the saint that establish his bona fides as such: when he was in his mother's womb, for example, it is said that he killed a serpent that his mother had accidentally consumed. Mahbub Subhani, who started speaking when he was only five days old, also brought the dead back to life. According to an interview conducted by Obeng with Imam Kareemsab Siddi of Gunjavatti in 2001, Mahbub Subhani is a mediator between human beings and God. "He understands a human heart better, as he was one of us," the imam said. Kareemsab, whose son is often possessed by the spirit of the saint, decided to build a shine to Mahbub Subhani "because it is much easier to ask favors and forgiveness from Mahbub Subhani than Allah." Although mosques are predominately male spaces, shrines devoted to Mahbub Subhani are mixed gender. Both men and women approach the saint for help with practically any problem. Kareemsab Siddi said that he asks for the saint's help when he needs a favor or is ill. He sacrifices animals in the saint's honor and vows to beautify his shrine. In addition, the imam helps to conduct his ʿurs, or death anniversary, every year. Villagers sing and dance as they process through their town; they pray, drop flowers, and scatter water in order to ritually cleanse the entire village. Finally, some Siddis set up small shrines in their homes devoted to Mahbub Subhani. In these spaces, families can venerate and make supplications to the saint together.[60]

A third way that Siddi Muslims practice Islam in Karnataka is in their life-cycle rituals such as marriage. As observed in chapter 2, the ritual requirements of a marriage as dictated by fiqh are quite few. But Muslim practitioners do not always distinguish between religious rules and social customs, and they often consider both to be necessary components of a wedding. Although wedding rites vary among Muslim Siddis in Karnataka, many share the following components: For four days, the bride's house serves as the center of the wedding activities. During the first day of the celebration, women decorate with henna first the hands of the bride and then the hands of all other women present—a prophetically sanctioned practice, performed in many places. Turmeric is used on the second day for the same purpose. The signing of the marriage contract occurs on the third day. The groom's parents often take a lead role in arranging the public engagement ceremony. The groom's family visits the house of the bride, often bringing gifts such as "a sari, betel leaves, areca nuts, bananas, dry coconut, bangles, [and] flowers," according to Obeng. An imam recites the Fatiha, the opening chapter of the Qurʾan, and the parents of the bride provide the groom with new clothes. The groom puts on the clothes and often goes to a nearby mosque to make salat, or prayer. The groom then returns and his family shows the gifts to all assembled. As more prayers are offered, five married women adorn

Siddis and Habshis in South Asia 105

the bride with a wedding necklace and then present her to the crowd outside the house. She sits with the groom as guests toss rice to celebrate the couple. The bride changes clothes and dons a veil. Guests then eat and dance. The next day, guests visit the house of the groom, where his parents give new clothes to the family of the bride. Guests once again enjoy a meal, and afterward sandal paste is applied to their chins.[61]

Some Siddi Muslim marriages in Karnataka incorporate the rituals of Hindu and other religious traditions. During a wedding in the village of Mainalli in 2000, for example, Sulemansab Patil, who self-identified as a Muslim, told Obeng that "he and his family had . . . to propitiate their family Hindu deity before he could go to the mosque to get married."[62] An icon of Lakshmi, the mother goddess, had come into the possession of the family several generations before. When the family had provided a good home to the deity, she had offered the family protection. But when she was forgotten, the family experienced various problems. The groom's mother, for example, nearly lost her sight when she failed to feed the deity. So, as one of the family's sons prepared to enter into marriage, it was only fitting—no, it was necessary—for him to ask for Lakshmi's blessings. Thus, his friends and family joined him at the household shrine devoted to Lakshmi to perform *puja*, or worship. Patil's brother split coconuts and placed them in front of her image. Green cloth, candles, a camphor, horse figurines, bananas, and rice were also offered to the deity. The older brother tapped the groom's shoulders three times with peacock feathers that had been incensed and immersed in coconut juice. Sulemansab then bowed to the goddess. His sisters entered the room followed by the parents. The family patriarch said prayers in Urdu and recited the Fatiha. Then all the women present sang songs to Lakshmi and threw rice on the floor. They sang to the groom and applied sandal paste to his legs, arms, and face. Other guests did the same. More food was given to Lakshmi, and the father of the bride smeared ashes on the groom's chin. Only then, after Lakshmi had been worshipped, could the groom set off to perform prayers at the mosque.[63]

While there are other life-cycle rites that involve Islam in Karnataka, the final ritual in the life of the Siddi Muslim is a funeral. The body of the deceased is generally put on a bed or perhaps on a veranda. Sandalwood sticks are lit, new clothes are purchased, and flowers are placed beside the body. The body is bathed by persons of the same gender. Milk, sandal paste, and sacred water are sprinkled on the body, which is wrapped in a burial shroud. Incense is burned as the body is placed on a funeral bier of some sort. There is a viewing of the body. Members of the deceased's family will not eat, work, or bathe until the body has been buried. An imam offers prayers, and then male members of the deceased take the body to the cemetery. Women do not generally attend the burial, as is the case in many other Muslim funerals around the world. The body is placed in a grave in the direction of Mecca. A stone is set near the grave, and then men at the burial walk backward for forty steps. The imam recites the Fatiha and men turn their heads away from the grave. They are not supposed to look back. Families share a meal, perhaps made with mutton, with all those who come to the house of the deceased in order to mourn. Three days later, family members go to visit the grave. They gather some dirt and add some lime to it, applying this cleansing solution to the floor of the house. Mourners will visit the grave on the eleventh and fortieth days after the death, decorating it with flowers and sandal sticks.[64]

The funeral, along with other life-cycle rites, the veneration of the saints, and the celebration of holidays are all essential components of religious practice among Siddi Muslims. These religious practices express a Siddi emphasis on communal solidarity in the face of sectarian religious division among various religious groups in India. Not only do Hindu, Muslim, and Christian Siddis participate in one another's rituals, but they also combine elements from various traditions into their own household and community practices. This religious pluralism is remarkable in a global age in which religious lines can be essential to political activism and social organization not only in India but across the globe. The incorporation of non-Muslim people and non-Islamic religious elements into the religious practice of Muslim Siddis also indicates how the African jamat, or community, matters to the lives of some Muslims in India. It is only by including non-Muslims in the Islamic rituals, or sharing one's wealth with non-Muslims, that some Muslim Siddis consider their ethical commitments to Islam to be fulfilled. Compassion for all, regardless of religious community, is acted out inside of the ethnic community of people of African descent.

CONCLUSION

Like Muslims with sub-Saharan roots in North Africa and the Middle East, some Muslim Siddis in South Asia have claimed their black African past as a form of spiritual authority in the present. The so-called cult of saints that characterizes traditional Islam in the region is present among

South Asians of African descent, and it works simultaneously to integrate *and* differentiate its worshippers from other Indians and Pakistanis. On one hand, many non-Siddi Muslims, Hindus, Parsis, and others visit the shrines of Gori Pir and seek the religious services, including the trial by ordeal and the dhikrs, of his Siddi devotees. These activities integrate Siddis into the diverse religious and social landscapes of South Asia. On the other hand, the veneration of Gori Pir, Mai Mishra, and Bava Habash can also function to distinguish Muslim Siddis from Muslim non-Siddis. Devotees of these saints construct a shared sense of diasporic community by remembering their collective origins in Africa. Using their malunga, or musical bow, and singing of Gori Pir's journey over the waves, they also dress and dance in ways that are understood by both performers and audience members as aspects of their shared African past. The contemporary construction of Siddi identity as a form of African ethnicity serves the political, economic, and cultural interests of both Siddis and non-Siddis. It has been encouraged, for example, by the Indian government, which has claimed Siddis as part of their foreign policy outreach to Africa. It has been spurred by European and American scholars, who have sought to map the Siddis as part of a larger African diaspora. And it is deployed by Indian and non-Indian activists as a way to obtain government aid and create entrepreneurial opportunities for musicians and dancers of African descent in India.[65] While some scholars worry that these activities are imposing an African identity on people who are, in their view, really Asian, other scholars see such developments as part of a process of globalization in which Siddis are both joining and being swept into Africanizing movements.[66]

But the politics of Siddi religious cultures are not limited to debates over whether Siddis are really African or not. They have a distinct South Asian ethnic and racial identity and a communal solidarity that transcends religious divisions. In rural settings such as the villages of Karnataka, Islamic religious holidays are made into communal occasions in which Muslim and non-Muslim Siddis participate. The 'ids celebrated at the end of both Ramadan and the hajj become occasions for thanksgiving and sharing among all Siddis, helping to create a sense of social solidarity across religious lines. Even if Muslim Siddis are married and buried according to the rules of fiqh, such occasions sometime blur distinct sectarian lines as Siddis adopt and adapt rituals from each other's religious traditions.

Muslim Siddis in India and Pakistan construct their belonging to an African diaspora in several different ways. For those devoted to Gori

Pir, the diaspora is simultaneously a historical and spiritual community linked by its access to the healing powers of African ancestors, both male and female. Their songs about their frizzy hair represent claims on a proud African past and a special role in Islamic history that stems from Bilal ibn Rabah and Gori Pir. This Africana Muslim diaspora is imagined, felt, and experienced not only in the bodies of believers and in earthly shrines but also in the spiritual spaces that are created by remembering the mythological conquest of Mai Mishra over Makhan Devi, by becoming possessed by a saint, and by feeling his or her healing or ecstatic power. These are not just physical happenings; these diasporic practices are metaphysical transactions. For other Siddi Muslims living in villages in Karnataka, the African diaspora is defined by their lateral relationships to one another as people of black African descent—as Indian nationals who are treated differently because of their perceived racial difference and who, in response, take care of one another across religious boundaries. Finally, there are some Siddis who have become part of a commercial African diaspora, emphasizing or even developing the African aspects of their music, their dance, and their costume in order to make products that might be purchased and patronized in South Asia and on the world market.

South Asian Muslims who consciously construct their religious and ethnic identities are examples of a larger phenomenon in the African diaspora: the importance of black African Muslim saints. In Paris, it is Ahmadu Bamba; in Tunis, it is Sidi Sa'ad or Sidi Frej; and in India and Pakistan, it is Gori Pir. These saints have different powers—whereas Gori Pir is able to inhabit someone's body, Ahmadu Bamba does no such thing for most members of the Murid Sufi order. But all of these saints do function to create a sense of diasporic connection between people of African descent, an African place of origin, and a metaphysical or spiritual realm. Africa itself may be configured differently: in the case of the Murids, followers point back to Touba, Senegal. Muslim Siddis on Gori Pir Hill look back more simply to "Africa," to a more generic place of origins for their patron. Sidi Sa'ad's devotees may see their saint as coming from Bornu by way of Istanbul. All of these black Africana Muslims embrace their saints as ones who can link them not only to a history of belonging to the sacred land of Africa but also to the sacred abode of the spirits and the unseen. Thus, a triangular relationship, one both horizontal and vertical, is created between these believers, their saints' place of origin, and the heavens above.

5

ISLAMIC JIHAD OR JUST REVOLT?

African Muslims in Latin America and the Caribbean

Pacífico Licutan, a Malê or Muslim religious teacher of Yoruban descent, was a beloved figure in Salvador, Bahia, Brazil. Muslims from his community had twice attempted to purchase his freedom from Antônio Pinto de Mesquita Varella, a physician who made money from Licutan's work as a tobacco roller on Dourado Wharf in Salvador. Varella refused, and when the doctor could no longer service his debts, this esteemed preacher was confiscated as a piece of property to be sold to pay off Varella's creditors. Pacífico Licutan awaited his imminent sale in prison during the month of Ramadan, the month in which Muslims fast from dawn to sunset as demanded by the Qur'an. This was November 1834. As he prayed and fasted in jail, fellow Muslims were plotting a complicated revolt that included an attempt to free this *alufá*, or religious teacher, once and for all. On January 25, 1835, the revolt began, but it was quickly put down. When Licutan heard the bad news, according to one witness, "he bowed his head and never raised it. He became upset and cried." But as historian João José Reis notes, "The old Malê's spirit was not entirely broken." When he was interrogated by Bahian authorities on February 11, 1835, he denied his inquisitors' demand that he give up the names of his students and fellow practitioners. He refused to cooperate even with a judge's request for his own name. When asked, he told the official that his name was Bilal—referring not only to the person of Bilal ibn Rabah but also to the generic West African term for prayer-caller. The judge became enraged, but Licutan said that "he could call himself whatever

(opposite)
Jama'at al-Muslimeen leader Yasin Abu Bakr surrenders to Trinidad and Tobago authorities on August 1, 1990, after an unsuccessful coup attempt. Their form of jihad, or Islamic struggle, focused on political change inside Trinidad and Tobago. Photograph by Mark Lyndersay. Courtesy of the *Trinidad & Tobago Guardian*.

he wanted." As Reis points out, "The revolt was still alive in Licutan's (or Bilal's) heart, despite its failure on the battlefield."[1]

For Licutan and hundreds of thousands of Bilal's heirs in the Americas, Islamic practice has long been associated with the struggle against racism and with other forms of resistance. Islamic practice has existed in the minds, bodies, and spirits of many African-descended Muslim Americans as a form of political activity. In this sense, it is not different from many of the other religious expressions of African Americans, which have often sought to challenge slavery and antiblack racism.[2] In Latin America and the Caribbean, however, enslaved Muslims of African descent, whether of Iberian, North African, or West African provenance, were singled out at an early stage as troublemakers by Spanish and Portuguese authorities. In 1530 and again in 1532, for example, the further importation of Moorish slaves was banned by authorities in Santo Domingo.[3] The ban did little over time to prevent the enslavement of African Muslims, and by the end of the Atlantic slave trade in the nineteenth century, more than one million of the twelve million Africans who endured the Middle Passage may have been Muslim. While tens of thousands landed in British North America and the United States, the vast majority were transported to colonies and countries throughout the Caribbean and Latin America.[4]

Despite the fears of the colonizers, most enslaved Muslims were not revolutionaries. Their history is one characterized more by the extraordinary lengths to which they would go to preserve and continue their practice of Islam. Some of them were among the most educated Americans in the Western Hemisphere, and many preserved their literacy by writing down verses from the Qurʾan or other Islamic texts on wooden tablets and using Arabic letters to transliterate African and creolized languages.[5] Some Muslims wrote letters to one another and even penned their memoirs.[6] Only in a few instances were African American Muslims able to erect the formal religious institutions necessary to sustain the literary traditions and educational specialization that produced this class of learned teachers and preachers in West Africa. The practice of Islam among African-descended Muslims depended instead on the continual importation of Africans, mostly men. After the slave trade ended, the public practice of Islam and the association of African-descended Americans with Islam as a public form of social identity all but disappeared in the Americas.

But the practice of Islam among African-descended people would be revived in the twentieth century as African Americans formed new groups dedicated to what they believed was their original religion, Islam. African and other Muslim missionaries arrived in both South and North America and played an important role in this Islamic revival from the 1920s onward.[7] The combined effect of these efforts was to reestablish various forms of Islam as an important religious tradition in African America. Some of the groups established by American-born Muslims began to proselytize in other parts of the Americas. For example, in Belize and Jamaica, Muslim missionaries from the Nation of Islam, a group established in Detroit, Michigan, in 1930, successfully founded chapters by the 1960s.[8] Then, during the late twentieth century, the increased presence of Muslim immigrants, especially from South Asia and the Middle East, led to the conversion of Latinos and Latinas, including those of African descent, in countries such as Colombia, Argentina, and Brazil. Today thousands of African-descended people throughout Latin America and the Caribbean once again claim a Muslim identity.[9]

While a great temporal divide exists between the era of slavery and that of freedom, one question linking the history of African American Muslims across both time and space is how to achieve self-determination and communal betterment in spite of the negative effects of antiblack racism on one's community. This is true even in countries such as Trinidad and Tobago, where antiblack racism is perpetuated in a nation in which nonwhite people are the majority. Like African Americans more generally, African American Muslims have responded in a variety of ways to oppression and injustice. One of those responses has been to rebel, violently, against political orders that they believe are responsible for their dehumanization.[10] This chapter examines two specific instances of violent revolt. Its goal is to probe the extent to which these revolts were inspired, informed, and/or sustained by the revolutionaries' understanding of Islamic religion. Put too simply, the chapter scrutinizes the use of what is sometimes called political Islam—that is, an Islam that expresses itself not only in personal pietistic terms but also in explicitly political ones.

Today political Islam can be found across the globe as Muslims utilize Islamic traditions as resources for constructing their nations' constitutions and shaping their legal systems, among other political activities. In examining the political Islam of Africana Muslim people in an accurate and scholarly way, it is necessary to acknowledge that political Islam is associated overwhelmingly with violence and terrorism in European and U.S. media, popular culture, and political discourse.[11] This assumption is a manifestation of Islamophobia, a form of both personal and institutional prejudice with deep roots in Western history that most scholars of Islam, Muslim and non-Muslim, attempt to correct.[12] The goal of widespread scholarly efforts to challenge Islamophobic readings of politics in Islam is not to obscure the political aspects of Muslim religious behavior but to develop a more accurate understanding of such phenomena.[13] Political Islam can be violent and apocalyptic, as can be seen in the 9/11 attacks by Muslim terrorists who were members of al-Qaeda.[14] But political Islam can also become a mundane and more peaceful aspect of politics in democratic nation-states, as it is in both Turkey and Indonesia. Moreover, political Islam can assume a great many governmental forms—to see the range, simply compare the radically different state institutions and foreign policies of the Islamic Republic of Iran and the Kingdom of Saudi Arabia.[15] The point is that political Islam is as much a *style* of thought as anything else. It has no necessary content but acts as a label under which we can group and differentiate different political platforms and ideas inspired by various Islamic interpretations.

Another assumption often made in Islamophobic discourse is that political violence committed by Muslims is a form of jihad, or struggle. Throughout history, many Muslims have considered jihad to be the sixth pillar of Islamic practice.[16] It can be a potent and vital aspect of Islamic religious practice. As one might guess, however, the idea of "struggle" can be applied in numerous ways. It can be violent or nonviolent; it can focus on battling one's own weaknesses or on battling other people. Most Muslims also argue that any violent jihad must be defensive rather than offensive in nature.[17] But what is often lost in popular discussions of jihad and is most relevant to the discussion below is this: not all political violence committed by Muslims is a form of jihad. While al-Qaeda has made famous its call for violent jihad against the "Crusaders," "Zionists," and other "infidels," there are many instances throughout history in which Muslims participated in war without calling it jihad. This is an essential aspect of the story below, as there is an important case to be made that the revolt of 1835 among Muslims in Bahia, Brazil, was no violent jihad.

The goal of the chapter is thus to show two different ways in which Muslims of African descent have looked to Islam as a resource in their political lives and struggles. The first section examines the Muslim-led revolt of African-born slaves and freedmen in Bahia in 1835. It asserts that rebels sought to protect their freedom to practice Islam and that Islam played a role in the revolt as a form of spiritual protection and social solidarity but that other factors, including pan-Yoruban consciousness and protodiasporic racial resistance, are just as important in explaining this act of political violence. The second section interrogates the attempted coup d'état launched by black Muslim members of Jama'at al-Muslimeen in the Caribbean nation of Trinidad and Tobago in 1990. In this second instance, the concept of violent jihad was important to the actions of the Muslims in question, though this jihad was one focused very much on the national politics of Trinidad and Tobago, not of the United States or the West more generally. In neither case was religious motivation the sole determinant of whether the people involved decided to use violence in politics. Instead, other political, social, and economic factors were inextricable from the reasons why these Muslims of African descent decided to revolt against the political order.

AFRICAN MUSLIMS AND THE BRAZILIAN REVOLT OF 1835

African-born Muslims, mostly from the Yoruba, or Nagô, ethnic group, planned a major revolt against the political status quo in the Brazilian province of Bahia on Sunday, January 25, 1835. It was timed to coincide with the Catholic celebration of Our Lady of Guidance and also took place at the end of Ramadan, the Muslim month of daily dawn-to-sunset fasts. In fact, the date on the Islamic calendar was the twenty-fifth of Ramadan, 1250 A.H., which the plotters knew was either on or near the date for Layla al-Qadr, the Night of Power or Destiny. For many Muslims, Layla al-Qadr is the night during which angels descend to earth and the presence of God can be felt in a most tangible form. It is the night when the Qur'an, the Word of God, was revealed to the Prophet Muhammad. The Muslim leaders of the revolt may have seen this as the most auspicious time to launch the revolt; they could call on the immanent presence of the Divine to help them. The leaders of the rebellion, who were Muslim, primarily used word of mouth to call on others to join in, but in at least one instance they communicated with each other by writing in Arabic. One letter found after the rebellion directed that "everyone should come out between 2:00 and 4:00 A.M. stealthily . . . and after doing what they could, they should gather at Cabrito . . . in a large hollow."[18]

But this plot was foiled before it really began. A freed slave let a white neighbor know what was about to happen, and when word got to the provincial president, Francisco de Souza Martins, he put the military on full alert, doubled patrols, and even sent a navy ship into Salvador's bay to catch any escaping rebels. As conspirators celebrated an early breakfast as part of Ramadan observance, authorities stormed the basement from which these revolutionaries planned to launch their attacks in the city of Salvador. Rebels escaped and began to fight with authorities, launching an attack against Salvador's jail. But the authorities possessed superior arms, including artillery and cavalry, and the revolt was put down in a day. The authorities set out to make an example of the revolutionaries, and more than five hundred people were flogged, deported, imprisoned, or executed. More than two hundred hearings were held to document the conspiracy.[19]

One of the major questions tackled by the investigators was whether Islamic religion was to blame for this challenge to proper authorities. As one might expect in the context of a Latin America whose heritage was shaped in no small part by the history of the Reconquista and fear of Muslim revolt in the New World, Brazilian officials wanted to know whether the revolutionaries were inspired by their belief in the necessity of jihad, or struggle. The answer, to this day, is still unclear. The insurgents never explained exactly why they revolted or what they hoped to achieve, although some government officials, the same ones responsible for taking eyewitness accounts and gathering evidence, thought that the religious motivations of the revolt were apparent. In the words of the provincial president, "there was religious fanaticism mixed up in this conspiracy."[20]

There seems to be little dispute about the events that most immediately led up to the revolt. In the two months before, African-descended Muslims, both slave and free, saw the authorities arrest two of their leaders and, perhaps most important, put a stop to one of their most meaningful and joyous ritual celebrations. To understand how these actions had an impact on the African-descended Muslims in Salvador, it is necessary to know more about their hopes and expectations for the growth of their community. In the three decades before the revolt, the continual influx of African-born slaves from the Bight of Benin, most of whom were ethnic Yoruba, reshaped the human geography of Bahia. The number of slaves transported from the Bight of Benin from 1801 to 1830 was 183,700. As a result, in 1835 perhaps one-third of Salvador's population, including both slaves and freedpeople, was African-born. There were likely more African-born than Brazilian-born blacks in the city at the time. Among the tens of thousands of enslaved Africans in Bahia was a significant population of Muslims.[21]

Though Muslims were likely a minority among people of color in Brazil, they represented a critical mass who had the means to establish the institutions necessary for the public performance of their faith and its perpetuation.[22] The institutionalization of Islam required religious meeting places, teachers, ritual specialists, and prayer leaders in addition to leisure time and financial resources. All of these elements were available in Salvador. In Salvador, freed African-born residents earned wages as domestic servants, porters, masons, tailors, butchers, barbers, tanners, and cooks, among other jobs. They also owned small stores and street stands. Some Islamic specialists set up shop on street corners in areas of town with heavy African populations; for a fee, they offered to teach people how to read and write Arabic and sold skullcaps and *abadás*, long white frocks. Free people of African descent used their homes and shops to hold communal meals, congregational prayer, and Islamic holiday celebrations. This community included people of Yoruban and non-Yoruban descent. For example, a Hausa Muslim scholar by the name of Dandará taught Arabic in his tobacco shop and held daily prayers there. Muslims used both wooden slates and paper to practice writing out verses from the Qur'an and various prayers. Basic writing errors in some of the documents discovered after the 1835 investigation show that some residents of Salvador were "beginners," as one witness dubbed them. This fact indicates that more-educated students of the Islamic religious sciences were attempting to pass along their knowledge to other Afro-Brazilians.[23]

Alufás, or Muslim religious specialists, were key participants in this burgeoning religious scene. These specialists were experts in the making of powerful talismans, which played a central role not only in the revolt of 1835 but also in Bahian culture more generally. Such talismans, called *breves* in 1830s Brazil, were similar to those found throughout much of the Islamic world, African-influenced or not. They are like those still used by people in the Jordan Valley today and bear even greater resemblance to those found in contemporary West Africa. Both non-Muslims and Muslims wore them, in the words of one nineteenth-century non-Muslim Brazilian, to "be free from wagging tongues"—that is, to avoid the ill effects of gossip. Another said that talismans provided protection against the wind, likely meaning that they protected the bearer from the whimsical or ill effects of spirit beings such as the Islamic *jinn* and Hausa *iska*. One police investigator in Bahia described these talismans as "little bundles or leather pouches" that contained seashells, cotton, and pieces of paper. The scraps of paper stuffed inside of them often featured Arabic script and geometric shapes with numerological significance. One amulet, for example, contained 143 separate squares filled with Arabic letters. The letter inside each square symbolized a number that was spiritually powerful. Below the squares were written Qurʾanic verses arranged and repeated to bring the wearer success in the revolt: "God's help and imminent triumph gives the good news" (61:13) was repeated three times. Similar verses discussing victory were found in other amulets.[24]

In addition to passing along knowledge of Arabic, Islamic prayer, and Islamic amulets, community leaders also hosted celebrations of the Islamic ritual calendar. Muslims gathered together to sacrifice goats and sheep for religious holidays such as ʿId al-Adha, the festival of sacrifice held at the end of the annual hajj. They also commemorated Layla al-Miʿraj, which celebrated the Prophet Muhammad's night journey from Mecca to Jerusalem and, from there, to the heavens and back.[25]

To celebrate the Prophet's night journey on November 29, 1834, some Muslims from this burgeoning and increasingly confident community gathered quite publicly in a hut behind an Englishman's house on Victória Road. What happened next changed Brazilian history. Having heard complaints about the gathering, police inspector Antônio Marques broke up the ritual celebration, and as word of this "disturbance of the peace" was circulated, the owner of the property ordered that the hut where the Muslims had gathered be torn down. In addition, the month of November saw the arrest of two prominent alufás, including the preacher Pacífico Licutan, who dramatically called himself Bilal in his February 1835 trial.[26]

Was this enough to inspire a revolt? There is little else in the way of direct evidence that would help explain the motivations of the rebels. But even if we assume that these slights to Muslim elders and the suppression of an Islamic holiday were enough to encourage the planning of the actual rebellion, we still need to explain the underlying causes of the decision of the rebel. Why turn to rebellion as a response to these incidents? Members of the Bahian military, freedmen, and slaves had tried unsuccessfully to overturn the political order several times since the country had achieved independence in 1822. As recently as 1830, slaves had attempted a revolt that led only to the massacre of the insurgents.[27] Why would things be different this time?

The answer for many scholars has been that the militants believed they were obligated to wage Islamic holy war.[28] Many of the African-born slaves transported to Brazil in the first three decades of the nineteenth century were familiar, some intimately so, with the violent jihad of the West African mystic and militant Uthman dan Fodio. He utilized religious appeals, especially for the purification of Islam from innovation and non-Islamic elements, to establish the Sokoto caliphate in northern Nigeria from 1804 to 1812. Slaves transported from the Bight of Benin, including those from Yorubaland, would have been well versed in this militant form of Islam. While there is no "indisputable evidence linking their activities to jihad and the creation of a theocracy," as historian Michael Gomez writes, this cultural background may have played a key role in the political consciousness of the rebels.[29]

But attributing the rebels' behavior solely or even primarily to a tradition that emerged in West Africa seems to ignore the Brazilian contexts that also influenced them. When migrants self-consciously attempt to preserve what they perceive to be the original traditions of their homeland, they often end up altering those very traditions. Even if a tradition is somehow preserved—for example, the teaching of Arabic grammar—its meaning and function inevitably change as the tradition is performed in new circumstances. João José Reis, who has written the most authoritative account of the 1835 revolt, insists the rebellion can be understood only inside of the multiple and overlapping socioeconomic, cultural, and political contexts of 1830s Bahia.

One of the primary contexts in which the rebellion needs to be understood is that of the racial divisions of Brazil's slave society. Brazil was a racialized society in which race, defined partly by the color of one's skin, influenced one's life opportunities. People who were *preto*, or black, had limited life opportunities, even if they were free. Racial categories in Bahia also included the terms *pardo*, or mulatto, a person of mixed race; *cabra*, a person whose skin color was perceived to be in between black and tan; and white, although some who called themselves white would have had troubling passing for such at the time in North America. One's racial identity in Bahia depended not only on physical characteristics such as skin color but also on the continent of one's birth. Native-born blacks had their own separate racial category; called *crioulos*, they were considered to be different from African-born blacks, and there was significant tension between the two groups. Brazilian-born blacks lived and worked in different social networks and saw themselves as having different political interests: throughout Brazilian history, they were far less willing to participate in slave revolts.[30]

Islamic Jihad or Just Revolt?

As much as anything else, the rebellion of 1835 seemed to be an attempt to overturn the political order that put whites on top and African-born blacks on bottom, though once again the available evidence points to differing interpretations of what this meant in practice. One testimony given in the post-rebellion hearings indicates that the point of the uprising was to kill whites; another witness said the purpose was to kill "all whites, mulattos, and native-born blacks"; still another said that blacks were to be killed only if they did not side with the militants. According to this last witness, the rebels "would keep the mulattos as their slaves and lackeys." The only thing common to all the testimonies was the idea that "the rebels certainly planned to end white domination."[31]

The idea that insurgents might have enslaved or killed other people of color points to a second domestic context in which the rebellion must be understood—namely, that of ethnic difference. Not all people of color were the same, and they did not always see themselves as sharing the same interests. Explaining how people joined across various social dividing lines is essential to comprehending the revolt. In addition to being divided along racial lines, Bahian society in the 1830s was structured around a framework of national ethnic groups, or *nações*. African-born blacks in Salvador were primarily from various West African ethnic groups, especially the Nagô or Yoruba, the Jejes or Ewe/Fon, the Hausas, and the Tapas or Nupe.[32] These identities were not merely transported from Africa; they were constructed anew in the context of Bahian society. The very term "Nagô" was a word derived from the Fon language. The consolidation of Nagô identity in Bahia was noted, at least implicitly, by Nagôs themselves. During the investigations of the rebellion, various witnesses tried to explain the differences among the Yoruba. They pointed out that one person might be referred to as "Nagô-Jabu, that is, an Ijebu, one of the Yoruba subdivisions," while another might be known as "Nagô-Ba, that is, a Yoruba from the kingdom of Egba." As one man testified, "Even though they are all Nagôs, each one has his own homeland." Whatever differences there were among these various groups, they were successfully bridged or put aside for the sake of the revolt. Reis calculates that "Nagôs made up 68.1% of all defendants" prosecuted for the rebellion. But Nagô rebels also reached out to African-born Bahians from other nações. Hausas composed 10 percent of all rebels, and twelve other distinct ethnic groups were also prosecuted for participating in the revolt.[33]

The bridging of ethnic difference as well as the creation of ethnic identity—in this case, involving the Nagôs—was one form of political solidarity created by the experience of diaspora. Importantly, the creation of ethnic solidarity did not preclude the creation of interethnic bonds. Nagô rebels were willing and anxious to unite with people from different ethnic identities in order to overturn a racial order that enslaved Africans and placed African-born freedmen and freedwomen at the bottom of the political order. The rebels shared common interests, even when there were important cultural differences among them based on the languages that they spoke and the social networks in which they lived and worked. The experience of African diaspora led simultaneously to ethnic differentiation and political solidarity.

But there was also another form of social solidarity—Islamic religion—working to unite many of the rebels. On one hand, Muslims in Bahia made distinctions between themselves and *gaveré*, meaning unbelievers, pagans, or infidels. Like Muslims throughout the Americas, they were known to be haughty and proud, which was partly a product of the prestige that they commanded as a result of their literacy and perceived ritual power.[34] Muslims rebels from the Yoruba, Hausa, Nupe, and several other ethnic groups shared the religious cultures and practices already described, and this form of solidarity was another axis along which the rebellion was formed. In fact, some previous interpreters of the revolt have concluded that the Muslims involved in the rebellion were religious exclusivists, unable to imagine cooperating with people of other religious backgrounds.

On the other hand, the very inclusion of non-Muslim Nagôs in the Muslim-led revolt indicates that the Islam of the rebels was not politically exclusivist. This was no jihad against the unbelievers. It was a holy war against a racist, slave society. Their plan depended on recruiting non-Muslims to join the revolt, and many non-Muslim Yoruba did so, making this an African, not an Islamic, struggle. Further, many of the non-Muslim Nagôs likely believed that their Muslim elders offered the rebellion their *baraka*, a spiritual power that would help to make the rebellion a success. It is no surprise that Islamic amulets were found on the bodies of Muslim and non-Muslim insurgents. The texts stashed inside these gris-gris quoted popular Qur'anic verses promising victory against the unbelievers—which in this case meant their enemies, the white overlords and their allies of color.

There is further evidence to suggest that the Islam of the rebels might have been viewed by the insurgency's non-Muslim participants as a blessing rather than as a curse. Like the Muslim Siddis of Karnataka, African Muslims in Brazil often lived alongside and maintained close relationships with non-Muslims of African descent, especially those from their same class and ethnic group. The Africana religious scene in 1830s Bahia was extremely diverse: in addition to Muslims, there were practitioners of Orisha religions, Fon traditions of Voodum, Catholicism, and other religions. Religious practitioners often freely borrowed spiritual technologies, rituals, healing practices, and other forms of religious culture from one another. For example, Muslims of Hausa descent, like the Stambali of Tunis, performed rituals to propitiate the Bori, or spirits/ancestors. Yoruba practitioners of an Orisha religion may have thought of Muslims as allies of the deity Oxalá, as they did in Africa. Most African-born residents of Salvador, Muslim or not, seemed to use Islamic talismans to ward off evil, illness, and bad luck. In the rebellion, many used them to try to achieve success.[35]

Did the Muslim leaders of the revolt hope to return to Africa, which they sometimes referred to as the "black man's land"? Whether they wanted to return or not, some of them were forcibly resettled there. Weary of another revolt, the government stepped up its repression of all African-born people and deported hundreds, both guilty and innocent, to Africa. A number of them had to pay their own way, and even after arriving in what today is Benin or Nigeria, some of them petitioned the Brazilian government for the right to return to Bahia.[36]

Islam played a variety of roles in the revolt. Perhaps for some Muslims, Islam was a utopian hope for a religious state, but even so, its central role in the revolt was likely something other than an ideological commitment to violent jihad or religious exclusivism. For many more, non-Muslim and Muslim, Islam was a form of spiritual power. To Muslim and non-Muslim rebels alike, Islam promised sacred protection from profane threats. Its political meaning was something other than the dream of a theocracy. Instead it was the means to political liberation—not from non-Muslims but from Brazilian whites and their accomplices, the real infidels. Given the relative success that Muslims had achieved in organizing a vibrant and public community, it is tempting to conclude that before the revolt, many of them had high hopes for their lives. While many African-born Muslims remained enslaved, they had seen numerous examples of manumission among other African-born people. Having achieved some success in the trades, freedmen were able to establish the religious institutions necessary to living an Islamic life. When the community's success was threatened and its religious institutions were attacked, they may have felt forced to respond with a violent uprising. Their hope may not have been to return to Africa or even to create a Bahian caliphate; it may have been more simply to preserve the life that they had managed to create for themselves in spite of the odds.

JIHAD IN TRINIDAD

To see a revolt in which ideas of jihad were more directly involved, we need to turn to a different example. On July 27, 1990, 114 Muslims, mainly but not exclusively of African descent, occupied Trinidad and Tobago's parliament and the headquarters of Trinidad and Tobago Television (TTT). Using rifles and other firearms, the Jama'at al-Muslimeen, literally meaning "group of Muslims," took hostages, including the country's prime minister, A. N. R. Robinson, and nineteen other government officials. At TTT, the group held twenty-six hostages. Yasin Abu Bakr, the leader of the gunmen, took to the air from the studios at TTT to announce that he had overthrown the government of Robinson, who was being held in the Red House, the name of Trinidad and Tobago's parliament building. As the imam, or religious leader, explained his actions, he said that the people of Trinidad and Tobago had had enough of the government's failure to put a halt to poverty, rape, cocaine addiction, prostitution, child abuse, murder, and other social problems. Outlining other reasons for the coup, he also detailed various examples of government corruption and what he considered to be ineptitude. "We want to assure the public at large," Abu Bakr said, "that their safety is our prime concern at the moment." He also attempted to reassure diplomats and foreigners of the same. Though he was now in charge, Abu Bakr promised to hold new elections in ninety days. It was not military might that allowed him to seize power, he said; "one had to depend solely on love, good deeds, and the will of Allah" for this opportunity to set the country on the right course.[37]

Reacting quickly to Abu Bakr's coup, the police surrounded the Red House and started shooting indiscriminately at the building. Jama'at officials directed Prime Minister Robinson to order them to stop. Instead, the prime minister shouted, "Attack with full force!" He was then shot in the leg. Later that night, Robinson changed his mind and ordered the police to stand down, but by this point they ignored him and continued to fire. It took the regular army to restore order to the scene. On the second day of the standoff, the army opened up with machine guns on both the TTT headquarters and the Red House. The Jama'at returned fire. Prepared, they said, to meet their maker, Jamaʿat members managed to keep up their regular prayers during the ordeal. Journalist Raoul Pantin and other hostages remarked afterward that it was curious how the terrorists, so capable of brutality, also treated the hostages at the TTT headquarters with courtesy and respect, even reassuring them that they would protect them in case of an army raid. Finally a ceasefire ensued, and by the third day of the coup, July 29, negotiations for the surrender of the Jamaʿat began in earnest. Brokered by Anglican canon Knolly Clarke, an agreement was drawn up between Abu Bakr at the TTT headquarters and Prime Minister Robinson at the Red House. It offered unconditional amnesty to the rebels, the resignation of the prime minister, and new elections. The acting president of the country, Emmanuel Carter, signed it in the presence of the Anglican priest. The only problem was that the army outside the Red House refused to recognize the agreement. In the meantime, the army and police continued to try to restore law and order to the nation's capital, which had been plagued by riots and looting since the insurrection began. By the end of the third day, approximately fifty people were dead, most of them shot by the army and the police. Six rebels were also killed.[38]

On the fourth day of the coup, the army tried once again to force the rebels to surrender unconditionally. It turned out that the army's previous assault was for the purpose of probing the military capabilities of the rebels. Now it would bring hell not only upon the rebels but also upon the hostages, who were terrorized by the experience, according to Raoul Pantin. Despite the assault, the Jamaʿat refused to return fire. Instead, the rebels and some of their hostages began working the telephone, trying to expose what they believed was a countercoup. The health of the prime minister was deteriorating, as he suffered not only from his gunshot wound in the leg but also from glaucoma—without his medication, he was going blind. Yasin Abu Bakr wanted to release him, but the army refused to allow his release, saying it would not engage in any further negotiations. With the help of the journalists inside the TTT headquarters, however, Abu Bakr was able to reach a BBC reporter and then other foreign journalists. The resulting press coverage put pressure on the army to abide by the civilian government's agreement. Robinson was freed, and the next day, August 1, 1990, the insurgents laid down their arms and peacefully surrendered to the army. "Rebels in Trinidad Free All Hostages," proclaimed the headline of the *New York Times*. The government continued to assert that it had made no deal with the

Jamaʿat al-Muslimeen and took all of its members into custody—though they would be let out of jail by Trinidad's courts two years later.[39]

In retrospect, the most palpable consequence of the revolt was the suffering of the hostages and all those who were injured or killed as a result of the army's crackdown on the looters and others. In December 1991 Prime Minister Robinson's government also fell from power, but it had already been highly unpopular before the coup attempt. Per capita gross national product had fallen from $7,560 USD in 1982 to $3,480 in 1987, and a poll taken one month before the coup attempt determined that 53 percent of those interviewed in Trinidad and Tobago gave the prime minister a negative job rating. Working-class Afro-Trinidadians were particularly dissatisfied with Robinson's party: only 14 percent of them said that they would vote for the incumbents, while 51 percent said that they would vote for their main rivals.[40] Popular discontent with the Robinson government remained in place after the coup, though most people opposed the violent assault of the Jamaʿat. While 60 percent of those polled after the rebellion said that they sympathized with the goals of the Jamaʿat, 75 percent said that it was wrong to overthrow the government by force.[41]

From 1990 until today, various government officials, scholars, journalists, and others have tried to explain more fully exactly why such a revolt occurred in the "Callaloo nation," the nation that in theory embraces religious, racial, and ethnic mixing with pride and enthusiasm.[42] Was the coup attempt first and foremost the result of a violent jihadist interpretation of Islam, yet another example of the global spread of Islamist violence? The increase of Muslim religious activity more generally in Latin America and the Caribbean has sparked just this fear among some in the U.S. military, though the U.S. Department of State has pointed out that there are no known al-Qaeda terrorist cells in the region.[43] If, on the other hand, one insists that the actual underlying causes of the revolt were poverty, lack of education, social maladjustment, racism, and other political, social, or economic factors, then one might simply dismiss the religious aspects of the story as some veneer or exotic clothing for what is really a social or political movement. The problem with all of these one-dimensional explanations is that they do not work hard enough to bring together the multiple explanations of the rebels themselves, the different reasons for their actions, the events that preceded the revolt, and the underlying conditions and contexts in which all of these explanations and events have meaning and significance.

Understanding the revolt requires a better sense of the history of the country in which the revolt took place. Since the end of the nineteenth century, Trinidad and Tobago's society has been characterized by a number of group tensions, including those that exist between those who identify as black and those who identify as (Asian) Indian. Many Indian-descended people insist that, while they embrace diversity, they do not "mix" with blacks—socially or sexually. This is one of the consequences of a society and economy founded upon the enslavement of Africans and the indentured labor of South Asians. The ideology of separate social and domestic spaces is a powerful myth often belied by the actual encounters of the people of Trinidad and Tobago of all racial backgrounds. The development of ethnicity as a strategy for claiming power and prestige within Trinidad and Tobago had important religious implications as Indo-Trinidadians in the post–World War II era built Muslim mosques and Hindu temples as a sign of their arrival as citizens with an ethnic and cultural heritage worthy of recognition.[44] The development of Islamic religion as a public sign of identity among Indo-Trinidadians, when combined with the racial hierarchies of the society, marginalized Muslims of African descent within the various mosques and Muslim associations dominated by those with South Asian roots, who greatly outnumbered Muslims of African descent. This marginalization resulted in greater tensions between the two groups during the 1960s and 1970s, as Trinidad and Tobago, like many other countries in Africa and the African diaspora, experienced social movements associated with black power, black consciousness, and pan-Africanism.[45]

As in other English-speaking countries in the region, including Jamaica and Belize, African Americans were part of a black Anglophone religious culture in which the Islamic revival was buoyed by the proliferation of a number of Muslim American groups focused on black liberation. The ideas of Elijah Muhammad's Nation of Islam, Malcolm X, and a U.S.-based group called Darul Islam, or the House of Islam, were influential far beyond the shores of the United States as North Americans founded missions in the Caribbean and Caribbean people traveled to and from North America. In the 1970s, for example, former police officer Lennox Phillip, the man who became Yasin Abu Bakr, was exposed to Darul Islam while in Canada.[46] Bilaal Abdullah, who was in charge of the crew that eventually took over the Red House, was another figure involved with Darul Islam in the 1970s.[47] Darul Islam helped to popularize the idea that residential communities of Muslims should be committed to the uplift of black society and culture. The key to success was residential living in Muslim communities, away from mainstream culture, that would be governed instead by the rules of *fiqh*, or Islamic jurisprudence.[48] For these Muslims, living according to Islamic law meant, among other things, that a man could have up to four wives—a fact that later made the Jama'at vulnerable to charges that it violated accepted norms of sexual propriety and gender equality.[49]

Another major influence on Abu Bakr and the Jama'at al-Muslimeen was the Islamic Party of North America (IPNA), a group established by Yusuf Muzaffaruddin Hamid in 1971.[50] In 1977 Hamid visited Port of Spain, Trinidad, and inspired some Muslims from Trinidad and Tobago to establish a branch of the IPNA in the Caribbean. By 1978 many in Darul Islam were becoming members of the IPNA—and by the 1980s they would become followers of Yasin Abu Bakr's Jama'at al-Muslimeen. The IPNA contributed much to the local spread of a modern, reform-oriented interpretation of Islam that opposed racial and ethnic divisions in Islam, emphasized the meaning of Islam as an agent of social and political change, and focused on liberation for the poor and oppressed.[51] It stressed the role of struggle in any social progress: "In Islam, struggle (Jihad) holds a position before even prayer, fasting and charity. . . . Faith in God and struggle for justice are the things which make a people or a nation superior."[52] Quoting Mawlana Mawdudi, the leader of the Jama'at-i Islami (or Islamic Society) of Pakistan, the organization seemed to indicate that its ultimate goal was to bring about a world revolution in which all un-Islamic governments were replaced with Islamic ones.[53] But its methods for achieving the revolution were apparently gradualist. Like Darul Islam, it created residential communities and economic cooperatives. The group was to be organized around what it called collective intention, worship, living, education, work, economics, and struggle.[54] But its decision making was not collectivist: "Obedience to and full cooperation with the leadership in the organised struggle will be given in all things that are right," declared its official publication, the *Faithful Struggler*.[55] The Trinidad and Tobago chapter of the IPNA failed by the early 1980s, but some of its members would join with Yasin Abu Bakr to make the Jama'at al-Muslimeen, which also drew on some of the IPNA's teachings, one of the premier organizations among African-descended Muslims in Trinidad and Tobago.[56]

In 1982 the Jama'at brought together various elements of the Afro-Trinidadian Sunni Muslim community in its residential headquarters on

Mucurapo Road in the capital city, Port of Spain. This land was originally promised by the government to the Islamic Missionaries Guild (IMG) in the late 1960s for the building of an Islamic cultural center. But in the face of controversy over the land grant, the IMG apparently halted its effort to erect the structure. The Jamaʿat al-Muslimeen filled the void, reclaiming what had been a swampy property for the purposes of building residences in addition to a mosque. In 1983 Abu Bakr began to build a mosque on the site, and in 1984 the city council offered to rent the land to the group. Abu Bakr declined.[57] By 1985 the police were conducting a series of raids on the compound, and Yasin Abu Bakr spent twenty-one days in jail for contempt of court.[58] In turn, the Jamaʿat claimed a right to defend itself against what it considered to be unlawful attacks against its property. In so doing it appealed to the authority of Islamic scripture: "The Qurʾan," it said in a statement to the press, "commands us to prevent people from pulling down Mosques. . . . If forced to choose between submitting to Allah and submitting to an unjust order to demolish the house of Allah, we would choose confrontation [with the court] rather than with Allah." In response to the arrest of the imam, the statement also warned that war could be fought to defend him.[59] On April 3, 1985, Yasin Abu Bakr declared that the group was now "in a state of war."[60]

During the second half of the 1980s, the Jamaʿat's campaign to interdict illegal drug trafficking exacerbated the tensions between the government and the Jamaʿat. In the 1980s Trinidad and Tobago became both a transfer point and niche market in the trans-American trade in crack cocaine and other illegal drugs. A 1986 report of a special commission chaired by Justice Garvin Scott determined that police officers had become involved in the drug trade. Officers used drugs, confiscated and then sold drugs, and operated protection rackets. "Lamentably," the report concluded, "there is not the slightest doubt that many members of the Police Service in every one of its divisions, including some of the most senior personnel, are engaged in the illegal drug trade in one way or another."[61] The Jamaʿat, like other African American grassroots organizations that identified crack cocaine as a community scourge, sought to stem the flow of drugs. Unlike many other groups, however, the Jamaʿat quite literally declared war on the dealers; some drug dealers apparently blamed the Jamaʿat for the murder of dealer Shazard "Teddy Mice" Khan during the Muharram festival in 1988. The Jamaʿat amassed an impressive cache of small arms, apparently smuggled in from Miami, Florida. Some Jamaʿat members also became implicated in the drug trade itself.

As a result, the police continued to raid the Jama'at's compound and investigate its members, quite literally establishing a camp next to the compound on Mucurapo Road. The Jama'at said that it was the victim of its own success—it was having an effect on the drug trade and getting close to revealing government officials and police who were complicit in drug dealing. By 1990 members of the Jama'at came to believe, probably correctly, that the security services were committed to the dismantling of the organization, by one means or another. They expressed these fears publicly but were frustrated by the media's lack of interest in their side of the story.[62]

Two days before the Jama'at launched its coup d'état on July 27, 1990, a ruling by the Trinidad and Tobago Court of Appeals denied the Jama'at's request for protection from the city's attempt to evict the group and tear down unauthorized structures at Mucurapo Road. This was apparently the final straw. As one member of the group put it, "What promoted the uprising was when the Imam realized that we would not get any justice from the courts of this nation."[63] Bilaal Abdullah, who was the Jama'at official in charge of the gunmen at the Red House, equated the police's coming assault as a matter of life and death. After having served almost two years in prison, Abdullah reflected on the reasons for his violent jihad: "Unless I change my understanding of the moral threat that I felt," he told the *Trinidad Guardian* on May 29, 1994, "it's difficult to talk about apologizing for what, in my mind, was self-defense."[64]

But this was a jihad as a form of nationalist resistance, not global hegemony. The imagined polis was not a region or a continent or a globe, but a nation. It was the nation of Trinidad and Tobago for which the jihadis were struggling. This belief was reflected in public opinion at the time: in the immediate aftermath of the revolt, 38 percent thought that Abu Bakr's goal was to establish an Islamic state in Trinidad and Tobago, while 45 percent of those polled said that Abu Bakr's aim was to remove the ruling party and hold new elections.[65] When Abu Bakr took over the national television station and announced that he had overthrown the government on July 27, 1990, he was engaging in a rhetorical performance meant to establish his political authority and to engender support among the people of Trinidad and Tobago. He had launched a jihad, to be sure, but it was a jihad more akin to nationalist resistance movements such as Hamas in Palestine than to transnational networks such as al-Qaeda. That is, it sought to free the nation, not the world, from occupation and injustice.[66] As Jama'at member Kwesi Atiba later wrote in a letter to his wife from prison: "People suggest that we want a state which will deny others their rights. No! We want a state that is just so that our rights can be guaranteed."⁶⁷ Bilaal Abdullah, who broke away from the Jamaʿat in 1993, also rejected the idea that the true goal of the group was to establish some "feudal" Islamic state, explaining that "I was born and bred in the West. My travels in the Middle East have shown me both much that I admire and many things that I either loathe or am uncomfortable with. My goal is the reform of my society using insights that I have gleaned from Islam. To my mind, this is precisely what the prophets have sought to do. There are Muslims whose concept of the Islamization process is their creation of some particular society that flourished in another time and place. This is not the dominant perspective in Jamaat al Muslimeen."⁶⁸ For Abdullah and other members of the Jamaʿat, then, Islam mandated jihad to ensure this-worldly justice, but Islam did not dictate a particular political order. The political imagination of the Jamaʿat operated with references to the existing political order, as evidenced in Imam Yasin Abu Bakr's demands for new elections. The nationalism of these Muslims could be observed even in the midst of the coup attempt itself; at one point in the siege, for example, Abu Bakr was said to have been listening to the radio when he decided to pretend as if his AK-47 were a microphone and to lip-synch along to the popular national calypso song: "Trinidad is my land and to love it I'm proud and glad."⁶⁹ Later, insurgent Kwesi Atiba wrote, "We are the most patriot[ic] citizens of Trinidad and Tobago."⁷⁰

Just as the religious imaginations of Jamaʿat members were not focused on establishing some kind of global Islamic order, they were not acting primarily out of political commitment to pan-African ties. Nor did they invest Africa or African-derived material culture, symbols, or ideas with any spiritual meaning or significance. Imam Yasin Abu Bakr blatantly rejected Rastafarianism and Yoruban traditions as inferior religions.⁷¹ According to ethnographer Aisha Khan, this stance toward non-Abrahamic religions is widespread among many Muslims of African descent on the islands: "When discussing their ideas about Islam, the Afro-Trinidadian Muslims I spoke with did not invoke Africa as a particular kind of cultural space. . . . [They] seem much more likely to see place (as a site of culture and race) and religion as distinct."⁷² The fact that the African Muslim presence in Trinidad and Tobago preceded that of South Asian Muslims is a claim not about the essential Africanness of Trinidadian Islam but about their belonging to the land and their rightful place in Trinidadian society. Their Islam, like the Islam of many Trinidadians of South Asian descent, is a strategy for power-making within the nation-state. Afro-Trinidadian Muslims have created a "Muslim identity oriented toward critique of, and resistance to, political and economic oppression."[73] Muslims of African descent often challenge the Islamic authenticity of South Asian–descended Muslims based on the notion that the latter accept the injustice of the social and political order—an unacceptable view for those Muslims who believe that "authentic Islam" challenges structural inequalities that "go against the grain of Islamic egalitarianism."[74]

Members of the Jamaʿat interpret the meaning of the African diaspora through notions of justice or its absence. Slavery, racism, structural inequality, and governmental corruption, all of which affected and continue to affect Afro-Trinidadians, are examples of the human failure to act in accordance with virtue. The solution to the problem of Trinidad and Tobago is not to recover an African heritage that has been lost or even to create cultural space for the expression of African-derived traditions and black pride. The Jamaʿat's political activities instead constitute a different form of nostalgia, one that mourns the lost innocence of all human beings who stray from the straight path of Islam. For the Jamaʿat, investing the African diaspora with spiritual meaning and significance can offer no salvation or hope for human renewal. Hope comes only from God and from the traditions of the Prophet Muhammad as acted out in everyday practice.

CONCLUSION

One of the reasons that this chapter has focused on two examples of political violence among African-descended Muslims is because there is limited current scholarship on the modern and contemporary practice of Islam among Muslims of African descent in Latin America and the Caribbean. The fact that there is, in contrast, an ample body of scholarship covering the topic of Islam and violent revolt is, at least in part, a legacy of English-language orientalism. That is, it reflects the fascination of Anglophone writers, readers, and publishers with what is framed as Islam's special ability to inspire violent assaults against the political status quo—and also their fear of the same. This is a legacy that deserves to be critiqued and challenged, not only because it is factually incorrect but also because it continues to fuel Islamophobia in international politics, popular culture, and scholarship. The practice of Islam among hundreds of thousands of people in Latin America and the Caribbean, including Muslims of African descent, cannot and should not be understood as particularly bellicose or bloody.

At the same time, violent political resistance is an important chapter in the story of Islamic practice among the heirs of Bilal. Rather than simply explaining it as some innate impulse among all Muslims, this chapter more carefully sifts through the available evidence to try to understand what role, if any, violent interpretations of jihad have played in fueling political violence. As observed in the analysis of the 1835 rebellion in Bahia, Brazil, the Islamic practice of insurgents can incorporate far more than a devotion to jihad. In this instance, the Muslim rebels understood the material arts of Islam such as talismans to offer them protection against their enemies; they sought to defend their ability to practice Islam in public; and they may have believed that their timing of the revolt, coming at it did near or on the Layla al-Qadr, the Night of Power, would help them achieve victory. Over a century and a half later, the Jamaʿat al-Muslimeen in Trinidad and Tobago similarly fought against what they considered to be social injustice and a threat to their life and property. But the role played by their commitment to jihad—interpreted here as the necessity of defending oneself against those who prevented the free practice and spread of Islam—was far more obvious. Even then, the point of the rebels was not to establish a Caribbean caliphate or to kill unbelievers. It was to work within the parliamentary political system of Trinidad and Tobago to establish a more just and moral government for a country to which the rebels felt attached.

The focus in this chapter on Islamic practice in politics reveals another perspective on the meaning of the black African diaspora to Bilal's heirs. The Muslim communities that African-descended Muslims built in nineteenth-century Brazil and twentieth-century Trinidad and Tobago constructed meaningful spaces within the New World for the practice of Islam and the economic and political enfranchisement of African-descended Muslims. Generally speaking, neither group expressed a sense of displacement; there was no widely shared communal dream of returning to Africa. Instead, most African-descended Muslims wished to take their rightful place as valued members of the New World communities in which they found themselves. For Muslims in Salvador, their stake in Bahian society could be seen not only through their religious belonging but also in their identification with the ethnic Yoruba identity that linked them to non-Muslims and in the racial identity that tied their social and political fates to all African-born slaves and freedmen. For members of the Jamaʿat al-Muslimeen, the symbol of Africa and its diaspora held no spiritual meaning. The turn of some Afro-Trinidadians to African traditions such as Orisha religions held no allure. Their violent jihad against the government of Trinidad and Tobago stemmed not from a commitment to black nationalism, black power, or pan-Africanism but from a belief in the promise of a multiethnic and multiracial nation in which opportunities for all were equal. Their sense of universal justice for all citizens sought inspiration from an interpretation of Islam that required the taking up of arms in order to make their country a just and good society.

Nation of Islam rally, 1964. Nation of Islam members listen to the Honorable Elijah Muhammad (1897–1975), whom they believed to be God's Apostle. Embodying the Messenger's commands to dress in a respectable manner, women wore officially sanctioned white robes and head scarves, while men wore suits and ties. *World Telegram & Sun* photograph by Stanley Wolfson.

6

AFRICAN AMERICAN MUSLIMS IN THE UNITED STATES

Making Physical and Metaphysical Homelands

> I was once a slave
> who was very brave.
> I was a man without fear
> who gave the first prayer
> in a land where Arabia lay
> and though there were great odds
> I was not afraid
> to proclaim the religion of God.
> Who am I?
> —*Bilalian News* children's puzzle, 1975[1]

The answer is Bilal. For a period of time in the 1970s, Bilal ibn Rabah not only was the object of historical pride among members of the Nation of Islam but also was seen as a moral exemplar whose name might provide a new ethnic label for people of African descent. When W. D. Mohammed took the reins of the Nation of Islam from his father, Elijah Muhammad, in February 1975, he sought new ways of recognizing the contributions of people of African descent to Islam. Mohammed suggested that his followers and all African Americans call themselves "Bilalians" instead of "blacks," "Afro-Americans," and so on. During this period, the name of the Nation of Islam's newspaper was also changed from *Muhammad Speaks* to *Bilalian News*.[2] Though these changes in nomenclature did not last into the 1980s, they symbolized a larger transition in the diasporic imagination of many African American Muslims, both inside and outside the Nation of Islam. Increasing emigration from African countries and stronger commercial and cultural ties between Africans and African Americans led to a multiplication of the ways that African American Muslims experienced, felt, and interpreted their connections to black

Africa and its history, languages, and cultures. In this case, as will be demonstrated further below, the linking of African American Muslim ethnic and religious identity to a close companion of the Prophet Muhammad signaled a shift in Muslim notions of "thick blackness"—that is, the black identities that Muslims themselves constructed. Rather than imagining a primordial and mythological origin for blacks/Muslims as the "original man" as Elijah Muhammad had done, celebrating Bilal was a way to link black people to the earthly history of the religion of Islam while also carving out a particular ethnic identity inside that larger story. It was a theme that would continue to echo across the black Atlantic over three decades later among some British- and Caribbean-born Muslims in the United Kingdom, as shown in chapter 3.

But the ethnic and religious identity engendered by the figure and symbol of Bilal is only one way that African American Muslims in the United States have constructed their peoplehood since the 1970s. Since then, the number of black Muslims in the United States has continued to increase due to the conversion of American-born people of African descent, the immigration of Africans to the country, and the raising of the children of both groups as Muslims. About one-third of all Muslims in the United States identify as black, meaning that there are approximately one to three million Muslims of African descent in the United States.[3] Today they are almost a microcosm of global Islam itself in that they represent an enormous variety of Islamic practice.[4] African-descended Muslims in the United States are members of a variety of Sufi groups, including the Muridiyya, the Tijaniyya, and homegrown orders such as the Bawa Muhaiyaddeen Fellowship.[5] There are also African-descended Muslims who follow one of the four major Sunni schools of *fiqh*, or Islamic jurisprudence, and there are those who do not subscribe to any school of fiqh at all, saying that they simply try to live out the meaning of the Qur'an and the Sunna, or traditions of the Prophet Muhammad, as well as they can in their daily lives.[6] Since the 1970s there has been a growing, if relatively modest, number of African American Shi'a Muslims.[7] There are African-descended Muslims who align themselves with the thought of the modern Muslim reformer Ghulam Ahmad, those who call themselves Salafi Muslims, and those who follow one of the several heirs to Elijah Muhammad, including Minister Louis Farrakhan.[8] It is also important to keep in mind that these group labels—Sunni, Shi'a, Sufi, and so on—are themselves dynamic; they have been and continue to be debated by African American Muslims themselves.

More has been published about African American Muslims in English than about any other group of African-descended Muslims in the world. Rather than summarize all of that literature, this chapter seeks to point out the diversity of Islamic practice among African-descended Muslims by focusing on three case studies of African American Islamic expression. Each of these case studies, like every other case study in the book, is examined with regard to questions about how these African-descended Muslims practice Islam, how those practices are connected to what they understand to be their black or African identities, and how African American Muslims think about and experience diaspora, or dispersal. The chapter shows how this embodied, symbolic, and sometimes contentious discourse affects the formation of African American Muslim groups and congregations, the forms of rituals that African American Muslims practice, and the culture that they create.

The chapter begins with an exploration of the enslaved Muslims who represented the first significant population of Muslims in the United States. The extraordinary efforts of a few of them to return to Africa is an important moment in the history of the African American Muslim diaspora, and it speaks to the idea that, for them, belonging to their particular homeland or country and also the larger continent of Africa precluded a similar political attachment to the United States, which was foreign land. Though most African-born Muslim slaves never returned home, the available evidence suggests that many continued to practice Islam in some way and dreamed that they would one day be reunified with their ancestors and their native land.

Next, the chapter explores the African American Muslim movement that has been the most consequential for U.S. history overall, the Nation of Islam. Messenger Elijah Muhammad, Minister Malcolm X, and boxer Muhammad Ali were the faces of a movement in the 1960s that opposed the civil rights movement, supported black separatism and pan-Africanism, and opposed U.S. involvement in the Vietnamese civil war. But going beyond this political history, this chapter shows that the Nation of Islam was also significant in the ways that it culturally and religiously imagined and embodied the connection between Islamic religion and the recovery of black dignity and power. The diaspora of the Nation of Islam was a metaphysical one; it explained the fracturing of black/Muslim self through a complicated and original myth of the "fall of man."

Finally, I examine the religious practices of African-born Muslim immigrants whose numbers have increased especially quickly in the past decade. The exile of Sierra Leonean refugees in the Washington, D.C., area during the 1990s evokes themes and questions that were already examined in chapter 3 in the discussion of Ahmadu Bamba's followers from Senegal in Turin and Paris and of the Mandinga people from Guinea-Bissau who have settled in Portugal. The diaspora of Sierra Leoneans in the United States is a more recent one, and since their displacement was shaped in no small part by their nation's civil war, many of them inevitably ask when and if they and their American-born children will return home. Like the Mandinga in Portugal, these emigrants and refugees from Sierra Leone meet Muslims from around the world in their new land and thus encounter new Islamic norms. As a result, the traditional link between what they come to see as Sierra Leonean culture and normative Islamic religious practice is challenged. Their decision about how to practice Islam in this new setting is often split along gendered lines as men and women come to understand their African cultural heritage in a new light.

AFRICAN AMERICAN MUSLIM SLAVES AND DIASPORIC IDENTITY

Though over a million Africans with Muslim backgrounds may have been transported against their will to the Americas, historians still disagree about how many of them landed in the United States. Allan Austin has figured that approximately 5 to 10 percent of all first-generation Africans who arrived between 1711 and 1808 in the thirteen colonies and the United States were Muslim. According to Austin, these 30,000–40,000 enslaved Africans were largely former residents of Senegambia.[9] Michael Gomez notes that 255,000 of the 481,000 first-generation Africans brought to Anglophone North America had come from places in Africa where Muslims were politically ascendant, but he largely agrees with Austin's estimate that, of these Africans in the United States, thousands or perhaps tens of thousands were Muslim.[10]

Among the thousands of Muslims to be brought to the United States were elite and literate Muslims educated in Arabic, the Qur'an, the Sunna, and fiqh, or Islamic jurisprudence. In addition to attending Islamic schools in West Africa, they had often been raised in the context of a local Islamic culture influenced deeply by beliefs in Islamic saints and by various Sufi orders.[11] The most celebrated of these Muslims in the antebellum United States was likely Abd al-Rahman Ibrahima, who hailed from the mountainous area of Guinea called Futa Jalon. An ethnic Fulbe, Ibrahima came from a group of people central to the story of Islamization in West Africa. The Fulbe constructed a potent state by trading slaves, farming lands near the Senegal and Gambia Rivers, and waging war against rival powers. Merchants and political leaders supported mosques and Islamic institutions of learning in Timbo, the capital of Futa Jalon. Raised in this city, Abd al-Rahman said that he was the son of an *almamy*, or Muslim noble. Born around 1762, Abd al-Rahman was educated not only in Timbo but also in the regional educational centers of Timbuktu and Djenné. He gained proficiency in Arabic and also learned several different West African languages. After finishing his education, Abd al-Rahman joined his country's military and helped his regime in its successful bid to achieve regional dominance. But as Abd al-Rahman was returning from battle in 1788, a rival ethnic group captured him, had him taken north to the Gambia River, and then sold him to slave traders from Europe. From the coast of West Africa, Abd al-Rahman traveled to the Caribbean and then to New Orleans, finally settling almost two hundred miles north in Natchez, Mississippi. As Abd al-Rahman tried to explain his noble background, the man who purchased him decided to call him "Prince," a name that would stick with him the rest of his life. Abd al-Rahman, like so many slaves, tried to run away from his owner, but after weeks of hard travel through the wilderness of Mississippi, he voluntarily came back to Natchez. In the 1790s he married an African American Baptist woman named Isabella. Tending to his owner's livestock, he settled into an American life. He and his family grew their own vegetables and raised livestock, earning extra money by selling their goods at a local market.[12]

This enslaved father and farmer is known by us today because he was discovered at his local market in 1807 by John Coates Cox, a white man who claimed to have been aided by Abd al-Rahman's father when he was lost on an adventure in Timbo. For many years afterward, Cox would work to free Abd al-Rahman. Cox wrote to the governor, attempted to purchase the freedom of Abd al-Rahman, and told the story of this lost prince to local newspapers. But none of these strategies worked, and Abd al-Rahman and his family continued to be enslaved for almost two more decades. In 1826, however, another miraculous happenstance changed the destiny of Abd al-Rahman. A letter that he had composed in Arabic to his father came to the attention of a U.S. senator, who then sent it to the U.S. consul in Morocco, who then passed it along to U.S. secretary of state

Henry Clay. Clay was interested in assisting Abd al-Rahman as a gesture of goodwill toward the North African "Barbary" states with whom the United States had engaged in battle from 1801 to 1805 and again from 1815 to 1816. Clay was operating on a false assumption, but the reasons he did so are important. Thinking that Prince Abd al-Rahman was from North Africa as opposed to West Africa reflected not only a challenged sense of geography but the assumption that Arabic writers belonged not to black Africa but to the more "Oriental" world of Moors, Turks, and Arabs. Like other slaveholders, Clay assumed that Muslim slaves were from racial backgrounds that differed from non-Muslim slaves. For Henry Clay and many other believers in the inherent inferiority of African people, Abd al-Rahman could not possibly be of pure "Negro" origins. And this was an assumption held in the North as much as in the South. It was an assumption that Abd al-Rahman, like other slaves who claimed a Muslim background, could use to his advantage among both white and black Americans. An 1828 article in New York's *Freedom's Journal*, perhaps penned by African American abolitionist John Russwurm, argued that "it must be evident to everyone that the Prince is a man superior to the generality of Africans whom we behold in this country."[13]

Henry Clay offered Abd al-Rahman free transportation back to Africa, and Abd al-Rahman desperately wanted to return to Futa Jalon. But he was unwilling to do so without his wife and children. Friends in Mississippi donated the two hundred dollars that would be required to purchase the freedom of Isabella. To free the children would require financial resources that Abd al-Rahman could never hope to find locally. So, with the help of abolitionist allies, the prince began a nationwide fund-raising tour. Secretary of State Henry Clay gave his approval, and American merchants, politicians, and philanthropists offered their living rooms and connections to their social networks to help him. Abd al-Rahman toured up and down the East Coast of the United States, often donning a Moorish costume as he spun his autobiographical tale of the tragic prince in exile. His story was lauded by some of the nation's most prominent citizens—people such as Francis Scott Key, the author of "The Star-Spangled Banner"; Thomas Gallaudet, a pioneer of education for the deaf; Charles and Arthur Tappan, rich Christian businessmen, evangelicals, and abolitionists; and David Walker, the African American activist who would soon publish his *Appeal to the Colored Citizens of the World* (1829). Abd al-Rahman tailored a message that appealed to each of them and their interests. He praised the idea of transferring all black people to Africa when he was raising money from the American Colonization Society. He pledged to spread Christianity in West Africa when he was speaking before evangelicals. Abd al-Rahman was single-minded in his efforts to free his family, and he used whatever strategies were effective to achieve his goals. And it worked. After ten months of speaking to various audiences Abd al-Rahman, who was around sixty years old at the time, was able to collect $3,400 toward the freeing and transportation of his family to Africa. In 1829 this Muslim noble and his spouse departed for Liberia, from which they planned to travel to Abd al-Rahman's home, Timbo. Some of their children followed on a later voyage.[14]

It was a truly unusual moment in the history of slavery in the United States. Very few Muslim slaves could conceive of returning to their homes in Africa, much less make concrete plans to do so. Even among literate and educated Muslim slaves, the best one could hope for was to use such resources to improve one's status in the pecking order of slaves, sometimes by claiming superiority over one's fellow slaves. For most first-generation Africans, the idea that they were different from one another was a given: they often spoke different languages, came from competing nations, and did not claim a shared sense of belonging in some sort of unified African political identity. But many first-generation Africans, including Muslims, did dream of returning home.

To understand the nature of this diasporic longing and its relationship to the ways that some Muslim men and women practiced Islam, there is suggestive evidence from the coastal areas of Georgia and South Carolina. Along the Atlantic Ocean on relatively isolated coastal plantations, African American Muslims observed various forms of Islam throughout the nineteenth century. On Sapelo Island, Georgia, where African Americans raised cotton, sugarcane, and rice, an enslaved first-generation African called Bilali, also known as Belali Mahomet, Ben Ali, and Bu Allah, became known as a highly successful overseer. He was captured in Futa Jalon, which was also Abd al-Rahman's home, and transported to the Bahamas. There he wed a woman and had children but was separated from them when he was sold to a new owner. Once he arrived in Georgia he started over, married again, and had more children. His wealthy owner, Thomas Spaulding, appointed Bilali to oversee the work of hundreds of slaves, and his unusual assignments included not only supervising their agrarian pursuits but also preparing for a possible British invasion during the War of 1812 and evacuating them to safety during the hurricane of 1824. Bilali's success allowed him certain privileges, including the protection of his wife, his twelve sons, and his seven daughters from the threat of sale and separation. In the late 1850s a woman from Broughton Island, Georgia, met Bilali's children. She wrote that that they were "tall and well-formed" and communicated in a language, perhaps Fula, that was incomprehensible to her. She said that Bilali's family "worshipped Mahomet," or Muhammad, suggesting that the religious identity of Bilali was public and, furthermore, that he was passing on some form of it to his children.[15] Two of the daughters were named Medina and Fatima, names both African and Muslim in origin. Bilali penned various Arabic manuscripts throughout his life. He likely began his education by memorizing parts or all of the Qur'an and by studying the Sunna. He then would have gone on to study Islamic theology, Arabic grammar, and Qur'anic commentary. Based on one of the manuscripts that he wrote, he seemed to be familiar with the Maliki school of fiqh, the most popular school of Islamic legal interpretation in Africa. There is no evidence that he passed on his literacy in Arabic or his Islamic education to his children, but he did seem to encourage them to practice at least some form of Islamic religion.[16]

During the 1930s some of Bilali's descendants were interviewed by members of the Savannah unit of the Georgia Writers Project, which was part of the Work Projects Administration (WPA). Created by President Franklin D. Roosevelt, the WPA offered employment to workers in various professions during the Great Depression. Unemployed writers and others were hired in Georgia and other states to record information about what many identified as the disappearing ethnic traditions of many rural and immigrant Americans. These remarkable interviews included the voices of women as well as men, and while oral history is not the same kind of historical source as a written document, these documents give us a sense of how, at least in this corner of the United States, both men and women practiced various forms of Islam in the nineteenth century. For example, according to one of these interviews, Bilali and his wife, Phoebe, prayed three times a day—which, notwithstanding the textbook notion that all pious Sunni Muslims are supposed to pray five times a day, is not unusual among some Sunni Muslims. Like Muslims around the world, they would prostrate their bodies on rugs faced toward Mecca. They "was very particular about the time they pray," said their great-granddaughter Katie Brown, a Sapelo Island native. "And they was very regular about the hour; [they prayed] when the sun come up, when it straight over the head, and when it set." Brown did not witness these rituals herself but told the Georgia writers that her grandmother and one other relative had passed on the information to her. In addition, "Bilali and his wife Phoebe prayed on the bead," Katie Brown said. This likely meant that they used a string of beads to recite *dhikr*, a litany that can include repeating certain short pietistic phrases or the name of God. According to Brown, Bilali pulled on each bead as he did so. She also remarked that the string of beads was very long, perhaps meaning that his particular string of beads was the same type that members of the Qadiri Sufi order used in West Africa. The use of prayer beads was apparently not limited to Bilali's family since another descendant of Bilali named Shad Hall recalled that not only his grandmother Hester but also others used the beads when they prayed.[17]

In addition to praying, coastal residents also celebrated African holidays associated with Islam. Katie Brown recalled that her grandmother often prepared "funny flat cake she call 'saraka'" for a holiday of the same name. The annual celebration of *saraka* or perhaps *sadaqa*, which comes from the Arabic word for "charity," took place in West Africa to offer gratitude for one's ancestors, to remember them, and to ask them for help. In America, Brown's grandmother adapted an old African recipe for the holiday. She soaked rice overnight and then used a wooden mortar and pestle to pulverize the rice into a paste. Adding honey or sugar, she then formed flat cakes out of the dough. "She make them same day every year," said Brown, "and it a big day. When they finish, she call us in, all the children, and put in hands little flat cake. And we eats it." Hester, the grandmother of Shad Hall, said a blessing before the children consumed them, uttering, "Ameen, ameen, ameen," the Arabic word for "Amen."[18]

African Muslim sartorial traditions were also practiced on the coast. Margaret, one of Katie Brown's grandmothers, donned a head scarf. This woman, who was born in the Bahamas, wore "a loose white cloth that she throw over her head like veil and it hang loose on her shoulder." Whether this head scarf had a particularly Islamic meaning for Grandmother Margaret was not clear to Brown: "I ain't know why she wear it that way, but I think she ain't like a tight thing round her head."[19] Using the head scarf does not necessarily mean that Margaret was attempting to observe Islamic teachings on modesty. One of the hallmarks of all religions, not just the religion of African American slaves, is that the meaning of material culture can change over time. Old traditions can meet new social needs or can be combined to make new meanings. One white southern preacher, the Reverend Charles Colcock Jones, noted that some enslaved African Americans saw Christianity and Islam as manifestations of the same religious impulse: "God, they say, is Allah, and Jesus Christ is Mohammed—the religion is the same, but different countries have different names."[20]

Even if some enslaved Africans were combining their Islam with Christianity, the majority of black American slaves living along the coasts of South Carolina and Georgia were probably prone to combining elements of West African Islamic traditions with those of Orisha and other West African religious traditions, sometimes referred to as conjure or hoodoo. Isolated from Christian churches and missions, the residents of these out-of-the-way places did not likely convert en masse to Christianity until after the Civil War.[21] That these African Americans were more likely to practice a variety of West African traditions, including Islam, is suggested by the memories of Nero Jones, another of those interviewed by members of the Georgia Writers Project. During harvest, for example, Jones said that his parents would sing and pray throughout the night, and then after the sun rose they danced, beat drums, shook gourd rattles, and fell into a trance. They moved in a counterclockwise fashion, performing what became known as the ring shout. But these same family members would also recite Islamic prayers. Jones's aunt and uncle were "mighty particular about praying." They seemed to recite Arabic words and also use prayer beads, much like Bilali and Phoebe.[22]

Some Muslims wanted to draw distinctions between what they deemed to be proper Islamic practice—the kind of Islam they had learned about in Qurʾan school or the seminary in Djenné—and the Islam that combined praying, beating drums, and dancing—that is, the stream of Islamic practice that was more popular. Salih Bilali of St. Simons Island, Georgia, was one such Muslim. James Hamilton Couper, his owner, described Salih Bilali as a strict Muslim who "abstains from spirituous liquors, and keeps the various fasts," including Ramadan. He added that this Muslim was "singularly exempt from all superstition; and holds in great contempt the African belief in fetishes and evil spirits." It is not clear exactly where the line between proper and improper Islam may have rested for someone like Salih Bilali. Certain practices that today would be labeled superstitious among most reform-minded Muslims were perfectly orthodox to many of those educated Muslims who had completed advanced education at a West African Islamic seminary. For many Islamic authorities, for example, it was fine to use an amulet that contained Qurʾanic verses to ward off illness or the evil eye.

Whether or not such practices were acceptable to Salih Bilali, he almost certainly would have opposed the religious practices of Rosa Grant's grandmother Ryna.[23] Based on Rosa Grant's recollections, it seems clear that Ryna was indeed a Muslim. "Every morning at sun-up," said Grant, "she kneel on the floor in a room and bow over and touch her head to the floor three time. Then she say a prayer. I don't remember just what she say, but one word she say used to make us children laugh.... When she finish praying, she say, 'Ameen, ameen, ameen.'" Ryna called Friday "her prayer day," likely signifying the Islamic practice of Friday congregational prayers. But these were not the only Africana religious practices that she observed. "She talk plenty about conjure," remembered Grant. "She say that when a person been made to swell up from an evil spell, they got to have somebody to pray and drag for them. If you have a pain or a misery in the leg or arm, you kill a black chicken and split it open and slap it where the pain is, and that will cure the pain." Whatever someone such as Salih Bilali thought about such things, it is likely that more enslaved African Americans practiced Islam in Ryna's way.[24]

Like many enslaved persons along the coast, Ryna also believed in the ability of slaves to fly back to Africa. She told her granddaughter how it happened. Ryna was a little girl when she had been captured with her mother, Theresa, and sent to America. After "they been here a while," recalled Rosa Grant, "the mother get to where she can't stand it and she want to go back to Africa. One day my gran, Ryna, was standing with her [mother] in the field." Theresa spun around twice. "She stretch her arms out"; then she "rise right up and fly back to Africa." Another woman had heard the same kind of story. Her grandmother Rachel Grant was a Muslim who prayed three times a day. "She always face the sun," said her granddaughter, "and when she finish praying she always bow to the sun. She tell me about the slaves what could fly too. If they didn't like it on the plantation, they just take wing and fly right back to Africa."[25]

For Rachel Grant and others, the stories of flying back to Africa, when combined with the ritual of daily prayer, seem to have been a powerful form of diasporic longing. Perhaps the eastward-facing prayers of Muslims such as Rachel Grant embodied submission to God's will and at the same time the hope that, one day, God would return them home. When they prostrated their bodies to the east, they prayed in both the direction of their African homeland and the religious center of the worldwide community of Muslims. Whether one believed in the ability of slaves to fly, the practice of Islam among scholars such as Abd al-Rahman and

Salih Bilali as well as among women practitioners like Ryna and Rachel was, deliberately or not, a tenacious attempt to perform the rites of one's home. The religious and cultural elements of Islam became a means to establish a sense of place in a hostile land.

This form of diasporic consciousness for both Islam and Africa would be expressed by later African American Muslims. But it was not the only kind of diasporic practice that developed among African-descended Muslims in the United States. There were other diasporas that African American Muslims embraced, including a form of black diaspora that had very different religious and political meanings.

THE NATION OF ISLAM IN THE TWENTIETH CENTURY

When the mysterious peddler W. D. Fard established the Temple of Islam, later better known as the Nation of Islam, in 1930, there were already several mosques and Muslim organizations across the country that were attempting to recruit African Americans. The first successful effort to bring thousands to the Islamic fold was the Ahmadiyya group, organized in British India in the late nineteenth century around the prophetic teachings of modern Muslim reformer Ghulam Ahmad. In 1921 missionary Muhammad Sadiq established his headquarters in Chicago in order to spread Ahmad's teachings in the United States. Emphasizing that Islam was a religion of racial equality, Sadiq's mission attracted African Americans throughout the country. Sadiq told his black American followers that Islam was an African religion and that Arabic was the original language of black people. This idea, which would later be repeated by Fard (often pronounced Fuh-RAHD), recast black American racial identity as a shadow in a cave, a mask that hid black people's true communal belonging to the larger Muslim world. Sadiq preached that the Qur'an guaranteed social as well as spiritual equality and promoted African Americans to leadership positions in the organization. By the middle 1920s over a thousand men and women had become Muslims under his guidance.[26]

Sunni traditions of Islam were also reestablished as an institutional presence among African Americans in the 1920s, and African missionaries played a key role. The most important was Satti Majid, a Sudanese preacher who worked mainly in Detroit, Buffalo, Pittsburgh, and New York City. Having arrived in the United States perhaps as early as 1904 in the port of New Orleans, Majid seems to have been itinerant for more than a decade, searching for a role as a community organizer and religious leader. He was active in both Detroit and New York City, where one of his students, Daoud Ahmed Faisal, went on to become the most prominent Sunni leader of the postwar era. Majid also found success in Buffalo, New York, in 1924, when he cofounded the Buffalo Moslem Welfare Society, which attracted over five hundred members in a matter of three months. Called the "high priest of the Buffalo Mohammedan colony" by the *Buffalo Morning Express*, he went on to establish the African Moslem Welfare Society of America in Pittsburgh in 1927. Though the Pittsburgh group named African Muslims in its title, its members included Arab immigrants and people of African descent from both the United States and the Caribbean. One of its goals was to eradicate both racial and national differences among Muslim Americans. Other Muslim welfare societies associated with Majid may have included those in Detroit, New York City, Chicago, Cincinnati, and Washington. Majid attempted to bring all of them together, both foreign- and American-born, in the first nationwide Sunni Muslim organization in the United States called the United Moslem Society. Claiming a membership perhaps in the low thousands, this network of believers associated with Satti Majid was especially important to the flowering of African American–led Sunni congregations in the 1930s.[27]

Finally, another important precursor to the Nation of Islam was the Moorish Science Temple of Noble Drew Ali, a North Carolina native who taught a metaphysical version of Islam based not on the Qur'an but on the teachings about Islam found in Freemasonry and particularly in the Ancient Egyptian Arabic Order of the Nobles of the Mystic Shrine, or the black Shriners. It remains disputed exactly when the movement was established, though the best explanation seems to be that Noble Drew Ali was part of a religious and civic group before World War I in Newark, New Jersey, and then in the 1920s established his national Moorish Science Temple headquarters in Chicago. One of several metaphysical groups emphasizing the efficacious effects of New Thought, the larger American trend toward using the power of the human mind to master the potential of the human body, Noble Drew Ali's organization argued that racial discrimination against black Americans was the result partly of their ignorance of their true identity. The group's English-language scriptures, which contained no excerpts from the Arabic Qur'an, commanded black Americans to stop calling themselves "black," "colored," or "Negro," all of which were incorrect self-understandings. Noble Drew

Ali taught that African Americans were in reality descended from the nation of Morocco (hence the label "Moors"), the larger race of Asian peoples (or Asiatics), and the religion of Islam. Ali imagined that all non-European people were, by nature, Muslim and that they were also of the same Asiatic race. This was a dramatic recasting of black identity as Noble Drew Ali proudly embraced a thick notion of black ethnicity that aligned the interests of Moors (or African Americans) with those of other nonwhite people who had been the victims of imperialism and white supremacy. Like African American Liberian nationalist Edward Wilmot Blyden and the pan-Africanist Dusé Ali, Noble Drew Ali saw Islamic religion as a form of political empowerment.[28]

The orienting of black Americans as Asian and Muslim was a theme picked up by W. D. Fard and the Nation of Islam. It would have important consequences for the political and religious teachings of the postwar Nation of Islam led by Elijah Muhammad. As Fard peddled silks door-to-door and established a small temple devoted to these ideas in Detroit, Georgia-native Elijah Poole emerged as one of his most eager supporters. By 1934 Fard left Detroit, and Poole, who came to be known as Elijah Muhammad, claimed leadership of the movement. Muhammad was on the move for much of the 1930s as he attempted to consolidate his power in the relatively small organization. It was only after he was released from federal prison on a draft evasion conviction in 1946 that the Nation of Islam in the Wilderness of North America emerged as the preeminent national Muslim organization among African Americans.[29]

It is noteworthy that the most important Muslim group among black Americans in the postwar period articulated a version of Islam with which most other Muslims in the world disagreed. Elijah Muhammad proclaimed himself the Messenger of Allah, and he revealed that the mysterious stranger, W. D. Fard, was actually God Incarnate, Allah in the flesh. These pronouncements violated Sunni doctrines that Muhammad of Arabia was the final prophet of God and that God had never appeared in the flesh on earth (which the Qur'an makes clear in talking about Jesus, whom the scripture explains was human, not divine). While such beliefs may have rendered the faith of the Nation of Islam unacceptable to many of the world's Muslims, Elijah Muhammad's followers thought that they were a vanguard people who had discovered a truth that the rest of the Islamic world would eventually come to know. As far as they were concerned, they were indeed real Muslims.[30] As followers of Muhammad Sadiq and Noble Drew Ali had done in the 1920s, they oriented their religious, political, and cultural imagination toward all people of color and not just Africans. This was part of a larger Afro-Asian alliance of color that had taken root among various intellectuals in the era of nineteenth-century imperialism and came to have institutional power after World War II in the nonaligned movement's response to the Cold War.[31] Such Afro-Asian political solidarity had religious meaning for many members of the Nation of Islam. Like Noble Drew Ali of the Moorish Science Temple, Elijah Muhammad argued that all nonwhite people were, by nature, Muslims.

This ontological identity originated trillions of years ago, according to Elijah Muhammad. His mythic explanation posited that sixty-six trillion years ago an explosion separated the moon from the Earth, leaving only the tribe of Shabazz alive. These original inhabitants of the Earth were Arabic-speaking black Muslims. They ruled the earth until a mad scientist created an inferior and brutish race of white people six thousand years ago. Blacks/Muslims forgot their original language and their religion, and their civilization went into decline. God sent the Prophet Muhammad, whom Elijah Muhammad considered to be black/Muslim, to stem the tide, but it was not possible to stop the march of white dominance at that time. Fortunately, according to this messenger, the dispensation that allowed white rule was finally about to end: God Himself had appeared in the person of W. D. Fard and commissioned him, a man of humble origins, to mentally resurrect the so-called Negro from the death of a false religion and an enslaved sense of self. This messenger was to prepare blacks/Muslims for an apocalypse in which a mother plane, like Ezekiel's wheel, would appear and destroy white supremacy and its sinful consequences on the black psyche. Blacks/Muslims would again rule the earth, saved from their exiled selves, restored to their true place as the original leaders of the world. This was what God had promised in the Qur'an and the Bible, said Elijah Muhammad, when God talked about the Day of Judgment and the rewards of the righteous. God was no spook in space, and heaven did not exist above. Echoing the metaphysical leanings of other American religious groups, Elijah Muhammad said that heaven and hell were states of being on the earth. "Stop looking for anything after death—Heaven or hell," he wrote. "These are in *this* life."[32]

This explanation of black suffering and the promise of salvation had important consequences for the construction of black identity within the Nation of Islam. Though it did not blindly determine the ways in which members of the organization imagined their connections to African history and identity, it did suggest that, as Anna Burks Karriem put it, "our boundaries are not those of Africa." Karriem, a former student at Tuskegee University and a member of Mosque No. 5 in Cincinnati, insisted in a column for the *Muhammad Speaks* newspaper that she was "neither an Afro-American nor am I a Negro." Instead, she said, she was part of the "original Asiatic Black nation of the universe." That identity was much older and more significant than anything to be found in Carter G. Woodson's Negro History Week or even the glorious past of great African kingdoms. As Nation of Islam minister Angelo 3X of Pensacola, Florida, explained, "What young and old Black people need today is the 'knowledge of self,' which is more than 66-trillion years of history; this is the history of the 'Original Man.'" For those readers of the newspaper unfamiliar with Elijah Muhammad's myth of black origins, the *Muhammad Speaks* cartoonist put the words in the mouth of one of his many figures, in this case a young male member explaining the origins of the black man to a classmate: "You and I are from the original people—the Asiatic Black Man, the Maker, the Owner—Cream of the Planet Earth, and God of the Universe! We have no beginning and no ending. Our people built civilization millions of years *before* white people were made!"[33]

But the identification of black Muslim ontology with the original rulers of the universe did not preclude an identification with the earthly achievements of black/Muslim people. Inside the Nation of Islam's many primary and secondary schools, in its congregational meetings, and on the pages of its popular newspaper, students, members, and readers learned about various parts of Islamic history—from Khawlah bint Azdar's assistance in the battle to conquer Damascus in 634–635 C.E. and the glorious conversion of Umar ibn Khattab, the second caliph of Islam, to Songhay emperor Sunni Ali and Baghdad caliph Harun Ar-Rashid. And the historical black achievements discussed were not limited to Muslims in the sixth century and thereafter. They included the accomplishments of any non-Christian person of color, "Black, brown, red, and yellow descendants of the Original Black Man, the maker and owner of the planet Earth," as Edward L. Truitt of Ann Arbor, Michigan, wrote in *Muhammad Speaks*.[34] No matter whether referring to Africans, Indians in the Americas, Tibetans, Chinese, or Polynesians, Nation of Islam poet William E. X insisted that they were all "Black Man / Giant of Giants."[35]

It was not enough, however, to laud past accomplishments. As Elijah Muhammad's myth of restoration warned, blacks/Muslims had become unmoored from their original moral underpinning. If they were to achieve heaven on earth, they would need to follow the Messenger's strict program of black uplift. To turn North America from a wilderness to a homeland would mean that blacks/Muslims would have to create their own communities devoted to institutional, economic, educational, cultural, political, and religious independence. Thus, Elijah Muhammad and his lieutenant Malcolm X called on all black people to renounce the desire to integrate with whites, to form separate black schools and businesses, to leave churches and join the Nation of Islam, and, if possible, to establish political independence in a few black-belt southern states given up by the federal government for a black nation.[36] The political rhetoric of the Nation of Islam may have been radical, but in reality the actual organizing of congregations, businesses, and schools around the teachings of Elijah Muhammad did not directly challenge the political status quo of 1960s America. It was the symbolic protest of people like Malcolm X and boxer Muhammad Ali that the U.S. Federal Bureau of Investigation feared most—not any armed insurrection.[37]

Much religious devotional activity in the Nation of Islam was directed toward self-improvement and personal moral reform. In order to know the true self and to achieve worldly success, Elijah Muhammad preached, Muslims would need to eschew the "slave behaviors" that they had acquired when they converted to the white man's religion. Properly embodied blackness should be manifested in punctuality, thrift, sexual modesty, temperance, proper manners, industry, respectable attire, and a healthy diet. In addition, men were required to guard against their emasculation and women were to be honored and protected as mothers, daughters, sisters, and wives. In short, being a real Muslim meant exhibiting those behaviors so often associated in the United States and black America with middle-class respectability and being "civilized." For members of the Nation of Islam, these Protestant-like habits did not signify a capitulation to the norms and ideals of American Protestantism but instead became evidence of a properly Islamized and mentally resurrected black person.[38]

Arguing that blacks/Muslims had been poisoned, weakened, and fattened by a slave diet, Elijah Muhammad issued commandments in speeches, articles, and his book *How to Eat to Live* (1972) that Muslims were not only to avoid chitterlings and all other parts of the swine but also to give up smoking, liquor, and all the other things that slave masters used to give their slaves. The Messenger also banned "water scavengers" or shellfish, corn bread, collard greens, and raccoon, all of which he associated with the lifestyle of slavery. Sounding what turned out to be a prophetic call, he named diabetes as a major health problem among African Americans, told his followers to stop eating processed sugar, and directed them to eat wheat bread in place of white bread—the darker the better, he said. In place of old habits, Elijah Muhammad proclaimed, his followers should control their calories by eating only once a day and by eating foods prepared in accordance with Jewish dietary law. *Muhammad Speaks* also featured healthy recipes, and women were taught about healthy cooking in Muslim Girls Training–General Civilization Class, which was a centerpiece of women's activities in the movement. He also told Muslims to observe the daily dawn-to-sunset fasts of Ramadan but changed the timing of the month to coincide with Yuletide. He said that he needed to focus his people's attention on Islam rather than on Christianity and that the Christmas season was an invitation to return to old slavish customs. Acknowledging that Muslims outside the Nation of Islam practiced Ramadan during the ninth month of the Islamic calendar, Elijah Muhammad explained that he had "set this up for you and me to try to drive out of us the old white slavemaster's way of worship of a false birthday." Believers responded positively to the effort, practicing Ramadan in their local congregations and in some cases in prisons, such as the federal penitentiary in Marion, Illinois. Brother Clifton 3X of Temple No. 27 in Los Angeles said that after trying several years, he finally succeeded in keeping the fasts in 1973. Ramadan, he said, "made me strong; it made me happy."[39]

Nation of Islam members also patronized hundreds of restaurants, groceries, and street vendors that were operated by its members. Some of these were owned by movement leadership, while others were the entrepreneurial efforts of rank-and-file members. Among the more prominent restaurants that prepared food in accordance with the dietary guidelines of Elijah Muhammad—at least much of the time—was the Salaam Restaurant in Chicago, located on Eighty-Third Street and South Cottage Grove Avenue. This was a place where Muslims and non-Muslim African Americans went to see and be seen. Featuring groovy drapes, wall-to-wall carpeting, and murals that depicted mosques and minarets, the Salaam hosted a weekly planning meeting for Rev. Jesse Jackson's Operation Breadbasket in 1968. In Washington patrons could enjoy dinner at the Shabazz Restaurant on Fourteenth Street, while in New York Harlemites could visit the Temple No. 7 Restaurant on 113 Lenox Avenue to "try our original bean pie and whole wheat muffins." In addition to the restaurants, Nation of Islam members opened butcheries and groceries, often near the local mosque. For example, Gordon X's meat market in Boston offered customers prime and choice kosher meats and poultry. In St. Louis there was a whole row of Muslim businesses along the 1400 block of North Grand Boulevard; it was called Little Egypt. The Nation of Islam was quite literally in the business of providing the healthy food and job opportunities that its leader said would be evidence of his successful program for black uplift. Elijah Muhammad invested in a number of food-related businesses, including a dairy and meat-processing plant, a large grocery store in Chicago, and farms in Georgia, Michigan, and Alabama. In the 1970s the organization developed a national sales force as part of a fish import business. Elijah Muhammad's lieutenants first imported fish from Japan but in 1974 began to purchase Pacific whiting fish from Peru. It became a multimillion-dollar business that employed dozens, if not hundreds, of people.[40]

The line between sacred obligations and secular responsibilities was blurred in the Nation of Islam since both were understood to be responses to the commandments of a prophet. In addition to eating a holy and healthy diet, members were directed to dress in a manner befitting their original status as rulers of the Earth. Men wore dark suits, crisply pressed shirts, bow ties, or sometimes movement uniforms; women often donned flowing gowns or at least modest skirts and blouses. They also wore head scarves at official movement functions.[41] Following the ethical and ritual directives of Elijah Muhammad was understood by many in the movement to be the surest path toward restoring heaven on earth for blacks/Muslims. To advance that goal, elite male and female organizations were established to model and enforce proper behavior. Male adults could join the Fruit of Islam, which was a cross between a security force, a fraternity, and a continuing education group. The Fruit of Islam protected female members, organized and provided security for mosque activities, drilled in formation, sold the movement newspaper, recruited new members, and enforced strict adherence to Elijah Muhammad's ethical directives. Adult females were invited to become members of the Muslim Girls Training–General Civilization Class. The functions of this group included many of those of the Fruit of Islam, even drilling in formation, but eschewed protection and security for home economics. Women also shared information in the class about family planning, negotiating with female leaders over Elijah Muhammad's ban on birth control and their needs to limit the size of their families and protect their own health.[42]

Being a member of the Nation of Islam could become a whole way of life, structuring not only one's religious beliefs but also one's daily activities. By the 1960s adult members could send their children to the University of Islam, the movement's growing system of parochial schools. Adults and children could participate in activities at the mosque nearly every night and weekend. Congregational meetings were generally devoted to studying the prophecies of Elijah Muhammad, to hearing lectures, and to other sorts of educational discussions. But there were also special events such as bazaars and a flurry of economic activity, in addition to special religious events, being conducted around many temples. Every February thousands of members traveled to Chicago to celebrate Savior's Day in honor of movement founder W. D. Fard. Movement members would also form caravans to hear Elijah Muhammad speak in different cities.[43]

The embodied quest to make a Muslim life had important implications for the diasporic consciousness of Nation of Islam members. In addition to the narratives of black/Muslim identity that oriented members toward black ontology, Islamic religion, and Asian geography, the daily commitment to living the directives of the Messenger focused the activities of the believers on building community, mainly at the local level. Though the networks of the Nation of Islam extended to countries such as Trinidad, Jamaica, and Belize, and Nation of Islam members might proudly cite some accomplishments of black people around the world, Nation of Islam members were not actively creating networks with people in Africa and were not making narratives that centered on Africa. The goal was not to return to Africa but to re-inherit the whole earth, which had been owned by black/Muslim people before the usurpation by white power. The "holy city" that the Nation of Islam sought was that which would take place, quite literally, when white supremacy would be destroyed and blacks would be restored to their rightful place as rulers of the whole earth, not just of Africa. Their mission was not to redeem only African people but to redeem all nonwhite people. Living according to the Islam of Elijah Muhammad was the path toward doing so, modeling a way of redemption based on the teachings of a prophet from Georgia that would change the history of the universe. The diasporic map of Nation of Islam members was not focused on the symbolic power of Africa but on that of racial and religious ontology. Coming home meant finding the true self.

But that would change for most members of the Nation of Islam starting in 1975, the year of Elijah Muhammad's death. His son and successor, Wallace D. Mohammed, began almost immediately on a different path of Islam—a Sunni path that in a few short years debunked the teachings about Fard's divinity and his father's prophecies and, in addition, required members to perform Sunni-style daily prayers, the pilgrimage to Mecca, and fasting during the Islamic lunar month of Ramadan. In addition, the Nation of Islam abandoned its support for racial separatism, its direct ownership of various businesses, and its wholesale criticism of both Christianity and the United States. It even changed its name, first to the World Community of al-Islam in the West in 1976 and then to the American Muslim Mission in 1980. Though Minister Louis Farrakhan and others devoted to a more traditional interpretation of Elijah Muhammad's religious and political thought broke away from W. D. Mohammed and formed their own version of the Nation of Islam in the late 1970s, most congregations remained loyal to Mohammed's new vision.[44]

In addition to aligning the movement's mosques with Sunni Islam, W. D. Mohammed altered the movement's orientation toward Africa. In November 1975 he announced a new religious-ethnic label, "Bilalian," for African Americans. Bilal, he said, was "a Black Ethiopian slave who was an outstanding man in the history of Islam. He was the first *muezzin* [prayer-caller] of Prophet Muhammad (may peace be upon Him). He was so sincere and his heart was so pure that the Prophet Muhammad and other leaders of Islam addressed him as 'Master Bilal.'" Mohammed explained that this African ancestor was a moral exemplar worthy to be emulated. African-descended Muslims had a "double connection with Bilal," Mohammed asserted, "because he was a Muslim and he was also a so-called African." In addition to changing the title of the group's newspaper from *Muhammad Speaks* to *Bilalian News*, Mohammed encouraged his followers to learn more about Bilal. Many responded positively. Samuel Ansari, who later became imam of the mosque in north St. Louis, said in a 1990s interview that "Bilalian" was still a better ethnic label for black Americans than "African American." For him, Bilal symbolized the larger moral and political journey of African Americans who needed to "come to the call that is calling you to dignity, to integrity, to live to employ principles [in] your life."[45]

This idea of seeking ethical inspiration from and adopting an ethnic label based on the story of an African Muslim ancestor paralleled larger shifts in U.S. history during the 1970s. Ethnic revivalism for African Americans—but also for white ethnics such as Irish and Italian Americans—was a strong cultural current perhaps best symbolized by the runaway best-selling 688-page book *Roots*. Alex Haley's 1976 ode to the black American journey from slavery to freedom began with the tale of his own African Muslim ancestor Kunta Kinte. Scholar Nathan Huggins notes that the book ended "with that onward, upward, progressive vision fundamental to the American faith. Through *Roots*, black people could find a collective memory and be mythically integrated into the American dream."[46] For Muslim followers of W. D. Mohammed, Bilal, not Kunta Kinte, was to be the ancestor to whom they could look for their roots, not only in Africa but also in Islam.

The story of Bilal promised to integrate members of the Nation of Islam into the *umma*, the worldwide community of Muslims. Bilal showed the way toward moral leadership and earthly success for those who were once enslaved. Instead of identifying with the tribe of Shabazz, whose origins could be dated to trillions of years ago, members of the Nation of Islam were asked to look to a companion of the Prophet Muhammad. They had a right to be proud of their heritage not because they were the original men of the universe but because their ancestor had endured great suffering as a slave and came through it to be a leader of the Muslim community and trusted confidante of the Messenger of God. Instead of looking to the primordial earth and a prehistoric Eden, members of the Nation of Islam were redirected to look at the African diaspora during the golden age of Islam, what is sometimes called the pristine Medina, city of the Prophet. In this mapping of black identity, Africa reappeared as the place from which a human dispersion had led to great human suffering but eventually to moral triumph.

THE NEW IMMIGRATION AND AFRICAN MUSLIM HOMELANDS

At the same historical moment that the Nation of Islam was becoming reoriented in Sunni Islamic time and space, Muslim America was being transformed by a new U.S. immigration law. Jettisoning old immigration quotas meant to favor certain groups of people from Europe, the Hart-Celler Act of 1965 permitted many more Latin Americans, Asians, and Africans to immigrate to the United States. Over a million Muslims, largely from Asia and Africa, did so by the end of the twentieth century.[47] These Muslims contributed enormous cultural and financial capital to the institutionalization of Islam in the United States. By the end of the Cold War, immigrant-led institutions had become the power brokers in Muslim America, sought after by government and the media to make pronouncements on behalf of the entire Muslim American community, especially on what was seen as the growing threat of political Islam abroad. Immigrant-dominated groups such as the Muslim Student Association, the Islamic Society of North America, and the Islamic Circle of North America struggled to maintain strong connections with American-born Muslims, most of whom were African Americans. First-generation Americans and American-born Muslims influenced one another, but sometimes *across* lines of racial division.[48]

Immigrant Muslim arguments about how much to assimilate to American culture reflected those of earlier waves of immigration.[49] But globalization, including a revolution in both communication and transportation, changed the terms of this debate. By the late twentieth century, it was possible to be "here" and "there" almost simultaneously, to participate in multiple communities and nations at the same time.[50] Some scholars noted that people's identities, including those of Muslims, were being increasingly figured as translocal.[51]

This was certainly the case for many immigrants, including those who sought refuge in the United States from civil conflict. For example, the 1991 Sierra Leone civil war displaced perhaps two million people; thousands came to the United States.[52] Many of them harbored a dream of returning to their homeland once the conflict was over. But their presence on American soil inevitably changed how they viewed their political, religious, and cultural identities. Even if many wanted to return from their diaspora to the homeland, they increasingly recognized that they would return as changed people. In her ethnographic study of Sierra Leonean Muslims in the greater Washington, D.C., area during the 1990s, anthropologist JoAnn D'Alisera found that Islam played a key role in forming ties among Sierra Leonean Muslims that were at once ethnic, national, and religious. These ties were shaped in response to the challenges of living as displaced persons while also connecting these Sierra Leoneans to an American Islam that was self-consciously universal and transnational. D'Alisera found that such identities and practices were created and debated not only in places such as mosques but also in the taxis that Sierra Leonean migrants drove and the food stands that they operated. Children's bodies, their upbringing, their education, and their choice of marriage partners all became symbolic sites where parents figured out what it meant to be living in America, participating in the worldwide community of Muslims, and preserving their connection to their home country of Sierra Leone. They also developed an African identity that simultaneously recognized their shared experiences with other immigrants from the African continent and differentiated them as Sierra Leonean nationals.[53]

Sierra Leoneans created a local diaspora in the neighborhoods of greater Washington, D.C., including northern Virginia and Maryland. Their mobile professions and shared religious spaces allowed them to maintain ties across the metropolitan area. A large number of men worked as taxi drivers, while a good number of women operated food carts on the well-traveled streets. Cab drivers frequently stopped to purchase food from the food carts and, while doing so, exchanged gossip about family and friends. These places of encounter became sites for the discussion of religion and politics as well. In many cases, drivers let the food vendors know what was happening at the mosque or shared a piece of wisdom that they gained there. Both food carts and taxis also acted as sites where Islamic religion was performed. Muslim cabbies might display an Islamic bumper sticker on the outside of the cab reading "I ♥ Islam" or put similar stickers featuring Qurʾanic verses inside. Recitations could be heard from the taxi's radio. Some cabbies, like Mustafa, even handed out religious pamphlets from the Islamic Center of Washington to Muslims and non-Muslims alike. These drivers knew that some passengers would feel uncomfortable about this open display of Islamic religious identity, but they proudly and piously claimed what was, even before 9/11, a contested religious identity in the United States. Female food-stand vendors such as Aminata also decorated their profane sites of employment with sacred symbols. Aminata's food cart featured a Sabrett Kosher Hot Dog sign—indicating that she served *halal*, or permissible food—and stickers with verses of the Qurʾan. Working the food stand also gave Aminata plenty of time to perform *salat*, or daily prayers. In order to make ablutions before the prayers, she and other vendors either kept a container of water nearby or went to a public restroom.[54]

Even in the middle of winter, drivers and food vendors sometimes hotly debated questions of Islamic practice and doctrine. For Sierra Leoneans, the competition over the boundaries of what constitutes proper Islamic religious practice were often influenced, on one hand, by the call of a universal Islam that transcended local variation and temporal contingency and, on the other hand, by the appeal of a local Islam that evoked and embraced an idealized Sierra Leone. At the Islamic Center of Washington, located on Massachusetts Avenue, Sierra Leoneans encountered Muslims, both Sunni and Shiʿa, from various national and ethnic backgrounds. These encounters and the impulse to find an Islam that was universal across social difference led to debate and ambivalence about Islam as practiced in Sierra Leone. For some immigrants, being in America offered a much more attractive form of Islamic piety. These Muslims pointed out that while America might be full of temptation, it was also a land where one could find one's true religious self. "It is here that I found Islam again," one of D'Alisera's informants told her. This man had been trained as a child to memorize certain portions of the Qur'an but had not prayed on a regular basis in Sierra Leone. However, at the Islamic Center "I learned that you pray and fast for God, not for yourself or material things. It is here that I learned to live every moment as a Muslim."[55]

Some Sierra Leoneans came to criticize Islam as practiced in the homeland. One man, Mustafa, said that "in Sierra Leone they do not go into details. They just tell you not to drink, but not why." The absence of a rational explanation for Mustafa ran counter to what he said was Islam's emphasis on knowledge. Like hundreds of millions of Muslims around the world, Mustafa felt that his fate in this world and the next depended on understanding the meaning of Islam's texts and traditions. It was not enough to repeat the traditions of one's predecessors—these practices should be grounded in proper interpretation of the sacred texts.[56] For Mustafa, this meant that much of the Islam practiced in Sierra Leone was not "pure Islam." Like so many other modern Muslims, including American Muslims, Mustafa insisted that the pure religion of Islam must be separated from the culture of the people who practice it. He labeled impermissible Islamic practices, such as the celebration of the Prophet's birthday, as "a mixing of culture with religion. You shouldn't celebrate your own birthday because it is like worship, and that means you are worshipping someone else besides Allah, and this is not good."[57]

But not all Sierra Leoneans agreed. In one exchange between a taxi driver and a food-cart vendor recorded by D'Alisera, a vendor demanded to know why celebrating the Prophet's birthday was forbidden. In doing so, she appealed to a sense of authenticity grounded in nostalgia for the homeland of Sierra Leone. "We do it at home! Are you saying we are not good Muslims at home?" she asked.

"They told me this at the mosque," responded the driver. "We make many mistakes at home but we can change this here [in the United States]."

"I like to celebrate the Prophet's birthday! We do it quiet here. We sit and recite Qur'an and ask the Imam questions. I have learned a lot this way."[58]

The debate continued, unresolved, for nearly an hour.

Another instance in which D'Alisera observed the boundaries of proper Islamic practice being negotiated against both American and Sierra Leonean cultural norms was a baby naming ceremony. Held in northern Virginia on Thanksgiving Day in 1991, this ceremony took place in a modest apartment whose walls were decorated with verses from the Qurʾan, masks from Sierra Leone, pictures of the Grand Mosque in Mecca, and even a photograph of former president Ronald Reagan and first lady Nancy Reagan. As participants prepared for the celebration, sounds of Qurʾanic recitation and those of a televised National Football League game—a U.S. Thanksgiving tradition—filled the room. The mother wore "Western" dress without a head scarf, while the father and the imam, or religious leader, donned shirts made out of African cloth. Immediately before the ceremony began, the mother covered her head and that of her daughter in a large piece of African cloth, making sure that they both embodied not only a sense of modesty but also a sense of place, the African homeland. The imam, with one eye on the football game, began to recite the Qurʾan to start the ceremony. His sermon, delivered in the Sierra Leonean language of Krio, asked everyone to equip their children with the tools that they needed to avoid "the evils of America," such as alcohol (but apparently not American football!). The mother then gave the baby to the imam, and he whispered into her ear that there is no god but God and that Muhammad is God's messenger. The parents then announced that the baby's name was Adana, meaning "the beginning of humanity." The ceremony was followed by a celebratory meal—or really two meals. The first, enjoyed more by the African-born parents and older people, featured Sierra Leonean cuisine: "*plasauce* [a leaf and palm oil–based stew] and rice, roasted *halal* meat on skewers, samosas, salad, fruit, and ginger beer." The second meal was traditional U.S. Thanksgiving fare—turkey and trimmings—and the American-born children consumed this meal with greater enthusiasm than they did the food with which their parents grew up.[59]

Sierra Leonean Muslims also negotiated the boundaries of proper Islamic practice, nostalgia for the homeland, and the pressures of U.S. society in their debates over gender roles, opposite-gender romantic relationships, child rearing, and other cultural practices. Even as Muslim women from Africa and Asia were (and continue to be) framed in media discourse as victims of a male-centered Islamic religion, scores of studies about Muslim women in the last two decades have established that women are active participants in arguments about their status, power, rights, and responsibilities. Muslim women's human agency also applies to debates over the controversial rite of initiation that is also known as female genital mutilation, female circumcision, and clitoridectomy. In the 1990s this practice became a major subject of public discourse in Washington, D.C., and Sierra Leoneans were almost forced to address publicly what is generally understood to be a secret initiation rite of adolescence practiced by African Muslims and non-Muslims alike. While some African female refugees filed for asylum to seek protection from the rite on behalf of their daughters, some of D'Alisera's informants protested the sense of powerlessness that these women were projecting to the public. One woman declared her fellow Sierra Leoneans to be dishonest, noting that it was women, not men, who conducted and perpetuated this ritual, often in secret. This woman, Khadi, also expressed ambivalence toward the ritual itself. She reported that her father in Sierra Leone had been strongly opposed to the act as un-Islamic but accepted his wife's decision to make her go through it. And when it came to her own daughter, who had been born in America, the burden was on Khadi to decide. Her husband told her that it was her decision since this is "women's business."[60]

Khadi's questioning of whether to initiate her daughter reflected a concern about whether she would be marriageable to a man from Sierra Leone if she did not go through with it. This key cultural tradition was wrapped around questions about the fate of Sierra Leonean identity—if the practice was simply eliminated, would this be one more step toward the end of a distinctive Sierra Leonean identity for American-born children? Even as men yielded this question to the mothers, they too expressed concern about the perpetuation of a Sierra Leonean identity among their children. But for many of the fathers, the answer did not rest with the question of whether to engage in clitoridectomy—this, after all, was "women's business." Instead, many of the men increasingly focused on education as a solution to the problem of disappearing national and religious affiliation. And this was something that many mothers and other women could agree on.

Both male and female parents in the 1990s constructed education as a solution to what they saw as the problem of their children's severed link to the homeland and an Islamic identity. In contrast to the views of some Sierra Leoneans who attended the Islamic Center of Washington and sought to purify their Islamic practice of cultural and specifically African accretions, the parents who in 1989 established the Fullah Progressive Union Islamic and Cultural Center, also called the Fullah Islamic

School, sought to preserve and inculcate among their children an identity that combined Sierra Leonean culture and Islamic religion. While named for only one of Sierra Leone's ethnic groups, the Fula, other members of the community attended. Some of the parents had previously sent their children to the schools that were dominated by South Asian Muslim Americans. But "we decided our kids needed something else," said one of D'Alisera's informants. "They needed Sierra Leonean culture as well as Islam." Parents worried that if and when their American-born children immigrated to Sierra Leone, which the parents saw as a homecoming, they would feel alienated from what the parents described as their indigenous culture, their roots. "Our kids are losing Krio and Fullah," said the same informant, referring to two of the indigenous languages of Sierra Leone. The solution was to combine cultural and religious education: "Our main goal is to have a community of Sierra Leoneans Muslims, a masjid [mosque], a center to teach our kids, and to have this all housed in one place," the man said.[61]

In the 1990s the Fullah Islamic School operated on the weekends, offering three different classes. Those in the first grade, which included young children and adults, were introduced to Arabic in addition to the pillars of Islamic practice and belief. Once students could recognize their Arabic letters and recite the basic teachings of Islam, they moved on to the second grade, which covered ʿibadat, or religious practices and worship. Finally, the third grade, which consisted mainly of teenagers, sought to achieve proficiency in Arabic reading and writing. Students studied the hadith, or reports of the Prophet's deeds and words, and engaged in basic interpretation of the Qur'an. Adult education was also available at the weekend school, and both teachers and adult students in these settings would sometimes debate the boundaries of proper Islamic practice. In one meeting that D'Alisera attended, for example, teacher and student argued about the position of the hands and the head during prayer—the issue of whether one needed to touch the ground hard enough to develop a callus on one's forehead was especially urgent.[62]

While the Fullah Progressive Union continued to sound many of the same themes into the twenty-first century, it is important to keep in mind that it is only one of dozens, if not hundreds, of schools, mosques, community organizations, study circles, and other religiously affiliated groups that have developed among African Muslim immigrants in the United States in the last two decades. Since the 1990s, the number of African Muslim immigrants has increased dramatically, and their presence has altered Islamic practice in the United States. By 2009 there were 1.5 million African-born immigrants in the United States; 965,300 of them were from West and East Africa. The top five countries of origin were Nigeria, Ethiopia, Egypt, Ghana, and Kenya.[63] Hundreds of thousands of Muslims were likely part of this cohort.

One of the better-known groups among these relatively recent immigrants is the Senegalese, most of whom are Muslim.[64] Many of them are part of a global diaspora: as already seen in chapter 3, for example, the Murid Sufi order is a networked group whose European members have a dramatic impact on what happens in their home country. In New York, these and other Senegalese Muslims are known for driving cabs, braiding hair, and operating food stands and restaurants, among other entrepreneurial activities. Around 116th and 117th Streets in Harlem they established an area called Little Africa or Le Petit Senegal. Senegalese Muslims successfully lobbied in the 1990s for an Ahmadu Bamba Day, honoring the Senegalese saint and national hero credited with establishing the Murid Sufi order. Every summer, Senegalese, Gambian, and other West African Muslims march down Seventh Avenue in Harlem to Central Park, exclaiming in Arabic that "there is no god but God." Honoring the saint, remembering him, and following his instructions are important parts of Islamic practice for many of these Muslims, who believe that the saint can intervene with God on their behalf both in this life and in the next. Other Sufi practices found among Senegalese Muslims in New York include the recitation of poems written by Ahmadu Bamba; the performance of Tijani dhikrs, or litanies, before sunset on Fridays; and the purchasing of "charms, amulets, and magic water on demand to people confronted with health, marital, or professional problems" from visiting spiritual healers. Senegalese and other West African Muslims have also established dozens of mosques in the city, including Masjid Aqsa, located at the corner of Frederick Douglass Boulevard and 116th Street in Harlem.[65]

When West African Muslims have spoken Pulaar or Wolof in their religious organizations, they have maintained strong boundaries between themselves and other Muslims, including African Americans. There has been noteworthy tension between American-born black Muslims and African-born black Muslims for other reasons, as well. But there has also been cultural exchange and cooperation among black Muslims, especially when English has become the vernacular language of religious interaction. In Cleveland, where African Muslim immigrants are fewer in number than in New York, many have integrated with the long-standing Sunni

African American Muslim community. In the 1980s religious teacher Masoud Laryea of Ghana became leader of the prayers on Islamic holidays when a number of Cleveland's Muslims, from a variety of backgrounds, would gather to pray. Religious leader Ali Omar of Nigeria became imam of Masjid al-Haqq, the "Mosque of Truth," in 1993 and then became principal of the school connected to the mosque. In 1997 he was appointed principal of the Cleveland Community Islamic School. As African Muslims integrated into existing Muslim schools and mosques in Cleveland, they influenced the shape of religious practice among American-born Muslims of African descent. As a result, Sufi Islamic religious traditions have blossomed in Cleveland. American-born black Muslim religious leader Daud Abdul Malick, for example, became interested in the Tijani Sufi order after Senegalese Muslims began attending Masjid al-Haqq, which he led. In the 1990s he went to the Tijani center at Kaolack, Senegal, and invited Tijani leader Hassan Cissé to visit Cleveland. In 1995 Malick employed seven teachers from Africa to work at the Islamic school that he directed.[66]

The emergence of an African Sufi Islam among American-born black Muslims and the institutionalization of Sufism among African-born Muslims represent important new trends in the practice of Islam among African-descended people in the United States. Identifying African Sufi masters as a source of Islamic legitimacy offers a potential tool of resistance to the authoritative claims of a reform-minded Islam that attempts to erase all racial and ethnic difference through Islam. It also signifies a very different form of diasporic consciousness from that offered by the Nation of Islam's mythology. Rather than locating the exile of black people from their true selves in a myth about the fall of man, the turn toward West African masters such as Ahmadu Bamba and Ibrahim Niassé, like W. D. Mohammed's use of Bilal's story, embraces historical Africa as the origin of healing and wholeness. While this form of Islam may be criticized by reform-minded Sunni Muslims who accuse Sufis of practicing impermissible innovations to the one true faith, it has certain structural defenses against such attacks. First, African Sufi Islam is sustained by global networks of believers whose economic and political lives are tied to this religious orientation and not likely to disappear anytime soon. Second, the Islam of the African saints provides intellectual responses to claims of illegitimacy. Fully conversant in the traditions of the Qur'an and the Sunna, as well as in the Islamic ethical and legal traditions that accompany them, West African Sufi Muslim leaders can seize, appropriate, and subvert the very traditions of authority to which their critics appeal.

CONCLUSION

Seeing the story of African American Islam through the lens of African migration challenges popular memories and narratives about the centrality of the Nation of Islam to the larger story of Islam in the United States. While the Nation of Islam may have been the most important black Muslim movement or group to date in terms of its impact on the larger story of U.S. society and culture, focusing on the long history of African American Muslims in both slavery and freedom forces us to look with new eyes on African American Islam itself. By doing so, we see the longing of Muslims such as Abd al-Rahman to return to Africa and the ways in which those who could only dream of doing so preserved some form of Islamic identity and practice in the Americas. We also notice networks, connections, and imaginative ties that have bound African Americans, Muslim or not, to the African continent for hundreds of years. The black Atlantic movement that was first set in motion by the transatlantic slave trade was but the beginning of a modern revolution that has pushed Africans and other colonized people to seek capital in the economically developed world. Slavery may have ended, but the forces that cheaply extract labor and raw materials from Africa have not. One of the consequences of this form of globalization is the continued landing on American shores of African Muslims. As they plant and nurture institutionalized forms of Islam that are connected to African histories, saints, and homelands, they challenge, at least implicitly, the claims to both a timeless Islam and a black metaphysic.

Seeing black Islam through the lens of its long history on North American soil reveals the diversity of Islamic religious practices among the differing "sects," or, perhaps, denominations, of Islam in the United States, including those of the Sunnis, the Shi'a, the Nation of Islam, and the Moorish Science Temple. Those groups are themselves diverse. Among Sunnis, who represent the majority, there are and have been debates about the boundaries of proper Islamic practice from slave times until the present. Just as Salih Bilali of St. Simons Island was said to condemn African beliefs in "fetishes and evil spirits," there are today heated discussions about what elements of African culture, including clitoridectomy and the observance of the Prophet's birthday, are permissible under Islamic fiqh, or jurisprudence. In addition, some American- and African-born Sunni Muslims have embraced a variety of Sufi interpretations and practices of Islam. Those Sufi traditions that were born in

Africa or are associated with African saints or sacred places have a special allure among some black Muslims. But there are also Sunni Muslims who condemn Sufi orders and their practices as un-Islamic.

The practice of Islam among African-descended Muslims has been embraced since slavery as a response to antiblack racism. Islam was the form of superior civilization cited by Abd al-Rahman Ibrahima as evidence of his racial distance from other slaves; for the Nation of Islam, Islam was a bold response to the psychological damage caused by white supremacy. In both of these cases and still others, Islam has been a resource in the political, religious, social, and economic responses of African Americans to both individual prejudice and structural racism from the 1800s until the present. Moreover, Islam has been a resource in the making of "thick blackness," those notions of black identity constructed by black people themselves as a form of solidarity. For some, including those who consider themselves to be Senegalese, Sierra Leonean, Moorish, U.S. American, or members of the Nation of Islam, Islam has been equated with various national identities. In addition, Islam has been associated closely with ethnic and cultural identities, whether those be Bilalian, African, black, or Asiatic. At times, these notions of thick blackness have themselves been seen as religious, as was the case when Elijah Muhammad linked black/Muslim identity to a special myth of origins and a salvation history involving his own prophecy.

But whether or not believers have articulated a sense of religious self that is connected to a black metaphysic, to a historically African Islam, or to a contemporary nation-state and the global dispersion of its citizens, the religious identity of many African-descended Muslims in the United States has been and remains diasporic in the broadest sense of that word. Islam is more often than not seen as a vehicle that will restore a self that is in some way broken and scattered. For members of the Nation of Islam, this meant being mentally resurrected to realize one's divine nature as the original man. For many enslaved Muslims and contemporary Sierra Leonean exiles, Islam has been a vehicle for a virtual return to the homeland from which one has been separated. And for those African-descended Muslims who speak neither of a black metaphysic nor of any African Islamic homeland, Islam has often become a way to survive and even prosper in the face of racism and other forms of oppression. In all these cases, reversing the dispersal of black and African selves becomes a restoration of mind, body, and spirit.

CONCLUSION

Echoes of Bilal across the African Diaspora

Bilal's *adhan,* or call to prayer, and the sound of his footsteps in heaven, first heard by the Prophet Muhammad in one of his dreams, still resonate across Africa and the African diaspora. In Essaouira, Morocco, Gnawa practitioners, the "children of Bilal," play a musical instrument, made from the soles of shoes, to evoke his presence in their night ceremonies. In London, the hip-hop group Mecca2Medina records a video for its song "Descendants of Bilal," and one of its members, cupping his hands next to his ears, acts out of the part of Bilal calling the believers to prayer. In West Africa, the very name for a prayer-caller is *bilal.* In Pakistan and India, those who see Bilal as their ethnic ancestor include his name in their songs of communal celebration.

The memory of Bilal echoes throughout the African diaspora in other ways as well. He is a saint who offers protection and authority for the healing ceremonies that are conducted at Islamic shrines. For members of the Dar Barnu, the Stambali group in Tunis, Tunisia, Bilal, also known as Jerma, sits atop the pantheon of "white" saints—those saints nearest to God whose spirits are present during the night ceremony but do not inhabit the bodies of participants. In a similar fashion, in India and Pakistan the followers of Bava Gor, also known as Gori Pir, see Bilal as a saint whose power can be accessed only through another saintly presence. But it is Saint Bilal who serves as the original link to the Prophet and to prophetic power.

As an ethnic symbol, Bilal often also has an important political meaning. Whether among black North Africans, African-descended South Asians, Afro-Europeans, or African Americans, the figure of Bilal has become a symbol in the struggle for self-determination and political autonomy. In all of these settings, African-descended Muslims have traced their lineage to Bilal or identified him as an important companion of the Prophet Muhammad in order to claim various forms of social power within their respective local and regional polities. For Pacífico Licutan, a Malê or Muslim religious teacher of Yoruban descent prosecuted for the 1835 revolt in Bahia, the name of Bilal was invoked as a symbolic protest against wrongful imprisonment. Refusing to identify himself to a judge as Pacífico Licutan, he said instead that his name was Bilal. For members of the Nation of Islam in the United States and the Caribbean, later the World Community of al-Islam in the West, the term "Bilalian" was an ethnic-religious label that was designed to combat the latent effects of slavery and racism among black Muslims in the United States. It was a proud ethnic and religious label that, for a time in this community, replaced the terms "black" and "Afro-American."

Of course, Bilal is not important to all Muslims of African descent—at least not as a symbol of their particular claims to or stake within the history of the *umma*, the worldwide community of Muslims. Bilal ibn Rabah may be valued as a companion of the Prophet and as a great historical figure in the Jordan Valley, but Muslims of African descent do not claim him as a racial or ethnic ancestor. Similarly, Imam Yasin Abu Bakr of the Jama'at al-Muslimeen in Trinidad and Tobago has not identified Bilal or any other African personage as an important racial or ethnic legacy within Islam. For him, and for all those who see Islam as a universalistic tradition that eliminates all particular ethnic or racial claims to personhood, Bilal is important not as a black man but as an excellent human being.

Bilal's various meanings and functions within Africa and the African diaspora also suggest the diversity of Islamic religious practices among African-descended Muslims more generally. In an effort to demonstrate that diversity, this book has used popular sectarian labels such as Sunni and Shi'a, among other group identifiers. By applying such labels to an incredible variety of religious practices, *The Call of Bilal* shows, at the very least, that any general discussion of Islamic religion among people of African descent must resist automatic associations with any one practice or ideology. Islam in the African diaspora is about much more than the practice of Islam by one group in one country. Like the majority of Muslims around the world, most African-descended Muslims are Sunni. But by placing such a diverse array of religious practices, including the celebration of Husayn's martyrdom by Siddi Muslims in rural Karnataka, India, under the label "Sunni," this book also shows that sectarian labels are limited in their abilities to describe the shapes and textures of Islamic practice among all Muslims, including Muslims of African descent. Besides the acknowledgment that the five pillars of Islamic practice are central to their religious practice, the mere fact that most Africana Muslims identify with or are connected historically to Sunni Islamic traditions tells us very little about the meaning and function of religion in their lives. Instead, tracing the story of Bilal's heirs in a global perspective has demonstrated the need to pay attention to the details of Islamic life-cycle passages, healing rites associated with dancing and music, Islamic holidays, pietistic exercises performed for African saints, study circles and weekend schools, the political impact of Islamic religion, the aesthetics of sacred spaces, the food and dress of Africana Muslims, doctrinal disputes, and transnational networks, among other elements of Islam in the African diaspora.

In looking at such phenomena, categories beyond Sunni and Shi'a have emerged for understanding Islam in the African diaspora. For example, many contemporary Africana Muslims, like Muslims more generally, debate the role of tradition and culture in their practice of Islamic religion. The ethnic or racial heritage that marks out particular ritual, social, and even theological space for Muslims of African descent is under pressure from those Muslims who believe that Islam should be standardized across racial, ethnic, national, and other sociological boundaries. The result is that the traditions that have tagged Africana Muslims as different are questioned, and those who practice them are often prompted to defend and sometimes abandon them. Those who see no place for ritual variety tied to racial and ethnic identities are part of a modern, reformist Islam that is self-consciously urban and suspicious of traditions associated with the village. The tensions between what some Muslims of African descent identify as "pure" Islam and that which is understood as "impure" Islam have been seen throughout this book. They exist in the criticisms of the healing rituals involving alum, salt, and talismans in Jordan, in the rituals performed by the devotees of Bava Gor and Mai Mishra in South Asia, in the spirit possession present in Stambali and Gnawa rites, and in the debates over how Sierra Leoneans in Washington, D.C., should celebrate the naming of a baby.

Criticism of cultural traditions labeled "backward" or "superstitious" comes from within Africana Muslim communities themselves. Many Muslims of African descent, including Imam Yasin Abu Bakr in Trinidad and some of JoAnn D'Alisera's Sierra Leonean informants on the streets of Washington, D.C., are the ones leading the charge against cultural practices that they see as un-Islamic. The attack against ritual variety is not some sort of conspiracy on the part of Saudi-funded missionaries, as some would have it, but instead is a modern reformist impulse that needs to be understood as a broad phenomenon indigenous to various Muslim locales. Wherever Muslims now live, it is typical to hear that "Islam is universal and clear, a coherent closed system, and that their representations of practice and tradition are stable and uniform."[1]

Gender also intersects with the debate over the role of pure and impure Islam in the African diaspora. Criticism of improper cultural influence on the practice of Islam is often leveled against the religious practices of Africana Muslim women. Though there is sometimes a dispute among male and female Muslims of African descent over what constitutes correct Islamic practice, there are also examples in which communities of both male and female Muslims of African descent are indicted by their critics as un-Islamic because of the special ritual tasks performed by women. For example, on Gori Pir Hill in Gujarat, the trustees of the shrine have scaled back the presence of women around the tomb of Gori Pir and have replaced rituals performed for him and his sister, the female saint Mai Mishra, with more Qur'anic recitation. Gori Pir has become increasingly popular among Muslims who are not Siddi or Habshi, at least judging by attendance at his annual ʻurs, or death anniversary, and ceremonies performed by Siddi men and women have taken a backseat to other ways of remembering the male saint. This new arrangement challenges the ritual power of the women who had been authorized in the past to perform special rites by virtue of their connection to the female saint. Criticism has also been waged against Africana Muslim practices in which women play a prominent role in the case of the Gnawa and the Stambali in North Africa. In these groups women are the ones who become the vessels of trance and spirit possession; even if men play the music and the rites are overseen by a man, women assume ritual roles critical to the successful performance of the *lila*, or night ceremony. These rituals continue but are always vulnerable to reformers who want to challenge their Islamic legitimacy.

In addition to the instances in which the Islamic legitimacy of religious practices associated with Muslims of African descent is challenged by outsiders, the debate over the proper role of African culture is part of the gendered dimension of Islamic practice *inside* Africana Muslim communities. The debate over the practice of clitoridectomy among Sierra Leonean Muslims in Washington, D.C., demonstrates that this is no simple matter of men asserting their power over women. Some Sierra Leonean women identify the rite as an evil, misogynistic practice, and some Muslim men come home from the Islamic Center of Washington assuring their wives and daughters that it is an un-Islamic practice that should not be performed. But some mothers, worried about their daughters' marriage prospects when they return to Sierra Leone and loath to relinquish authority over this realm of family life, challenge this teaching and insist on performing what is, to at least some of their American daughters, a cruel form of initiation.

Another example of the gendered dimension of Islamic practice in the African diaspora is the debate among Somali immigrants in London over whether or not to wear the hijab, or head scarf. Some Somali women point out that they did not wear the scarf at home but have come to do so in the United Kingdom because they want to demonstrate their Muslim identity. They see their particular identity within the UK not through the lens of Somali ethnicity but through their religious community. The hijab and modest dress become a universal symbol of this Islamic identity for women, even as some women complain that their less-modest dress, including the wearing of swimsuits, was accepted more often in Somalia than it is by Muslim community members in London. In this case, the social pressure to make dress a signifier of Muslim identity and to conform to Muslim community norms in the United Kingdom puts limits on the variety of dress styles associated with the "old country."

Despite challenges to various ritual practices associated either with Muslim women of African descent or with Muslim communities of African descent more generally, there is no sign that all such practices will disappear anytime soon. This is not to say that such practices are not transformed. No tradition is beyond transformation, and often a tradition's transformation is that which assures its relevance. Today, Africana Muslims play key roles in the contemporary practice of Islam. Africana Muslims are not merely attempting to preserve their traditions against the onslaught of some standardized, reformed Islam. They are creating new meanings and finding new functions for the terms of their participation in the global Islamic community.

The staking of particular territory within the umma for Africana Muslim communities is more often than not bounded by meaningful but diverse links to a diasporic space. The transnational Murid order's pilgrimage, the ceremonies performed by the Tunisian Stambali, the veneration of the female saint Mai Mishra in Afro-India, the Nation of Islam's myth of black origins, and the anticolonial, subaltern hip-hop of African-Caribbean Muslim converts begin to indicate the diversity of interpretations and practices of diaspora among these populations. Some Africana Muslims see their dispersion as a voluntary form of economic opportunity. For example, the *modou modou* followers of Shaykh Ahmadu Bamba of the Murid Sufi order fan out around the globe and successfully develop markets for various goods on the streets of New York, Paris, and Turin. Their economic success not only is an important individual achievement but also allows people to contribute financially to the global network of teachers and to the maintenance of the sacred ritual center at Touba, institutions at the heart of the Muridiyya communal life. Other Africana Muslims understand diaspora to be a mystical, ontological scattering of the soul, as Nation of Islam leader Elijah Muhammad taught when he explained that sixty-six trillion years ago the black Eden was ended by a massive explosion on the earth. In this case, the space of the fractured black self is not associated with the African continent but with a cosmic disturbance.

For a larger number of Africana Muslims, the experience of diaspora is seen through the lens of a historical tragedy that has its origins in physical dispersion from Africa. The injustice and cruelty of the slave trade is a shared memory of Africana Muslim converts in the United Kingdom, the Caribbean, and North America. For many of them, Islam is a heritage stolen by slavery; thus, they do not *convert* but instead *revert* to their original African religious identity. The power of this narrative is demonstrated by the fact that it can be observed across two centuries (the twentieth and the twenty-first) and on both sides of the Atlantic Ocean among Muslim groups with different theologies (from the Nation of Islam to various Sunni congregations). There is great variety within this narrative arc: the hip-hop group Mecca2Medina links the history of African diaspora to a larger struggle against European colonialism and white supremacy, while W. D. Mohammed adapts the biography of Bilal to tell an Islamic up-from-slavery story that might address African Americans' internalized racism and the black American identity crisis. In both cases, however, the cruel legacy of slavery is one that can be addressed through a religious rediscovery of Islam.

Even in cases in which African-descended Muslims do not understand Islam as a stolen heritage, there is often an acknowledgment of slavery's powerful role in their lives. Many attempt to battle the antiblack racism among Muslims by charting a special course for the African diaspora within Islam. For example, Gnawa in Morocco turn the trope of slavery on its head, insisting that real freedom comes only through enslavement to God and all the Muslim saints. Their ritual specialists have particular healing powers by virtue of their access to a pantheon of white saints and black spirits. The followers of Gori Pir in India and Pakistan sometimes say that their diaspora has its origins in a prophetic command for their patron saint and his family to move from Arabia and East Africa to South Asia, where they could defeat the forces of the troublesome Makhan Devi on behalf of God and God's Prophet. These Siddis and Habshis, like the Gnawa and the Stambali in North Africa, see Bilal ibn Rabah as the ancestor who links them to the very origins of the Prophet Muhammad's mission.

All of this mapping across the African diaspora challenges the notion that these Muslims are somehow marginal to the umma. Instead, it creates narrative space in the greater story of global Islam for the Muslims who are often most vulnerable to racial prejudice, both in Muslim and non-Muslim lands. Such stories, which demonstrate trust in God's will, make sense of painful memories. Reinterpreting the terrible dispersion of black bodies across the globe as a result of the African slave trade, these religious narratives and often-embodied ritual activities acknowledge the haunted black body while claiming alternate meanings, fates, or a sense of ultimate justice in confronting that past.

Of course, it is important to keep in mind that not all Muslims with a historical link to Africa or its many lands and nations see the continent, its diverse cultural heritage, or its modern national identities as valuable or important to their religious identity. For Imam Yasin Abu Bakr, any claim to a special role for African cultural tradition within Islam or within the lives more generally of black Americans is a form of *jahilliyah*, or ignorance. A harsh critic of Afrocentrism, the imam repeats the arguments of many modern reformists who see Islam as devoid of racial and ethnic particularity. In Trinidad and Tobago, where Muslims of South Asian descent control most of the institutions of the Muslim community, Yasin Abu Bakr and other reform-minded black Sunni Muslims identify race and ethnicity themselves as a cause of Indo-Trinidadian dominance over Afro-Trinidadian Muslims. Africanness has no spiritual or religious allure for them. Bilal's voice is a universal one calling all of humanity to Islam, and his Ethiopian heritage has no special meaning for black Muslims today.

Ongoing debates about the meaning of the Africana Muslim diaspora raise important questions for the entire Muslim umma, not just for black people. In addition to calling attention to the continued salience of prejudice and discrimination directed toward black Muslims, the story of the black Muslim diaspora invites discussion about the larger question of religion's relationship to culture in the making of Islamic norms. Muslim social conservatives and progressives alike often appeal to a critique of culture's corrupting influence on Islamic religion as a means to argue for reform of one kind or another. Culture rather than religion is fingered as the culprit or cause in producing discrimination against women, lax moral behavior, or improper ritual performance. Many feminist and progressive Muslims, for example, note that patriarchal interpretations of Islam are derived not from Islamic texts but from the tribal and ethnic practices of the men who had the right to interpret them.[2] But the story of the Africana Muslim diaspora may require those who would like to nurture religious diversity and pluralism in Islam to distinguish between cultural traditions that liberate and those that oppress. For the many cultural practices of Africana Muslims, those often colored as black and un-Islamic by their opponents, have been the vehicles not only of the powerful but also of the marginalized. Sustaining black minds, bodies, and spirits in the midst of racist oppression, the embodied and meaningful practices of some black Muslims often violate the modern, reform sensibility of a large number of Muslims. Is there room in their umma for such interpretations of Islam? Any response that hopes to acknowledge the pain of racism and the agency of black Muslims must grapple with the Islam that black people have actually practiced, the Islam that has been the vehicle of healing and wholeness in an often violent diaspora.

The diversity of Islamic practices among African-descended Muslims also raises questions for opinion makers around the world, whether Muslim or not. Experts, policy makers, legislators, and journalists in Europe and the United States have too often presented overly simplistic or antagonistic analyses of Islamic religious tradition and its impact on society, politics, and economics.[3] One-dimensional analyses can negatively affect the ways in which non-Muslim nation-states, nongovernmental organizations, businesses, and other institutions imagine the potential for cooperation with their non-Muslim counterparts. The need for such cooperation could hardly be more acute. One out of every four to five people on the planet is Muslim, and our collective future depends in no small part on how Muslim and non-Muslim people and institutions interact. It is not enough to know about the five pillars and the sectarian split between Sunni and Shi'a Muslims; the time has come for a much more concerted effort, especially among elites, to complicate notions of Islamic religion and Muslim populations. Studying Islam in Africa and its diaspora is an essential component of a functional understanding of

Islam that goes beyond stereotypes and overgeneralizations: "The Muslim population in sub-Saharan Africa is expected to grow by nearly 60% in the next twenty years, from 242.5 million in 2010 to 385.9 million in 2030."[4] Based on the numbers of Muslims in sub-Saharan Africa alone (exclusive of black Muslims in the diaspora), this is a population that cannot be ignored.

But beyond the obvious utility of developing a more accurate and three-dimensional view of Islamic religions and Muslim people, there is a more humanistic reason for a deeper exploration of Islam in the African diaspora. The legacy of Bilal and his heirs is one that speaks to a larger human quest for dignity and justice. A vulnerable, enslaved convert to the message of Muhammad, Bilal suffered at the hand of a cruel master. Even after he became the Prophet's prayer-caller in Medina, there were those Muslims who still questioned whether this man of such low social status could be so close to the Messenger of God. For his faithful service and loyal companionship, Bilal received his recompense on earth as well as in heaven. The sound of his voice rang out from atop the Kaʿba after Muhammad's triumphant return to Mecca. The sound of his footsteps could be heard in heaven. Those sounds reverberate across the African diaspora among the generations who keep the memory of them alive and among all who are willing to listen to them.

NOTES

Chapter One

1. "Kitab Fada'il al-Sahabah," in *Sahih Muslim*, book 31, hadith 6012, vol. 4, 1310. See also *Sahih Bukhari*, book 21, hadith 250.

2. Abdul-Rauf, *Bilal Ibn Rabah*, 5, 64. Others reported that Bilal's voice had a high pitch. See Qazi, *Bilal*, 90.

3. *Sahih Bukhari*, book 56, hadith 633; Abdul-Rauf, *Bilal*, 63–64. Translation of the call to prayer is mine.

4. Abdul-Rauf, *Bilal*, 51.

5. Lewis, *Race and Slavery in the Middle East*, 25.

6. Abdul-Rauf, *Bilal*, 19–23.

7. 'Arafat, "Bilal b. Rabah."

8. Abdul-Rauf, *Bilal*, 29.

9. Miles, "'Anaza," and compare *Sahih Bukhari*, book 8, hadith 373, and book 72, hadith 677.

10. *Sahih Bukhari*, book 56, hadith 767, and book 59, hadith 617.

11. 'Arafat, "Bilal b. Rabah"; Abdul-Rauf, *Bilal*, 48–52.

12. *Sahih Bukhari*, book 12, hadith 822; book 15, hadith 78 and 95; book 24, hadith 51; "Kitab al-Salat," in *Sahih Muslim*, book 4, hadith 1923 and 1926, vol. 2, 416, 417.

13. *Sahih Bukhari*, book 38, hadith 504; "Kitab al-Nikah," in *Sahih Muslim*, book 8, hadith 3463, vol. 2, 751; Abdul-Rauf, *Bilal*, 38–44.

14. 'Arafat, "Bilal b. Rabah."

15. Abdul-Rauf, *Bilal*, 31. Translation of the verse is by Abdullah Yusuf Ali.

16. "Kitab al-Hajj," in *Sahih Muslim*, book 7, hadith 2977, vol. 2, 654.

17. For an overview of this issue, see Robinson, *Muslim Societies in African History*, 60–73. See also Walz and Cuno, *Race and Slavery in the Middle East*; Lovejoy, *Transformations in Slavery*; and Lewis, *Race and Slavery in the Middle East*.

18. See, for example, Lindsay, *Captives as Commodities*.

19. Lewis, *Race and Slavery in the Middle East*, 25.

20. See Hourani, *History of the Arab Peoples*, 38–58; and compare Bulliet, *Conversion to Islam in the Medieval Period*.

21. Levtzion and Pouwels, *History of Islam in Africa*, 2–5.

22. Ibid., 5–8.

23. For an overview, see Gomez, *Reversing Sail*.

24. See, for example, Walz and Cuno, *Race and Slavery in the Middle East*; and Toledano, *As If Silent and Absent*.

25. See Hawley, *India in Africa*.

26. For overviews, see Gomez, *Black Crescent*; and Curtis, *Muslims in America*.

27. Brubaker, "'Diaspora' Diaspora." For other approaches, see Braziel and Mannur, *Theorizing Diaspora*; Dufoix, *Diasporas*; and Knott and McLoughlin, *Diasporas*.

28. See, for example, Judith Byfield, "Introduction"; Edwards, "Uses of Diaspora"; and Olaniyan and Sweet, *African Diaspora and the Disciplines*.

29. Safran, "Diasporas in Modern Societies."

30. See Gilroy, *There Ain't No Black in the Union Jack*; compare Gilroy, *Black Atlantic*.

31. Clifford, *Routes*, 250.

32. Clarke, *Mapping Yoruba Networks*.

33. For an exception, see Trost, *African Diaspora and the Study of Religion*.

34. Jonathan Smith, *HarperCollins Dictionary of Religion*, 373–74.

35. For a helpful overview of religious studies approaches to sacred space, see the introduction to Chidester and Linenthal, *American Sacred Space*, 1–42.

36. Tweed, *Crossing and Dwelling*.

37. Jonathan Smith, *Map Is Not Territory*.

38. Meier, "Per/forming African Identities," 87.

39. Renard, *Seven Doors to Islam*; J. Bowen, *New Anthropology of Islam*.

40. Pew Research Center, *World's Muslims*.

41. Ibid., 43.

42. Ibid., 59.

43. Ibid., 73.

44. For introductions to Sufism, see Karamustafa, *Sufism*; and Ernst, *Shambhala Guide to Sufism*.

45. The body of literature on modern reform movements in Islam is enormous. A good place to begin is "Reform," in Martin, *Encyclopedia of Islam and the Muslim World*, 2:574–83.

46. See Hesse, "Racialized Modernity"; King, *Orientalism and Religion*; Said, *Culture and Imperialism*; and Chidester, *Savage Systems*.

47. Lockman, *Contending Visions of the Middle East*, 59.

48. See further Said, *Orientalism*.

49. Clarke and Thomas, *Globalization and Race*.

50. Gordon, *Her Majesty's Children*, 53.

51. Shelby, *We Who Are Dark*, 207–8.

52. See, for example, Oliver and Shapiro, *Black Wealth/White Wealth*.

53. Young, *Haunting Capital*, 25.

54. Shelby, *We Who Are Dark*, 209–10.

55. See further S. Johnson, "Rise of the Black Ethnics"; and compare Wallerstein, "Construction of Peoplehood," 78, 84.

Chapter Two

1. El-Sawy, "Essaouira Report."

2. Paques, "Gnawa of Morocco," 319; El Hamel, "Constructing a Diasporic Identity," 250.

3. Waugh, *Memory, Music, and Religion*, 108–11.

4. I include North Africa as part of the entire African continent, as do most mainstream geographers and historians. See, for example, Fage and Oliver, *Cambridge*

History of Africa; UNESCO, *General History of Africa*; and Newman, *Peopling of Africa*; and compare Murdock, *Africa*.

5. The idea of the "Arab world" is a highly disputed one, and its meaning shifts in various circumstances. One official political definition can be found in the member states of the Arab League, which includes the Comoros, Morocco, Tunisia, Mauritania, Libya, Algeria, Egypt, Saudi Arabia, Djibouti, Palestine, Lebanon, Iraq, Jordan, Kuwait, Somalia, United Arab Emirates, Bahrain, Oman, Qatar, Sudan, Yemen, and Syria, whose membership was suspended during the civil war there.

6. Lewis, *Race and Slavery in the Middle East*, 48–61.

7. See, for example, Jankowsky, *Stambeli*, 16–17; and Walz and Cuno, *Race and Slavery in the Middle East*, 8–9.

8. Hunwick, "Same but Different."

9. For a discussion of black North African music and culture and "the blues," see Kapchan, *Traveling Spirit Masters*, 35–36; and El Hamel, "Constructing a Diasporic Identity."

10. Austen, "Mediterranean Islamic Slave Trade."

11. Toledano, *As If Silent and Absent*, 11–14. See further Erdem, *Slavery in the Ottoman Empire*.

12. Toledano, *As If Silent and Absent*, 23–25, 85.

13. John Hunwick, "The Religious Practices of Black Slaves in the Mediterranean Islamic World," in Lovejoy, *Slavery on the Frontiers of Islam*, 150–52.

14. Toledano, *As If Silent and Absent*, 71, 78, 108–52.

15. See Tremearne, *Ban of the Bori*.

16. Hunwick, "Religious Practices," 163–67.

17. Constantinides, "History of *Zar* in the Sudan." Maxine Rodinson may have coined the term; see "Le culte de 'zar' en Egypte."

18. Boddy, *Wombs and Alien Spirits*, xxi.

19. Toledano, *As If Silent and Absent*, 216–17, 222. See also Boddy, *Wombs and Alien Spirits*, 131; and Sengers, *Women and Demons*, 23, 65.

20. Jankowsky, *Stambeli*, 19.

21. Sengers, *Women and Demons*, 222–23.

22. See, for example, Khalifa, "African Influence"; Ashkanani, "*Zar* in a Changing World"; Toledano, *As If Silent and Absent*, 204–54; Jankowsky, *Stambeli*, 18; and Mirzai, "African Presence in Iran."

23. Montana, "*Bori* Colonies of Tunis," 164.

24. Ibid., 155–60.

25. Montana, "Ahmad ibn al-Qadi al-Timbuktawi," 181.

26. Hunwick, "Religious Practices," 153.

27. Montana, "Ahmad ibn al-Qadi al-Timbuktawi," 181–82.

28. Ibid., 182–83.

29. Montana, "*Bori* Colonies of Tunis," 161–62.

30. Ibid., 163–64. See also Jankowsky, *Stambeli*, 55–61.

31. Montana, "Ahmad ibn al-Qadi al-Timbuktawi," 179.

32. Montana, "*Stambali* of Husaynid Tunis," 176–78.

33. Ibid., 179, 181.

34. Montana, "Ahmad ibn al-Qadi al-Timbuktawi," 184–85.
35. Ibid., 185.
36. Montana, "*Stambali* of Husaynid Tunis," 180.
37. Ibid., 180–81.
38. Jankowsky, *Stambeli*, 66.
39. Hunwick, "Religious Practices," 158–59.
40. Jankowsky, *Stambeli*, 45–46.
41. Hunwick, "Religious Practices," 154–56.
42. Ibid., 156–58.
43. Jankowsky, *Stambeli*, 37–42.
44. Ibid., 68–71.
45. Ibid., 68–91.
46. Ibid., 131–48.
47. Ibid., 155–76.
48. Ibid., 177.
49. El Hamel, "Constructing a Diasporic Identity," 248–49.
50. Ibid., 247–48, 258.
51. Paques, "Gnawa of Morocco," 319–20; Kapchan, *Traveling Spirit Masters*, 36.
52. El Hamel, "Constructing a Diasporic Identity," 241.
53. Kapchan, *Traveling Spirit Masters*, 4–5, 176–95.
54. El Hamel, "Constructing a Diasporic Identity," 256. Compare Gilroy, *Black Atlantic*.
55. Waugh, *Memory, Music, and Religion*, 110.
56. El Hamel, "Constructing a Diasporic Identity," 257.
57. Ibid., 256.
58. Kapchan, *Traveling Spirit Masters*, 11–13, 39–41. Translations of the prayers to the Prophet are mine, not Kapchan's.
59. Ibid., 14–15, 33–34, 42, 64.
60. Ibid., 14–17.
61. El Hamel, "Constructing a Diasporic Identity," 254–55.
62. Quoted in ibid., 252.
63. Hunwick, "Religious Practices," 165–67; Kapchan, *Traveling Spirit Masters*, 26.
64. El Hamel, "Constructing a Diasporic Identity," 249; Hunwick, "Religious Practices," 165.
65. Kapchan, *Traveling Spirit Masters*, 26.
66. Paques, "Gnawa of Morocco," 60. See also Crapanzo, *Hamadsha*.
67. Andrew Shryock calls the Ghawarna people an "Afro-Arab" population. See Shryock, *Nationalism and the Genealogical Imagination*, 136. But some Ghawarna do not have black roots. On the Israeli Ghawarna, for example, see Khawalde and Rabinowitz, "Race from the Bottom of the Tribe."
68. Kareem, *Settlement Patterns in the Jordan Valley*, 11; Walker, "Role of Agriculture," 82, 84; Albright, "Archaeological Results."
69. Layne, "Production and Reproduction of Tribal Identity in Jordan," 86–87, 309–11. See also Burckhardt, *Travels in Syria and the Holy Land*, 388; Toledano,

Ottoman Slave Trade, 39; and Cohen and Lewis, *Population and Revenue in the Towns of Palestine*, 56–59.

70. See, for example, Shryock, *Nationalism and the Genealogical Imagination*, 45, 158–59.

71. Layne, "Production and Reproduction of Tribal Identity in Jordan," 311–12; Toledano, *Ottoman Slave Trade*, 29–30, 64.

72. Clarence-Smith, *Islam and the Abolition of Slavery*, 116; Layne, *Home and Homeland*, 51 (n. 29).

73. Gubser, *Politics and Change in Al-Karak*, 65–67.

74. Bani Yasin, "Critical and Comparative Study."

75. Layne, "Production and Reproduction of Tribal Identity in Jordan," 83–88, 318–20.

76. This is true of other black populations in the region; see, for example, Khalifa, "African Influence," 229.

77. Helal, "Muhammad Ali's First Army"; Beckerleg, "African Bedouin in Palestine," 290–91; Konanga-Nicolas, "African Palestinian Community."

78. Curtis, "Ghawarna of Jordan," 199–200.

79. Beckerleg, "African Bedouin in Palestine," 291.

80. Compare Pieterse, *White on Black*.

81. Curtis, "Ghawarna of Jordan," 199.

82. Gubser, *Politics and Change in Al-Karak*, 28, 65.

83. See "Ayn," in Martin, *Encyclopedia of Islam*; Sengers, *Women and Demons*, 254–73; and Donaldson, *Wild Rue*, 13–23.

84. Spooner, "Evil Eye."

85. Curtis, "Ghawarna of Jordan," 203–4.

86. Ibid., 204; and compare Jankowsky, *Stambeli*, 20.

87. For discussions of gender and healing in various Muslim communities, compare Flueckiger, *In Amma's Healing Room*; Boddy, *Wombs and Alien Spirits*; and Sengers, *Women and Demons*.

88. Bani Yasin, "Critical and Comparative Study," 47. See further Hilma Granqvist's many photographs of shrine visitation in 1920s Palestine in *Portrait of a Palestinian Village*, 150–54.

89. Curtis, "Ghawarna of Jordan," 204–5.

90. Ibid., 205.

91. See El Alami, *Marriage Contract*; and compare Mir-Hosseini, *Marriage on Trial*.

92. Curtis, "Ghawarna of Jordan," 205–6.

93. Ibid., 206.

94. Van Aken, "Dancing Belonging," 204. See also Van Aken, *Facing Home*.

95. Van Aken, "Dancing Belonging," 211.

96. Mauro Van Aken, e-mail message to author, May 17, 2011.

97. Van Aken, "Dancing Belonging," 211.

98. Ibid., 213–15.

99. Ibid., 217.

100. For an introduction to Islamic law and ethics, see Kamali, *Shari'ah Law*.

101. See Pew Research Center, *World's Muslims*.

102. For a critique of "Islam in the Eyes of the West" and an alternate view of Islamic "Spirituality in Practice," see Ernst, *Following Muhammad*.

Chapter Three

1. Mecca2Medina, "Descendants of Bilal," transcribed by author, January 15, 2013, http://www.youtube.com/watch?v=D-hAeHzkPpw. The ellipses indicate inaudible words.

2. Blyden, *Christianity, Islam, and the Negro Race*.

3. Lapidus, *History of Islamic Societies*, 309–19; Almond, *Two Faiths*, 13–38.

4. Almond, *Two Faiths*, 38–46; Gomez, *Black Crescent*, 5–6.

5. For an introduction to the idea of Oceanic history, see "The Ocean World and the Beginnings of American History," in Bender, *Nation among Nations*, 15–60.

6. I. Smith, *Race and Rhetoric*, 87–88.

7. Northrup, *Africa's Discovery of Europe*, 2.

8. I. Smith, *Race and Rhetoric*, 88.

9. Casares, "Free and Freed Black Africans," 248.

10. Ibid., 251; Lowe, "Introduction: The Black African Presence in Renaissance Europe," 5–6.

11. Lowe, "Introduction: The Black African Presence in Renaissance Europe," 7–8.

12. See further Earle and Lowe, *Black Africans in Renaissance Europe*, 227, 230.

13. Ibid., 286 (n. 17).

14. Northrup, *Africa's Discovery of Europe*, 7.

15. Ibid., 117.

16. Austin, *African Muslims in Antebellum America: Transatlantic Stories*, 50–62.

17. Bluett, *Some Memoirs of the Life of Job*.

18. Middleton, "Strange Story," 349.

19. See Northrup, *Africa's Discovery of Europe*, chap. 3; and Middleton, "Strange Story."

20. Wesseling, *European Colonial Empires*, 96. The colony in Senegal was founded in 1659.

21. Ibid., 148; Reid, *History of Modern Africa*, 135–37.

22. Wesseling, *European Colonial Empires*, 94; Reid, *History of Modern Africa*, 185.

23. Reid, *History of Modern Africa*, 135.

24. Ibid., 152, 158, 163, 201. See Wesseling, *European Colonial Empires*, 148, 156, for a periodization of the colonization process.

25. Reid, *History of Modern Africa*, 234, 245, 272.

26. Ibid., 245, 272; Shabazz, "Blacks in Portugal"; Northrup, *Africa's Discovery of Europe*, 7; Blakely, "Emergence of Afro-Europe," 15.

27. M. Johnson, "'Proof Is on My Palm,'" 51.

28. Loja, "Islam in Portugal," 193.

29. M. Johnson, "'Proof Is on My Palm,'" 54–55, 57.

30. Ibid., 50, 57–58, 61–63.

31. M. Johnson, "Death and the Left Hand," 99–100.

32. M. Johnson, "'Proof Is on My Palm,'" 65.
33. Ibid., 65–66.
34. M. Johnson, "Death and the Left Hand," 107, 110.
35. M. Johnson, "'Proof Is on My Palm,'" 68–70.
36. Dodgen, "Immigration and Identity Politics," 21, 29; "Cittadini Stranieri."
37. Babou, "Educating the Murid," 312.
38. D. Carter, *Navigating the African Diaspora*, 151, 167.
39. D. Carter, *States of Grace*, 18; D. Carter, *Navigating the African Diaspora*, 156.
40. D. Carter, *Navigating the African Diaspora*, 167.
41. More recently the migration trends have shifted, with an emphasis on family reunification and an increasing number of single women moving to Europe to work. See Timera, "Righteous or Rebellious?"
42. There are many alternate spellings of the saint's name, including Aamadu Bamba Mbàkka, Ahmadou Bamba, Ahmadou Bamba Mbacké, and Amadou Bamba.
43. Kaag, "Mouride Transnational Livelihoods," 272.
44. Diouf, "Invisible Muslims," 150–51. The dahiras often have thirty to fifty active members but an overall membership of perhaps one or two hundred participants. More people participate during major events or the visit of a marabout. See Sheff, "Problem with Eating Money," 49; and Kaag, "Mouride Transnational Livelihoods," 275.
45. See Bryceson and Vuorela, *Transnational Family*, 219, 253.
46. See further in ibid.
47. Diouf, "Invisible Muslims," 148.
48. Kaag, "Mouride Transnational Livelihoods," 275.
49. Ibid., 274.
50. Sheff, "Problem with Eating Money," 45–46.
51. Riccio, "Senegalese Street-Sellers," 233.
52. D. Carter, *States of Grace*, 64.
53. Ibid., 93.
54. See, for example, Bryceson and Vuorela, *Transnational Family*, 224.
55. Riccio, "Transnational Mouridism," 936.
56. D. Carter, *States of Grace*, 69, 95.
57. See, for instance, Buggenhagen, "Islam and the Media of Devotion," 85; and D. Carter, *States of Grace*, 84.
58. See Riccio, "From 'Ethnic Group,'" 594.
59. Riccio, "Transnational Mouridism," 932.
60. D. Carter, *States of Grace*, 61.
61. Kaag, "Mouride Transnational Livelihoods," 283.
62. Buggenhagen, "Islam and the Media of Devotion," 88, 90.
63. Ibid., 84, 87.
64. See, for instance, Diouf, "Invisible Muslims," 145; and Riccio, "Transnational Mouridism," 930.
65. Quoted in Andall, "Second-Generation Attitude?," 399.
66. Diouf, "Invisible Muslims," 145.
67. Sinatti, "Diasporic Cosmopolitanism," 32, 44.

68. Riccio, "Transnational Mouridism," 938.
69. Kaag, "Mouride Transnational Livelihoods," 282.
70. Sinatti, "Diasporic Cosmopolitanism," 33, 40.
71. Buggenhagen, "Islam and the Media of Devotion," 91.
72. Change Institute, *Nigerian Muslim Community*, 7; Ansari, "Black Muslims," 55.
73. Walvin, *Making the Black Atlantic*, 109.
74. Ibid., 113; Ansari, "Black Muslims," 54.
75. According to a 2010 Pew Research Center report, there are 2.869 million. Pew Research Center, *Muslim Networks*, 5. For mosques in the UK, see Peach and Gale, "Muslims, Hindus, and Sikhs," 470, 479.
76. Change Institute, *Summary Report*, 9.
77. Reddie, *Black Muslims in Britain*, 56–58.
78. See Adebayo, "Young, Muslim, and Black."
79. Change Institute, *Nigerian Muslim Community*, 5–6.
80. Change Institute, *Somali Muslim Community*, 24.
81. Ibid., 6.
82. The number of Muslim prisoners has increased from about 5 percent of the overall prison population in 1994 to 12 percent of the prison population in 2008. See HM Chief Inspector of Prisons, *Muslim Prisoners' Experiences*, 9. The report also indicates that there are proportionately more black Muslim prisoners than their numbers in the broader British population: 34 percent of Muslim prisoners in 2008 were black, compared to 7 percent of Muslims overall.
83. Change Institute, *Summary Report*, 20; Ansari, "Black Muslims," 54.
84. Tinaz, "Black Islam in Diaspora," 155–58.
85. Reddie, *Black Muslims in Britain*, 168, 170–73, 176–77, 193.
86. Melville, "New Brotherhood."
87. Muslim Belal, "Like a Soldier," http://www.youtube.com/watch?v=nzW3 GRbUd2w.
88. HM Chief Inspector of Prisons, *Muslim Prisoners' Experiences*, 23.
89. Berns-McGown, *Muslims in the Diaspora*, 72, 76.
90. Ibid., 84, 96, 224–25.
91. Ibid., 116, 125.
92. Ibid., 104.
93. Reddie, *Black Muslims in Britain*, 179, 155; Tinaz, "Black Islam in Diaspora," 159, 163.
94. Change Institute, *Somali Muslim Community*, 34, 37.
95. Reddie, *Black Muslims in Britain*, 218.
96. Change Institute, *Somali Muslim Community*, 37.
97. Change Institute, *Nigerian Muslim Community*, 31.
98. Change Institute, *Somali Muslim Community*, 44.
99. Berns-McGown, *Muslims in the Diaspora*, 109, 111.
100. Ibid., 5, 28.
101. Adebayo, "Young, Muslim, and Black."
102. Schick, "UK Duo on a Poetic Pilgrimage."
103. Reddie, *Black Muslims in Britain*, 162.

104. Jouili, "Beat-ification." Muslim hip-hop artists themselves vary in their use of instruments, from those who use only human voices to those who are accompanied by a variety of instruments.

105. In 2008 they featured Muslim Belal and Pearls of Wisdom (who appeared also in 2009).

106. Quoted in Reddie, *Black Muslims in Britain*, 209.

107. Shahrad, "Muslim Rap."

108. Ibid.; and see "Blind Alphabetz."

109. Muslim Belal, "I Can See Clearly," http://www.youtube.com/watch?v=oi817Hyb6oM.

110. David Drissel argues that South Asian youth have taken on "black-inflected identities," yet in that process they are "tending to avoid any explicit self-identification as black." Drissel, "Hybridizing Hip-Hop," 212. He claims that "much of the allure of Desi hip-hop is based on its intimate association with African diasporic imagery and angry defiance in the face of adversity" (218).

111. Fun-Da-Mental, "English Breakfast," http://www.satho.freeservers.com/fundamental.htm.

Chapter Four

1. Translation by Amy Catlin-Jairazbhoy with the assistance of Sidi Salam Jaffar, quoted in Catlin-Jairazbhoy and Alpers, *Sidis and Scholars*, 196.

2. See, for example, Bigelow, *Sharing the Sacred*.

3. Catlin-Jairazbhoy and Alpers, *Sidis and Scholars*, 195–96.

4. Basu, "Slave, Soldier, Trader, Faqir," 223.

5. The now classic English-language work on Africans in Asia is by Harris, *African Presence in Asia*. For a review of literature on the Siddis, see Catlin-Jairazbhoy and Alpers, *Sidis and Scholars*, 12–17.

6. Camara, "Siddis of Uttara Kannada," 102.

7. Meier, "Per/forming African Identities," 86.

8. Collins, "African Slave Trade to Asia and the Indian Ocean Islands."

9. Jayasuriya, *African Identity in Asia*, 37.

10. Collins, "African Slave Trade," 336–40.

11. Austen, "19th Century Islamic Slave Trade."

12. Machado, "Forgotten Corner," 26.

13. Campbell, "Slave Trades" and "Female Bondage and Agency."

14. Alpers, "Africans in India," 28.

15. Ibid., 32.

16. Eaton, "Rise and Fall of Military Slavery"; Alpers, "Africans in India," 32.

17. McLeod, "Marriage and Identity"; Oka and Kusimba, "Siddi as Mercenary"; Jayasuriya, *African Identity in Asia*, 67–71.

18. Obeng, *Shaping Membership*, 18–19; Alpers, "Africans in India," 34.

19. Eaton, "Malik Ambar."

20. Yimene, "African Cavalry Guards."

21. Obeng, *Shaping Membership*, 19.

22. Alpers, "Africans in India," 30–31.
23. Camara, "Siddis of Uttara Kannada," 102.
24. Kenoyer and Bhan, "Sidis and the Agate Bead Industry," 46.
25. Camara, "Siddis of Uttara Kannada," 103, 108–9.
26. Obeng, *Shaping Membership*, 10.
27. Quoted in ibid., 40–41.
28. Camara, "Siddis of Uttara Kannada," 103–4.
29. Obeng, *Shaping Membership*, 21, 50.
30. Camara, "Siddis of Uttara Kannada," 109.
31. Obeng, *Shaping Membership*, 30.
32. Camara, "Siddis of Uttara Kannada," 110–11.
33. Basu, "Theatre of Memory," 248–49; Basu, "Hierarchy and Emotion," 118; Amy Catlin-Jairazbhoy, "A Sidi CD," in Catlin-Jairazbhoy and Alpers, *Sidis and Scholars*, 181–82.
34. Basu, "Gendered Indian Ocean Site," 230–31.
35. Catlin-Jairazbhoy, "Sacred Pleasure," 77–82, 83–84, 92–95.
36. Catlin-Jairazbhoy, "Sidi CD," 184.
37. Basu, "Siddi and the Cult of Bava Gor," 294; Basu, "Hierarchy and Emotion," 123–24, 134; Catlin-Jairazbhoy, "Sacred Pleasure," 75.
38. Basu, "Slave, Soldier, Trader, Faqir," 244; Basu, "Hierarchy and Emotion," 119.
39. Basu, "Theatre of Memory," 249–50.
40. Basu, "Gendered Indian Ocean Site," 232.
41. Basu, "Hierarchy and Emotion," 120.
42. Ibid., 127–29.
43. Ibid., 129–30.
44. Basu, "Gendered Indian Ocean Site," 252.
45. Ibid., 248–52.
46. Basu, "Hierarchy and Emotion," 131.
47. Basu, "Siddi and the Cult of Bava Gor," 295.
48. *Ghusl* is distinguished from *wudu*, which is the washing of only certain parts of the body.
49. Basu, "Siddi and the Cult of Bava Gor," 296–97.
50. Catlin-Jairazbhoy, "Sacred Pleasure," 88–89.
51. Basu, "Siddi and the Cult of Bava Gor," 297–98; Basu, "Hierarchy and Emotion," 132–36.
52. Basu, "Theatre of Memory," 255–64.
53. Basu, "Redefining Boundaries."
54. David Pinault, "Muharram," in Martin, *Encyclopedia of Islam and the Muslim World*, 2:488–89.
55. Obeng, *Shaping Membership*, 95–98.
56. Ibid., 96–98.
57. Ibid., 95–96, 100.
58. Phone interview by author with Pashington Obeng, August 10, 2011.
59. Quoted in Obeng, *Shaping Membership*, 101–3.
60. Ibid., 103–8, 111.

61. Ibid., 160–61.
62. Ibid., 163.
63. Ibid., 161–63.
64. Ibid., 184–85.
65. See Meier, "Per/forming African Identities."
66. For a full-throated rejection of the idea that Siddis can be fruitfully understood as part of an African diaspora, see Campbell, "Slave Trades." The other side of the debate is represented in Obeng's *Shaping Membership*. John McLeod, who insists on self-identification as an example of roots in the African diaspora, shows how the Siddis of Janjira strongly identify with their African origins. See McLeod, "Marriage and Identity."

Chapter Five

1. Reis, *Slave Rebellion*, 130–32.
2. For helpful introductions, see Raboteau, *Canaan Land*; and Wilmore, *Black Religion*.
3. Gomez, *Black Crescent*, 15–16.
4. See Diouf, *Servants of Allah*.
5. See Dobronravin, "Literacy among Muslims"; and Addoun and Lovejoy, "Muhammad Kaba Saghanughu."
6. Austin, *African Muslims in Antebellum America: Transatlantic Stories*, 83–186.
7. Curtis, *Muslims in America*, 31–44.
8. Nunez, *History of Muslims*; Afroz, "Invisible Yet Invincible," 215–16; "Islam in Jamaica," *Muhammad Speaks*, January 17, 1975, 1, 2, 6–9, S1–S7.
9. See, for example, Oliveira and Mariz, "Conversion to Islam," 107–8; Pereira, "A discreta presença"; and Mesa, "El Islam."
10. See, for example, James, *Black Jacobins*; and Aptheker, *American Negro Slave Revolts*.
11. See Gottschalk and Greenberg, *Islamophobia*; and compare Said, *Covering Islam*.
12. For an account of institutional Islamophobia against African American Muslims, see Curtis, "Black Muslim Scare."
13. For a history of Islamic and Middle East studies, see Lockman, *Contending Visions of the Middle East*.
14. See Gerges, *Far Enemy*.
15. See further Ayoob, *Many Faces*; and Mandaville, *Global Political Islam*.
16. For a full consideration of the concept of jihad in Islamic history, see Kelsay, *Arguing the Just War in Islam*.
17. Sohail H. Hashmi, "Jihad," in Martin, *Encyclopedia of Islam and the Muslim World*, 1:377–79.
18. Reis, *Slave Rebellion*, 73, 89, 118–19.
19. Ibid., xiii, 73–92.
20. Ibid., 93.
21. Ibid., 6, 96, 139.

22. This situation was markedly different from that in British North America where formal institutions of Islamic learning and ritual practice do not seem to have been established and passed on from generation to generation. See further chapter 6.

23. Reis, *Slave Rebellion*, 93–115, 170.
24. Ibid., 99–102.
25. Ibid., 104–8.
26. Ibid., 109, 130–31.
27. Ibid., 66.
28. See, for example, Goody, "Writing, Rebellion, and Revolt."
29. Gomez, *Black Crescent*, 110–16.
30. Reis, *Slave Rebellion*, 5, 146.
31. Ibid., 116, 121–22.
32. Butler, "Africa," 138–39.
33. Reis, *Slave Rebellion*, 140, 146, 154.
34. Ibid., 98, 110.
35. Ibid., 97, 124.
36. Ibid., 220–23.
37. "Trinidad Rebels Threaten to Kill Premier and 11 Other Hostages," *New York Times*, July 29, 1990, A1; Forte, *Against the Trinity*, 19; Ryan, *Muslimeen Grab for Power*, vii, 52–55.
38. Pitt, "Accord Is Stalled"; Pantin, *Days of Wrath*, 1–69, 87. See also Ryan, *Muslimeen Grab for Power*, 131–88.
39. Pantin, *Days of Wrath*, 84–141; Pitt, "Rebels in Trinidad."
40. Ryan, *Muslimeen Grab for Power*, 17, 32, 35.
41. Ibid., 225.
42. Khan, *Callaloo Nation*, 1–26.
43. See, for example, Connell, *Understanding Islam and Its Impact in Latin America*; and Ramsey, "What Is the Real Threat of Islamic Terrorism in Latin America?"
44. Khan, *Callaloo Nation*, 9–10. See also Premdas, *Trinidad and Tobago*, 1–48.
45. See the polemical critique of "Indian Islam" in Figueira, *Jihad*, 1–54.
46. Ibid., 87.
47. Ibid., 67.
48. A. McCloud, *African American Islam*, 69–72.
49. Forte, *Against the Trinity*, 128–31.
50. Y. Carter, "Islamic Party of North America."
51. Figueira, *Jihad*, 66–71.
52. "No Progress without Struggle," *Faithful Struggler* 1, no. 2, quoted in ibid., 76.
53. *Faithful Struggler* 2, no. 1, quoted in ibid., 82.
54. *Faithful Struggler* 1, no. 4, quoted in ibid., 72.
55. *Faithful Struggler* 1, no. 5, quoted in ibid., 74.
56. Ryan, *Muslimeen Grab for Power*, 56; Figueira, *Jihad*, 82–83.
57. Ryan, *Muslimeen Grab for Power*, 55–58.
58. Figueira, *Jihad*, 55–59, 89–90.

59. Statement by Bilaal Abdullah in *Trinidad Guardian*, January 29, 1985, quoted in Figueira, *Jihad*, 101–2; Ryan, *Muslimeen Grab for Power*, 65–66.
60. Figueira, *Jihad*, 105.
61. Ibid., 128–29.
62. Ibid., 121–44.
63. Ryan, *Muslimeen Grab for Power*, 74–75, 79.
64. Figueira, *Jihad*, 146.
65. Ryan, *Muslimeen Grab for Power*, 226.
66. Compare Ayoob, *Many Faces*, 112.
67. Ryan, *Muslimeen Grab for Power*, 115.
68. Ibid., 311.
69. Pantin, *Days of Wrath*, 53, 65.
70. Ryan, *Muslimeen Grab for Power*, 116.
71. Forte, *Against the Trinity*, 138–40, 144–47.
72. Khan, *Callaloo Nation*, 191.
73. Ibid., 192.
74. Ibid. See also Ryan, *Muslimeen Grab for Power*, 84–104.

Chapter Six

1. *Bilalian News*, November 28, 1975, 25.
2. Ibid., November 1, 1975. The larger story of the transition is in Curtis, *Islam in Black America*, 107–27.
3. See Gallup, "Muslim Americans," 10.
4. For a survey of the many forms of Islamic practice among African Americans, see A. McCloud, *African American Islam*, 9–94.
5. On African American Murids, see Abdullah, *Black Mecca*, 114–15. On African American Tijanis, see Dannin, *Black Pilgrimage to Islam*, 248, 255–56. For a primary account of one African American woman's decision to join the Bawa Muhaiyaddeen Fellowship, see Simmons, "Are We Up to the Challenge?"
6. Bambach, "Shariʿa."
7. See Takim, *Shiʿism in America*.
8. African American Ahmadi Muslims are discussed in Turner, *Islam in the African-American Experience*, 109–46. For Minister Farrakhan's Nation of Islam, see Gardell, *In the Name of Elijah Muhammad*.
9. Austin, *African Muslims in Antebellum America: Transatlantic Stories*, 22.
10. Gomez, *Black Crescent*, 166.
11. See further Diouf, *Servants of Allah*.
12. My account of Abd al-Rahman is based on Alford, *Prince among Slaves*; Austin's 1984 sourcebook, *African Muslims in Antebellum America*; and Austin's 1997 monograph (which has the same title as the sourcebook), *African Muslims in Antebellum America: Transatlantic Stories*, 65–83.
13. "An Afro-American Recalls His Visit to Washington, D.C.," August 29, 1828, 29, quoted in Austin, *African Muslims in Antebellum America: A Sourcebook*, 159, 251 (n. 67).

14. Austin, *African Muslims in Antebellum America: Transatlantic Stories*, 65–83.

15. Georgia Bryan Conrad, *Reminiscences of a Southern Woman* (Hampton, Va.: Hampton Institute, n.d.), quoted in Austin, *African Muslims in Antebellum America: A Sourcebook*, 275, 304 (n. 14).

16. For a fuller account of Bilali, see Austin, *African Muslims in Antebellum America: Transatlantic Stories*, 85–113.

17. Georgia Writers Project, *Drums and Shadows*, 158–67.

18. Ibid., 162, 167.

19. Ibid., 162.

20. Raboteau, *Slave Religion*, 47.

21. See further ibid., 1–92.

22. Georgia Writers Project, *Drums and Shadows*, 166.

23. Austin, *African Muslims in Antebellum America: Transatlantic Stories*, 101–10.

24. Georgia Writers Project, *Drums and Shadows*, 144–45.

25. Ibid., 145.

26. For excerpts of Sadiq's writings, see Curtis, *Columbia Sourcebook*, 53–58.

27. P. Bowen, "Satti Majid"; Abu Shouk et al., "Sudanese Missionary."

28. For Noble Drew Ali's writings, see Curtis, *Columbia Sourcebook*, 59–64. For accounts of the movement, see Haddad and Smith, *Mission to America*, 79–104; Curtis, "Debating the Origins"; and Nance, "Mystery of the Moorish Science Temple."

29. For accounts of the emergence of the Nation of Islam, see Lincoln, *Black Muslims*; Essien-Udom, *Black Nationalism*; Clegg, *Original Man*; and Curtis, *Islam in Black America*, 63–84.

30. Curtis, *Black Muslim Religion*, 1–14.

31. For a discussion of Afro-Asian solidarity and African American Islam from a number of different angles, see Marable and Aidi, *Black Routes to Islam*, 49–119.

32. Elijah Muhammad's theological magnum opus, where his doctrines are best spelled out, is *Message to the Blackman*.

33. All quotations from Curtis, *Black Muslim Religion*, 72–76.

34. Ibid., 90.

35. Ibid., 67.

36. This political program, "What Muslims Want," was reprinted in the *Muhammad Speaks* newspaper on a weekly basis in the 1960s.

37. For more on the exaggeration of the threat posed by the Nation of Islam, see S. McCloud, *Making the American Religious Fringe*, 55–94.

38. Curtis, *Black Muslim Religion*, 96–98, 127–30.

39. Ibid., 98–99, 133–34.

40. Ibid., 102–5.

41. Ibid., 109–18.

42. Ibid., 136–53.

43. Ibid., 153–68.

44. Curtis, *Islam in Black America*, 107–27.

45. Curtis, *Black Muslim Religion*, 181.

46. Huggins, *Black Odyssey*, xlviii.

47. Nimer, *North American Muslim Resource Guide*, 24–25.

48. GhaneaBassiri, *History of Islam*, 272–326. For critiques of the racialized aspects of Muslim American immigrant institution building and religious culture, see further A. McCloud, *Transnational Muslims*; and Jackson, *Islam and the Blackamerican*. For a view of how women are confronting racialization, see Karim, *American Muslim Women*.

49. Sometimes the Muslim American experience is read primarily as the story of immigrant assimilation, a view that does not grapple with Muslims' participation in American history from the colonial era until today. See Jane Smith, *Islam in America*; Cesari, *When Islam and Democracy Meet*; and Haddad and Esposito, *Muslims on the Americanization Path?*

50. See, among other possibilities, Appadurai, *Modernity at Large*; and Clifford, *Routes*.

51. See, for example, Mandaville, *Transnational Muslim Politics*.

52. Carpenter, "Remembering the Homeland."

53. D'Alisera, *Imagined Geography*, 2–3.

54. Ibid., 77–92.

55. Ibid., 58.

56. Compare Eickelman, "Inside the Islamic Reformation."

57. D'Alisera, *Imagined Geography*, 74.

58. Ibid., 92.

59. Ibid., 52–57.

60. Ibid., 95–102.

61. Ibid., 133–34.

62. Ibid., 136–45. Since the 1990s the Fullah Progressive Union has remained devoted to teaching children both "African" and "Islamic" values. Unlike some other Muslim organizations in the United States, for example, it does not shy away from celebrating traditional African cultural practices. In fact, its annual fund-raiser in 2011 was a dance. Though some Muslim Americans associate any form of dance with un-Islamic behavior, this is simply not the case in the Fullah Progressive Union, which sponsors dancing and praying alike.

63. McCabe, "African Immigrants."

64. See, for example, Abdullah, *Black Mecca*; and Kane, *Homeland Is the Arena*.

65. Kane, *Homeland Is the Arena*, 67, 71, 102, 162. See also Abdullah, *Black Mecca*.

66. Lo, *Muslims in America*, 86–136.

Conclusion

1. D'Alisera, *Imagined Geography*, 59.

2. See, for example, Ahmed, *Women and Gender in Islam*; and Wadud, *Qur'an and Woman*.

3. See further Lockman, *Contending Visions of the Middle East*; Said, *Covering Islam*; and Ernst, *Islamophobia in America*. Opinions about Islam and Muslims in media, think tanks, and governmental offices may often be prejudicial, but they also have important cultural and political meanings and functions. For the history of U.S. interests, broadly defined, in the Middle East, see McAlister, *Epic Encounters*.

4. Pew Research Center, *Future of the Global Muslim Population*, 105.

BIBLIOGRAPHY

Abdullah, Zain. *Black Mecca: The African Muslims of Harlem*. New York: Oxford University Press, 2010.

Abdul-Rauf, Muhammad. *Bilal Ibn Rabah: A Leading Companion of the Prophet Muhammad*. Takoma Park, Md.: American Trust Publications, 1977.

Abu Shouk, Ahmed I., et al. "A Sudanese Missionary to the United States: Satti Majid, Shaykh al-Islam in North America, and His Encounter with Noble Drew Ali, Prophet of the Moorish Science Temple." *Sudanic Africa* 8 (1997): 137–91.

Addoun, Yacine Daddi, and Paul Lovejoy. "Muhammad Kaba Saghanughu and the Muslim Community of Jamaica." In *Slavery on the Frontiers of Islam*, edited by Paul E. Lovejoy, 199–218. Princeton, N.J.: Markus Wiener, 2004.

Adebayo, Dotun. "Young, Muslim, and Black." BBC Radio, 2010.

Afroz, Sultana. "Invisible Yet Invincible: The Muslim Ummah of Jamaica." *Journal of Muslim Minority Affairs* 23, no. 1 (April 2003): 211–22.

Ahmed, Leila. *Women and Gender in Islam: Historical Roots of a Modern Debate*. New Haven, Conn.: Yale University Press, 1993.

Albright, W. F. "The Archaeological Results of an Expedition to Moab and the Dead Sea." *Bulletin of American Schools of Oriental Research* 14 (1924): 2–12.

Alford, Terry. *Prince among Slaves*. New York: Oxford University Press, 2007.

Almond, Ian. *Two Faiths, One Banner: When Muslims Marched with Christians across Europe's Battlefields*. Cambridge, Mass.: Harvard University Press, 2009.

Alpers, Edward A. "Africans in India and the Wider Context of the Indian Ocean." In *Sidis and Scholars: Essays on African Indians*, edited by Amy Catlin-Jairazbhoy and Edward A. Alpers, 26–40. Trenton, N.J.: Red Sea Press, 2004.

Andall, Jacqueline. "Second-Generation Attitude? African-Italians in Milan." *Journal of Ethnic and Migration Studies* 28, no. 3 (2002): 389–407.

Ansari, Humayun. "Black Muslims." In *The Oxford Companion to Black British History*, edited by David Dabydeen, John Gilmore, and Cecily Jones, 54–56. Oxford: Oxford University Press, 2007.

Appadurai, Arjun. *Modernity at Large: Cultural Dimensions of Globalization*. Minneapolis: University of Minnesota Press, 1996.

Aptheker, Herbert. *American Negro Slave Revolts*. 6th ed. New York: International Publishers, 1993.

'Arafat, W. "Bilal b. Rabah." In *Encyclopedia of Islam*, CD-ROM ed., vol. 1.0. Leiden, Netherlands: Brill, 1999.

Ashkanani, Zubaydah. "*Zar* in a Changing World: Kuwait." In *Women's Medicine: The Zar-Bori Cult in Africa and Beyond*, edited by I. M. Lewis, Ahmed Al-Safi, and Sayyid Hurreiz, 219–29. Edinburgh: Edinburgh University Press, 1991.

Austen, Ralph A. "The Mediterranean Islamic Slave Trade Out of Africa: A Tentative Census." In *Slavery and Abolition* 31, no. 1 (1992): 214–48.

———. "The 19th Century Islamic Slave Trade from East Africa (Swahili and Red Sea Coasts): A Tentative Census." In *The Economics of the Indian Ocean Slave*

Trade in the Nineteenth Century, edited by William Gervase Clarence-Smith, 21–44. London: Frank Cass, 1989.

Austin, Allan D. *African Muslims in Antebellum America: A Sourcebook.* New York: Garland, 1984.

———. *African Muslims in Antebellum America: Transatlantic Stories and Spiritual Struggles.* New York: Routledge, 1997.

Ayoob, Mohammed. *The Many Faces of Political Islam: Religion and Politics in the Muslim World.* Ann Arbor: University of Michigan Press, 2008.

Babou, Cheikh Anta. "Educating the Murid: Theory and Practices of Education in Amadu Bamba's Thought." *Journal of Religion in Africa* 33 (2003): 310–27.

Bambach, Lee Ann. "Shariʿa." In *Encyclopedia of Muslim-American History*, edited by Edward E. Curtis IV, 2:512–15. New York: Facts on File, 2010.

Bani Yasin, Sheikh Raslan Ahmad M. El-Kayed. "A Critical and Comparative Study of the Dialectical Speech of the Ghawarna Community in the Jordan Valley in Jordan." PhD diss., University of Leeds, 1980.

Basu, Helene. "A Gendered Indian Ocean Site: Mai Mishra, African Spirit Possession, and Sidi Women in Gujarat." In *Journeys and Dwellings: Indian Ocean Themes in South Asia*, edited by Helene Basu, 227–55. Hyderabad, India: Orient Longman Private Limited, 2008.

———. "Hierarchy and Emotion: Love, Joy, and Sorrow in a Cult of Black Saints in Gujarat, India." In *Embodying Charisma: Modernity, Locality, and Performance of Emotion in Sufi Cults*, edited by Prina Werbner and Helene Basu, 117–39. London: Routledge, 1998.

———. "Redefining Boundaries: Twenty Years at the Shrine of Gori Pir." In *Sidis and Scholars: Essays on African Indians*, edited by Amy Catlin-Jairazbhoy and Edward A. Alpers, 61–85. Trenton, N.J.: Red Sea Press, 2004.

———. "The Siddi and the Cult of Bava Gor in Gujarat." *Journal of Indian Anthropology* 28 (1993): 289–300.

———. "Slave, Soldier, Trader, Faqir: Fragments of African Histories in Western India (Gujarat)." In *The African Diaspora in the Indian Ocean*, edited by Shihan de Silva Jayasuriya and Richard Pankhurst, 223–50. Trenton, N.J.: Africa World Press, 2003.

———. "Theatre of Memory: Ritual Kinship Performances of the African Diaspora in Pakistan." In *Culture, Creation, and Procreation: Concepts of Kinship in South Asian Practice*, edited by Monika Böck and Aparna Rao, 243–70. New York: Berghahn Books, 2000.

Beckerleg, Susan. "African Bedouin in Palestine." *Asian and African Studies* 6 (2007): 289–303.

Bender, Thomas. *A Nation among Nations: America's Place in World History.* New York: Hill and Wang, 2006.

Berns-McGown, Rima. *Muslims in the Diaspora: The Somali Communities of London and Toronto.* Toronto: University of Toronto Press, 1999.

Bigelow, Anna. *Sharing the Sacred: Practicing Pluralism in Muslim North India.* New York: Oxford University Press, 2010.

Blakely, Allison. "The Emergence of Afro-Europe: A Preliminary Sketch." In *Black Europe and the African Diaspora*, edited by Darlene Clark Hine, Trica Danielle Keaton, and Stephen Small, 3–28. Urbana: University of Illinois Press, 2009.

"Blind Alphabetz." Muslimhiphop.com. http://muslimhiphop.com/Hip-Hop/Blind_Alphabetz.

Bluett, Thomas. *Some Memoirs of the Life of Job, the Son of Solomon, the High Priest of Boonda in Africa; Who was a Slave About Two Years in Maryland; and Afterwards Being Brought to England, was Set Free, and Sent to His Native Land in the Year 1734*. London: Printed for R. Ford, 1734. http://docsouth.unc.edu/neh/bluett/menu.html.

Blyden, Edward Wilmot. *Christianity, Islam, and the Negro Race*. 1887. Edinburgh: Edinburgh University Press, 1967.

Boddy, Janice. *Wombs and Alien Spirits: Women, Men, and the Zar Cult in Northern Sudan*. Madison: University of Wisconsin Press, 1989.

Bowen, John R. *A New Anthropology of Islam*. Cambridge: Cambridge University Press, 2012.

Bowen, Patrick. "Satti Majid: A Sudanese Founder of American Islam." *Journal of Africana Religions* 1, no. 2 (2013): 194–209.

Braziel, Jana Evans, and Anita Mannur, eds. *Theorizing Diaspora: A Reader*. Oxford: Blackwell Publishing, 2003.

Brubaker, Rogers. "The 'Diaspora' Diaspora." *Ethnic and Racial Studies* 28, no. 1 (2005): 1–19.

Bryceson, Deborah, and Ulla Vuorela, eds. *The Transnational Family: New European Frontiers and Global Networks*. Oxford: Berg, 2002.

Buggenhagen, Beth. "Islam and the Media of Devotion in and out of Senegal." *Visual Anthropology Review* 26, no. 2 (2010): 81–95.

Bulliet, Richard W. *Conversion to Islam in the Medieval Period: An Essay in Quantitative History*. Cambridge, Mass.: Harvard University Press, 1979.

Burckhardt, John Lewis. *Travels in Syria and the Holy Land*. London: John Murray, 1822.

Butler, Kim D. "Africa in the Reinvention of Nineteenth-Century Afro-Bahian Identity." In *Rethinking the African Diaspora: The Making of a Black Atlantic World in the Bight of Benin and Brazil*, edited by Kristin Mann and Edna G. Bay, 135–54. New York: Frank Cass, 2011.

Byfield, Judith. "Introduction: Rethinking the African Diaspora." *African Studies Review* 43, no. 1 (2000): 1–9.

Camara, Charles. "The Siddis of Uttara Kannada: History, Identity, and Change among African Descendants in Contemporary Karnataka." In *Sidis and Scholars: Essays on African Indians*, edited by Amy Catlin-Jairazbhoy and Edward A. Alpers, 100–114. Trenton, N.J.: Red Sea Press, 2004.

Campbell, Gwyn. "Female Bondage and Agency in the Indian Ocean World." In *African Communities in Asia and the Mediterranean: Identities between Integration and Conflict*, edited by Ehud R. Toledano, 37–63. Trenton, N.J.: Africa World Press, 2012.

———. "Slave Trades and the Indian Ocean World." In *India in Africa, Africa in India: Indian Ocean Cosmopolitanisms*, edited by John C. Hawley, 17–51. Bloomington: Indiana University Press, 2008.

Carpenter, Shelby E. "Remembering the Homeland: Sierra Leone Refugees in Urban Gambia." *Inter-University Center on International Migration*, http://web.mit.edu/cis/www/migration/pubs/rrwp/Remembering%20the%20Homeland.pdf.

Carter, Donald Martin. *Navigating the African Diaspora: The Anthropology of Invisibility*. Minneapolis: University of Minnesota Press, 2010.

———. *States of Grace: Senegalese in Italy and the New European Immigration*. Minneapolis: University of Minnesota Press, 1997.

Carter, Youssef J. "Islamic Party of North America." In *Encyclopedia of Muslim-American History*, edited by Edward E. Curtis IV, 1:292–93. New York: Facts on File, 2010.

Casares, Aurelia Martín, "Free and Freed Black Africans in Granada in the Time of the Spanish Renaissance." In *Black Africans in Renaissance Europe*, edited by T. F. Earle and K. J. P. Lowe, 247–60. Cambridge: Cambridge University Press, 2005.

Catlin-Jairazbhoy, Amy. "Sacred Pleasure, Pain, and Transformation in African Indian Sidi Sufi Ritual and Performance." *Performing Islam* 1, no. 1 (2012): 73–109.

Catlin-Jairazbhoy, Amy, and Edward A. Alpers, eds. *Sidis and Scholars: Essays on African Indians*. Trenton, N.J.: Red Sea Press, 2004.

Cesari, Jocelyne. *When Islam and Democracy Meet: Muslims in Europe and in the United States*. New York: Palgrave Macmillan, 2004.

Change Institute. *The Nigerian Muslim Community in England: Understanding Muslim Ethnic Communities*. London: Communities and Local Government, 2009.

———. *The Somali Muslim Community in England: Understanding Muslim Ethnic Communities*. London: Communities and Local Government, 2009.

———. *Summary Report: Understanding Muslim Ethnic Communities*. London: Communities and Local Government, 2009.

Chidester, David. *Savage Systems: Colonialism and Comparative Religion in Southern Africa*. Charlottesville: University of Virginia Press, 1996.

Chidester, David, and Edward T. Linenthal, eds. *American Sacred Space*. Bloomington: Indiana University Press, 1995.

"Cittadini Stranieri. Popolazione residente per sesso e cittadinanza al 31 Dicembre 2010, Italia–Africa." http://demo.istat.it/str2010.

Clarence-Smith, William Gervase. *Islam and the Abolition of Slavery*. New York: Oxford University Press, 2006.

Clarke, Kamari Maxine. *Mapping Yoruba Networks: Power and Agency in the Making of Transnational Communities*. Durham, N.C.: Duke University Press, 2004.

Clarke, Kamari Maxine, and Deborah A. Thomas, eds. *Globalization and Race*. Durham, N.C.: Duke University Press, 2006.

Clegg, Claude Andrew, III. *An Original Man: The Life and Times of Elijah Muhammad*. New York: St. Martin's Press, 1997.

Clifford, James. *Routes: Travel and Translation in the Late Twentieth Century.* Cambridge, Mass.: Harvard University Press, 2007.

Cohen, Ammon, and Bernard Lewis. *Population and Revenue in the Towns of Palestine in the Sixteenth Century.* Princeton, N.J.: Princeton University Press, 1978.

Collins, Robert O. "The African Slave Trade to Asia and the Indian Ocean Islands." *Asian and African Studies* 5, nos. 3–4 (2006): 325–46.

Connell, Curtis C. *Understanding Islam and Its Impact in Latin America.* Maxwell Air Force Base, Ala.: Air University Press, 2005.

Constantinides, Pamela. "The History of *Zar* in the Sudan: Theories of Origin, Recorded Observation and Oral Tradition." In *Women's Medicine: The* Zar-Bori *Cult in Africa and Beyond,* edited by I. M. Lewis, Ahmed Al-Safi, and Sayyid Hurreiz, 83–99. Edinburgh: Edinburgh University Press, 1991.

Crapanzo, Vincent. *The Hamadsha: A Study in Moroccan Ethnopsychiatry.* Berkeley: University of California Press, 1973.

Curtis, Edward E., IV. *Black Muslim Religion in the Nation of Islam, 1960–1975.* Chapel Hill: University of North Carolina Press, 2006.

———. "The Black Muslim Scare of the Twentieth Century: The History of State Islamophobia and Its Post 9/11 Variations." In *Islamophobia in America: The Anatomy of Intolerance,* edited by Carl W. Ernst, 75–106. New York: Palgrave Macmillan, 2013.

———, ed. *Columbia Sourcebook of Muslims in the States.* New York: Columbia University Press, 2008.

———. "Debating the Origins of the Moorish Science Temple." In *The New Black Gods: Arthur Huff Fauset and the Study of African American Religions,* edited by Edward E. Curtis IV and Danielle Brune Sigler, 70–90. Bloomington: Indiana University Press, 2009.

———, ed. *Encyclopedia of Muslim-American History.* 2 vols. New York: Facts on File, 2010.

———. "The Ghawarna of Jordan: Race and Religion in the Jordan Valley." *Journal of Islamic Law and Culture* 13, nos. 2–3 (2011): 193–209.

———. *Islam in Black America: Identity, Liberation, and Difference in Islamic Thought.* Albany: State University of New York Press, 2002.

———. *Muslims in America: A Short History.* New York: Oxford University Press, 2009.

D'Alisera, JoAnn. *An Imagined Geography: Sierra Leonean Muslims in America.* Philadelphia: University of Pennsylvania Press, 2004.

Dannin, Robert. *Black Pilgrimage to Islam.* New York: Oxford University Press, 2002.

Diouf, Sylviane A. "Invisible Muslims: The Sahelians in France." In *Muslim Minorities in the West: Visible and Invisible,* edited by Yvonne Yazbeck Haddad and Jane I. Smith, 145–59. Walnut Creek, Calif.: AltaMira, 2002.

———. *Servants of Allah: African Muslims Enslaved in the Americas.* New York: New York University Press, 2013.

Dobronravin, Nikolay. "Literacy among Muslims in Nineteenth-Century Trinidad and Brazil." In *Slavery, Islam, and Diaspora,* edited by Behnaz A. Mirzai, Ismael Musah Montana, and Paul E. Lovejoy, 217–36. Trenton, N.J.: Africa World Press, 2009.

Dodgen, Justine. "Immigration and Identity Politics: The Senegalese in France." Claremont McKenna College senior thesis 284. Claremont, Calif.: Claremont Colleges, 2011.

Donaldson, Bess Allen. *The Wild Rue: A Study of Muhammadan Magic and Folklore in Iran*. London: Luzac, 1938.

Drissel, David. "Hybridizing Hip-Hop in Diaspora: Young British South Asian Men Negotiating Black-Inflected Identities." *International Journal of Diversity in Organizations, Communities and Nations* 10, no. 5 (2011): 199–222.

Dufoix, Stéphane. *Diasporas*. Berkeley: University of California Press, 2008.

Earle, T. F., and K. J. P. Lowe, eds. *Black Africans in Renaissance Europe*. Cambridge: Cambridge University Press, 2005.

Eaton, Richard M. "Malik Ambar and Elite Slavery in the Deccan, 1400–1650." In *African Elites in India: Habshi Amarat*, edited by Kenneth X. Robbins and John McLeod, 45–67. Ahmedabad, India: Mapin, 2006.

———. "The Rise and Fall of Military Slavery in the Deccan, 1450–1650." In *Slavery and South Asian History*, edited by Indrani Chatterjee and Richard M. Eaton, 115–35. Bloomington: Indiana University Press, 2006.

Edwards, Brent Hayes. "The Uses of Diaspora." *Social Text* 19, no. 1 (Spring 2001): 45–73.

Eickelman, Dale F. "Inside the Islamic Reformation." In *Everyday Life in the Muslim Middle East*, 2nd ed., edited by Donna Lee Bowen and Evelyn A. Early, 245–56. Bloomington: Indiana University Press, 2002.

El Alami, Dawoud. *The Marriage Contract in Islamic Law*. London: Graham and Trotman, 1992.

El Hamel, Chouki. *Black Morocco: A History of Slavery, Race, and Islam*. New York: Cambridge University Press, 2013.

———. "Constructing a Diasporic Identity: Tracing the Origins of the Gnawa Spiritual Group on Morocco." *Journal of African History* 49 (2008): 241–60.

El-Sawy, Tewfic. "Essaouira Report: The Gnaoua (Gnawa) Music Festival." http://www.photocrati.com/essaouira-report-the-gnaoua-gnawa-music-festival/.

Encyclopedia of Islam. CD-ROM ed., vol. 1.0. Leiden, Netherlands: Brill, 1999.

Erdem, Y. Hakan. *Slavery in the Ottoman Empire and Its Demise, 1800–1909*. New York: St. Martin's Press, 1996.

Ernst, Carl W. *Following Muhammad: Rethinking Islam in the Contemporary World*. Chapel Hill: University of North Carolina Press, 2003.

———, ed. *Islamophobia in America: The Anatomy of Intolerance*. New York: Palgrave Macmillan, 2013.

———. *The Shambhala Guide to Sufism*. Boston: Shambhala, 1997.

Essien-Udom, E. U. *Black Nationalism: A Search for an Identity in America*. Chicago: University of Chicago Press, 1962.

Fage, J. D., and Roland Oliver, eds. *The Cambridge History of Africa*. 8 vols. New York: Cambridge University Press, 1975–86.

Figueira, Daurius. *Jihad in Trinidad and Tobago, July 27, 1990*. Lincoln, Neb.: iUniverse, 2002.

Flueckiger, Joyce Burkhalter. *In Amma's Healing Room: Gender and Vernacular Islam in South Asia*. Bloomington: Indiana University Press, 2006.

Forte, Maximilian Christian. *Against the Trinity: An Insurgent Imam Tells His Story*. Binghamton, N.Y.: Polaris-Australis, 1997.

Gallup. "Muslim Americans: A National Portrait." http://www.gallup.com/strategicconsulting/153572/report-muslim-americans-national-portrait.aspx.

Gardell, Mattias. *In the Name of Elijah Muhammad: Louis Farrakhan and the Nation of Islam*. Durham, N.C.: Duke University Press, 1996.

Georgia Writers Project. *Drums and Shadows: Survival Studies among the Georgia Coastal Negroes*. Athens: University of Georgia Press, 1940.

Gerges, Fawaz A. *The Far Enemy: Why Jihad Went Global*. New York: Cambridge University Press, 2005.

GhaneaBassiri, Kambiz. *A History of Islam in America*. New York: Cambridge University Press, 2010.

Gilroy, Paul. *The Black Atlantic: Modernity and Double Consciousness*. Cambridge, Mass.: Harvard University Press, 1993.

——— . *There Ain't No Black in the Union Jack: The Cultural Politics of Race and Nation*. Chicago: University of Chicago Press, 1987.

Gomez, Michael A. *Black Crescent: The Experience and Legacy of African Muslims in the Americas*. New York: Cambridge University Press, 2005.

——— . *Reversing Sail: A History of the African Diaspora*. New York: Cambridge University Press, 2005.

Goody, Jack. "Writing, Rebellion, and Revolt in Bahia." *Visible Language* 20 (1986): 318–43.

Gordon, Lewis R. *Her Majesty's Children: Sketches of Racism from a Neocolonial Age*. Lanham, Md.: Rowman and Littlefield, 1997.

Gottschalk, Peter, and Gabriel Greenberg. *Islamophobia: Making Muslims the Enemy*. Lanham, Md.: Rowman and Littlefield, 2008.

Granqvist, Hilma. *Portrait of a Palestinian Village: The Photographs of Hilma Granqvist*. Edited by Karen Seger. London: Third World Centre for Research and Publishing, 1981.

Gubser, Peter. *Politics and Change in Al-Karak, Jordan: A Study of a Small Arab Town and Its District*. London: Oxford University Press, 1973.

Haddad, Yvonne Yazbeck, and John Esposito, eds. *Muslims on the Americanization Path?* New York: Oxford University Press, 1998.

Haddad, Yvonne Yazbeck, and Jane Idleman Smith. *Mission to America: Five Islamic Sectarian Communities in North America*. Gainesville: University of Florida Press, 1993.

Harris, Joseph E. *The African Presence in Asia: Consequences of the East African Slave Trade*. Evanston, Ill.: Northwestern University Press, 1971.

Hawley, John C., ed. *India in Africa, Africa in India: Indian Ocean Cosmopolitanisms*. Bloomington: Indiana University Press, 2008.

Helal, Emad Ahmed. "Muhammad Ali's First Army: The Experiment in Building an Entirely Slave Army." In *Race and Slavery in the Middle East*, edited by Terence

Walz and Kenneth M. Cuno, 17–42. Cairo: American University of Cairo Press, 2010.

Hesse, Barnor. "Racialized Modernity: An Analytics of White Mythologies." *Ethnic and Racial Studies* 30, no. 4 (July 2007): 643–63.

HM Chief Inspector of Prisons. *Muslim Prisoners' Experiences: A Thematic Review*. London: HM Chief Inspector of Prisons, 2010.

Hourani, Albert. *A History of the Arab Peoples*. Cambridge, Mass.: Harvard University Press, 1991.

Huggins, Nathan Irvin. *Black Odyssey: The African-American Ordeal in Slavery*. New York: Vintage Books, 1990.

Hunwick, John. "The Same but Different: Africans in Slavery in the Mediterranean Muslim World." In *The Africa Diaspora in the Mediterranean Lands of Islam*, edited by John Hunwick and Eve Trout Powell, xvii–xix. Princeton, N.J.: Markus Wiener, 2002.

Jackson, Sherman. *Islam and the Blackamerican*. New York: Oxford University Press, 2005.

James, C. L. R. *The Black Jacobins: Toussaint L'Ouverture and the San Domingo Revolution*. 2nd rev. ed. New York: Vintage, 1989.

Jankowsky, Richard C. *Stambeli: Music, Trance, and Alterity in Tunisia*. Chicago: University of Chicago Press, 2010.

Jayasuriya, Shihan de Silva. *African Identity in Asia: Cultural Effects of Forced Migration*. Princeton, N.J.: Markus Wiener, 2009.

Johnson, Michelle C. "Death and the Left Hand: Islam, Gender, and Proper Mandinga Funerary Custom in Guinea-Bissau and Portugal." *African Studies Review* 52, no. 2 (2009): 93–117.

———. "'The Proof Is on My Palm': Debating Ethnicity, Islam and Ritual in a New African Diaspora." *Journal of Religion in Africa* 36, no. 1 (2006): 50–77.

Johnson, Sylvester A. "The Rise of the Black Ethnics: The Ethnic Turn in African American Religions, 1916–1945." *Religion and American Culture* 20, no. 2 (2010): 125–63.

Jouili, Jeanette. "Beat-ification: British Muslim Hip Hop and Ethical Listening Practices." *Sounding Out!* http://soundstudiesblog.com/2012/05/21/beat-ification-british-muslim-hip-hop-and-ethical-listening-practices/.

Kaag, Mayke. "Mouride Transnational Livelihoods at the Margins of a European Society: The Case of Residence Prealpino, Brescia, Italy." *Journal of Ethnic and Migration Studies* 34, no. 2 (2008): 271–85.

Kamali, Mohammad Hashim. *Shari'ah Law: An Introduction*. Oxford: Oneworld Publications, 2008.

Kane, Ousmane Oumar. *The Homeland Is the Arena: Religion, Transnationalism, and the Integration of Senegalese Immigrants in America*. New York: Oxford University Press, 2011.

Kapchan, Deborah. *Traveling Spirit Masters: Moroccan Gnawa Trance and Music in the Global Marketplace*. Middletown, Conn.: Wesleyan University Press, 2007.

Karamustafa, Ahmet T. *Sufism: The Formative Period*. Berkeley: University of California Press, 2007.

Kareem, Jum'a Mahmoud H. *The Settlement Patterns in the Jordan Valley in the Mid- to Late Islamic Period.* Oxford: Archaeopress, 2000.

Karim, Jamillah. *American Muslim Women: Negotiating Race, Class, and Gender within the Ummah.* New York: New York University Press, 2009.

Kelsay, John. *Arguing the Just War in Islam.* Cambridge, Mass.: Harvard University Press, 2009.

Kenoyer, J. Mark, and Kuldeep K. Bhan, "Sidis and the Agate Bead Industry of Western India." In *Sidis and Scholars: Essays on African Indians*, edited by Amy Catlin-Jairazbhoy and Edward A. Alpers, 41–60. Trenton, N.J.: Red Sea Press, 2004.

Khalifa, Aisha Bilkhair. "African Influence on Culture and Music in Dubai." *International Social Science Journal* 58, no. 188 (2006): 227–35.

Khan, Aisha. *Callaloo Nation: Metaphors of Race and Religious Identity among South Asians in Trinidad.* Durham, N.C.: Duke University Press, 2004.

Khawalde, Sliman, and Dan Rabinowitz. "Race from the Bottom of the Tribe That Never Was: Segmentary Narratives amongst the Ghawarna of Galilee." *Journal of Anthropological Research* 58 (2002): 225–43.

King, Richard. *Orientalism and Religion: Postcolonial Theory, India and "the Mystic East."* New York: Routledge, 1999.

Knott, Kim, and Sean McLoughlin, eds., *Diasporas: Concepts, Intersections, Identities.* London: Zed Books, 2010.

Konanga-Nicolas, Dzouyi Therese. "The African Palestinian Community in the Old City of Jerusalem." *This Week in Palestine* 112 (August 2007). http://www.thisweekinpalestine.com/details.php?id=2215&ed=144&edid=144.

Lapidus, Ira M. *A History of Islamic Societies.* 2nd ed. Cambridge: Cambridge University Press, 2002.

Layne, Linda L. *Home and Homeland: The Dialogics of Tribal and National Identities in Jordan.* Princeton, N.J.: Princeton University Press, 1994.

———. "The Production and Reproduction of Tribal Identity in Jordan." PhD diss., Princeton University, 1986.

Levtzion, Nehemia, and Randall L. Pouwels, eds. *The History of Islam in Africa.* Athens: Ohio University Press, 2000.

Lewis, Bernard. *Race and Slavery in the Middle East.* New York: Oxford University Press, 1990.

Lincoln, C. Eric. *The Black Muslims in America.* 3rd ed. Grand Rapids, Mich.: Eerdmans, 1994.

Lindsay, Lisa A. *Captives as Commodities: The Transatlantic Slave Trade.* Upper Saddle River, N.J.: Pearson, 2007.

Lo, Mbaye. *Muslims in America: Race, Politics, and Community Building.* Beltsville, Md.: Amana, 2004.

Lockman, Zachary. *Contending Visions of the Middle East: The History and Politics of Orientalism.* New York: Cambridge University Press, 2004.

Loja, Fernando Soares. "Islam in Portugal." In *Islam, Europe's Second Religion: The New Social, Cultural, and Political Landscape*, edited by Shireen T. Hunter, 191–203. Westport, Conn.: Praeger, 2002.

Lovejoy, Paul E., ed. *Slavery on the Frontiers of Islam*. Princeton, N.J.: Markus Wiener, 2004.

———. *Transformations in Slavery: A History of Slavery in Africa*. 3rd ed. New York: Cambridge University Press, 2011.

Lowe, Kate. "Introduction: The Black African Presence in Renaissance Europe." In *Black Africans in Renaissance Europe*, edited by T. F. Earle and K. J. P. Lowe, 1–14. Cambridge: Cambridge University Press, 2005.

Machado, Pedro. "A Forgotten Corner of the Indian Ocean: Guajarati Merchants, Portuguese India, and the Mozambique Slave-Trade, c. 1730–1830." In *The Structure of Slavery in Indian Ocean African and Asia*, edited by Gwyn Campbell, 17–32. London: Frank Cass, 2004.

Mandaville, Peter. *Global Political Islam*. New York: Routledge, 2007.

———. *Transnational Muslim Politics: Reimagining the Ummah*. London: Routledge, 2001.

Marable, Manning, and Hishaam D. Aidi, eds. *Black Routes to Islam*. New York: Palgrave Macmillan, 2009.

Martin, Richard C., ed. *Encyclopedia of Islam and the Muslim World*. New York: Macmillan, 2004.

McAlister, Melani. *Epic Encounters: Culture, Media, and U.S. Interests in the Middle East since 1945*. Updated ed. Berkeley: University of California Press, 2005.

McCabe, Kristen. "African Immigrants in the United States." *Migration Information Source*. http://www.migrationinformation.org/USfocus/display.cfm?id=847#.

McCloud, Aminah Beverly. *African American Islam*. New York: Routledge, 1995.

———. *Transnational Muslims in American Society*. Gainesville: University Press of Florida, 2006.

McCloud, Sean. *Making the American Religious Fringe: Exotics, Subversives, and Journalists, 1955–1993*. Chapel Hill: University of North Carolina Press, 2004.

McLeod, John. "Marriage and Identity among the Sidis of Janjira and Sachin." In *India in Africa, Africa in India: Indian Ocean Cosmopolitanisms*, edited by John C. Hawley, 253–71. Bloomington: Indiana University Press, 2008.

Meier, Prita Sandy. "Per/forming African Identities: Sidi Communities in the Transnational Moment." In *Sidis and Scholars: Essays on African Indians*, edited by Amy Catlin-Jairazbhoy and Edward A. Alpers, 86–99. Trenton, N.J.: Red Sea Press, 2004.

Melville, Caspar. "New Brotherhood." *New Humanist* 120, no. 5 (2005): 12.

Mesa, Andrea Morales. "El Islam en la Actualidad Cubana." *Revista Académica para el Estudio de las Religiones*, no.4 (2002): 93–102.

Middleton, Arthur. "The Strange Story of Job Ben Solomon." *William and Mary Quarterly* 5, no. 3 (1948): 342–50.

Miles, G. C. "'Anaza." In *Encyclopedia of Islam*, CD-ROM ed., vol. 1.0. Leiden, Netherlands: Brill, 1999.

Mir-Hosseini, Ziba. *Marriage on Trial: A Study of Islamic Family Law; Iran and Morocco Compared*. London: I. B. Tauris, 1993.

Mirzai, Behnaz A. "African Presence in Iran: Identity and Its Reconstruction in the 19th and 20th Centuries." *Revue d'Histoire Outre-Mers* 89, nos. 336–37 (2002): 229–46.
"Mohammed Yahya." *Muslimhiphop.com*. http://muslimhiphop.com/index.php?p=Hip-Hop/Mohammed_Yahya.
Montana, Ismael Musah. "Ahmad ibn al-Qadi al-Timbuktawi on the Bori Ceremonies of Tunis." In *Slavery on the Frontiers of Islam*, edited by Paul E. Lovejoy, 173–98. Princeton, N.J.: Markus Wiener, 2004.
———. "The *Bori* Colonies of Tunis." In *Slavery, Islam, and Diaspora*, edited by Behnaz A. Mirzai, Ismael Musah Montana, and Paul E. Lovejoy, 155–68. Trenton, N.J.: Africa World Press, 2009.
———. "The *Stambali* of Husaynid Tunis: From Possession Cult to Ethno-Religious and National Culture." In *African Communities in Asia and the Mediterranean: Identities between Integration and Conflict*, edited by Ehud R. Toledano, 171–84. Trenton, N.J.: Africa World Press, 2012.
Muhammad, Elijah. *Message to the Blackman in America*. Chicago: Muhammad Mosque No. 2, 1963.
Murdock, George Peter. *Africa: Its People and Their Culture History*. New York: McGraw-Hill, 1959.
Nance, Susan. "Mystery of the Moorish Science Temple: Southern Blacks and American Alternative Spirituality in 1920s Chicago." *Religion and American Culture* 12, no. 2 (2002): 123–66.
Newman, James L. *The Peopling of Africa*. New Haven, Conn.: Yale University Press, 1995.
Nimer, Mohamed. *The North American Muslim Resource Guide*. New York: Routledge, 2002.
Northrup, David. *Africa's Discovery of Europe, 1450–1850*. 2nd ed. New York: Oxford University Press, 2009.
Nunez, Abdulmajeed Marin. *A History of Muslims in Belize*. Rev. ed. Privately published, 2010.
Obeng, Pashington. *Shaping Membership, Defining Nation: The Cultural Politics of African Indians in South Asia*. Lanham, Md.: Lexington Books, 2007.
Oka, Rahul C., and Chapurukha M. Kusimba. "Siddi as Mercenary or as African Success Story on the West Coast of India." In *India in Africa, Africa in India: Indian Ocean Cosmopolitanisms*, edited by John C. Hawley, 203–29. Bloomington: Indiana University Press, 2008.
Olaniyan, Tejumola, and James H. Sweet, eds. *The African Diaspora and the Disciplines*. Bloomington: Indiana University Press, 2010.
Oliveira, Vitória Peres de, and Cecília L. Mariz. "Conversion to Islam in Contemporary Brazil." *Exchange* 35, no. 1 (2006): 102–15.
Oliver, Melvin, and Thomas M. Shapiro. *Black Wealth/White Wealth: A New Perspective on Racial Inequality*. 2nd ed. New York: Routledge, 2006.
Pantin, Raoul A. *Days of Wrath: The 1990 Coup in Trinidad and Tobago*. Lincoln, Neb.: iUniverse, 2007.
Paques, Viviana. "The Gnawa of Morocco: The *Derdeba* Ceremony." In *The Nomadic Alternative: Modes and Models of Interaction in the African-Asian*

Deserts and Steppes, edited by Wolfgang Weissleder, 319–30. The Hague: Mouton, 1978.

Peach, Ceri, and Richard Gale. "Muslims, Hindus, and Sikhs in the New Religious Landscape of England." *Geographical Review* 93, no. 4 (2003): 469–90.

Pereira, Lenora. "A discreta presença dos muçulmanos em Porto Alegre: uma análise antropológica das articulações de significados e da inserção do islamismo no pluralismo religioso local." Master's thesis, UFRS, Porto Alegre, Brazil, 2001.

Pew Research Center. *The Future of the Global Muslim Population*. Washington, D.C.: Pew Research Center, 2011.

———. *Muslim Networks and Movements in Western Europe*. Washington, D.C.: Pew Research Center, 2010.

———. *The World's Muslims: Unity and Diversity*. Washington, D.C.: Pew Research Center, 2012. http://www.pewforum.org/uploadedFiles/Topics/Religious_Affiliation/Muslim/the-worlds-muslims-full-report.pdf.

Pieterse, Jan Nederveen. *White on Black: Images of Africa and Blacks in Western Popular Culture*. New Haven, Conn.: Yale University Press, 1992.

Pitt, David E. "Accord Is Stalled in Trinidad Siege." *New York Times*, July 31, 1990, A1.

———. "Rebels in Trinidad Free All Hostages." *New York Times*, August 2, 1990, A1.

Premdas, Ralph. *Trinidad and Tobago: Ethnic Conflict, Inequality, and Public Sector Governance*. New York: Palgrave Macmillan, 2007.

Qazi, M. A. *Bilal: The First Muadhdhin of the Prophet of Islam*. Lahore, Pakistan: Kazi Publications, 1978.

Raboteau, Albert J. *Canaan Land: A Religious History of African Americans*. New York: Oxford University Press, 2001.

———. *Slave Religion: The "Invisible Institution" in the Antebellum South*. New York: Oxford University Press, 1978.

Ramsey, Geoffrey. "What Is the Real Threat of Islamic Terrorism in Latin America?" *Christian Science Monitor*, August 14, 2012. http://www.csmonitor.com/World/Americas/Latin-America-Monitor/2012/0814/What-is-the-real-threat-of-Islamic-terrorism-in-Latin-America.

Reddie, Richard. *Black Muslims in Britain*. Oxford: Lion Hudson, 2009.

Reid, Richard J. *A History of Modern Africa, 1800 to the Present*. Malden, Mass.: Wiley-Blackwell, 2009.

Reis, João José. *Slave Rebellion in Brazil: The Muslim Uprising of 1835 in Bahia*, translated by Arthur Brackel. Baltimore: Johns Hopkins University Press, 1993.

Renard, John. *Seven Doors to Islam: Spirituality and the Religious Life of Muslims*. Berkeley: University of California Press, 1996.

Riccio, Bruno. "From 'Ethnic Group' to 'Transnational Community': Senegalese Migrants' Ambivalent Experiences and Multiple Trajectories." *Journal of Ethnic and Migration Studies* 27, no. 4 (2001): 583–99.

———. "Senegalese Street-Sellers, Racism and the Discourse on 'Irregular Trade' in Rimini." *Modern Italy* 4, no. 2 (1999): 225–39.

———. "Transnational Mouridism and the Afro-Muslim Critique of Italy." *Journal of Ethnic and Migration Studies* 30, no. 5 (2004): 929–44.
Robinson, David. *Muslim Societies in African History.* New York: Cambridge University Press, 2004.
Rodinson, Maxine. "Le culte de 'zar' en Egypte." *Comptes Rendues Sommaires des Séances de l'Institut Français d'Anthropologie,* 7e fasc (1953): 87–93.
Ryan, Selwyn. *The Muslimeen Grab for Power: Race, Religion, and Revolution in Trinidad and Tobago.* Port of Spain: Inprint Caribbean, 1991.
Safran, William. "Diasporas in Modern Societies: Mythos of Homeland and Return." *Diaspora* 1, no. 1 (1991): 83–99.
Sahih Bukhari. Translated by M. Muhsin Khan. n.d. http://www.hadithcollection.com/sahihbukhari.html.
Sahih Muslim. Translated by Abdul Hamid Siddiqi. Riyadh: International Islamic Publishing House, n.d.
Said, Edward W. *Covering Islam: How the Media and the Experts Determine How We See the Rest of the World.* Rev. ed. New York: Vintage, 1997.
———. *Culture and Imperialism.* New York: Knopf, 1993.
———. *Orientalism.* New York: Vintage Books, 1978.
Schick, Greg. "UK Duo on a Poetic Pilgrimage." *World Hip Hop Market,* March 29, 2012. http://worldhiphopmarket.com/uk-duo-on-a-poetic-pilgrimage/636.
Sengers, Gerda. *Women and Demons: Islamic Cult Healing in Egypt.* Leiden, Netherlands: Brill, 2003.
Shabazz, Maryam Sharron Muhammad. "Blacks in Portugal." In *Encyclopedia of Blacks in European History and Culture,* edited by Eric Martone, 421–22. Westport, Conn.: Greenwood, 2009.
Shahrad, Cyrus. "Muslim Rap: The Power of Verse." *Huck Magazine,* no. 32 (2012). http://www.huckmagazine.com/features/muslim-rap/.
Sheff, Rebecca F. "The Problem with Eating Money: Remittances and Development within Senegal's Muridiyya." Honors project, Macalester College, 2009. Paper 18, http://digitalcommons.macalester.edu/poli_honors/18.
Shelby, Tommie. *We Who Are Dark: The Philosophical Foundations of Black Solidarity.* Cambridge, Mass.: Harvard University Press, 2005.
Shryock, Andrew. *Nationalism and the Genealogical Imagination: Oral History and Textual Authority in Tribal Jordan.* Berkeley: University of California Press, 1997.
Simmons, Gwendolyn Zoharah. "Are We Up to the Challenge? The Need for a Radical Reordering of the Islamic Discourse on Women." In *Progressive Muslims: On Justice, Gender, and Pluralism,* edited by Omid Safi, 235–48. Oxford: Oneworld, 2003.
Sinatti, Giulia. "Diasporic Cosmopolitanism and Conservative Translocalism: Narratives of Nation among Senegalese Migrants in Italy." *Studies in Ethnicity and Nationalism* 6, no. 3 (2006): 30–50.
Smith, Ian. *Race and Rhetoric in the Renaissance: Barbarian Errors.* New York: Palgrave Macmillan, 2009.
Smith, Jane I. *Islam in America.* 2nd ed. New York: Columbia University Press, 2010.

Smith, Jonathan Z., ed. *HarperCollins Dictionary of Religion*. New York: HarperSanFrancisco, 1995.

———. *Map Is Not Territory: Studies in the History of Religions*. Leiden, Netherlands: Brill, 1978.

Spooner, Brian. "The Evil Eye in the Middle East." In *Witchcraft Confessions and Accusations*, edited by Mary Douglas, 311–19. London: Tavistock, 1970.

Takim, Liyakat N. *Shi'ism in America*. New York: New York University Press, 2009.

Timera, Mahamet. "Righteous or Rebellious? Social Trajectory of Sahelian Youth in France." In *The Transnational Family: New European Frontiers and Global Networks*, edited by Debroah Bryceson and Ulla Vuorela, 147–54. Oxford: Berg, 2002.

Tinaz, Nuri. "Black Islam in Diaspora: The Case of Nation of Islam (NOI) in Britain." *Journal of Muslim Minority Affairs* 26, no. 2 (2006): 151–70.

Toledano, Ehud. *As If Silent and Absent: Bonds of Enslavement in the Islamic Middle East*. New Haven, Conn.: Yale University Press, 2007.

———. *The Ottoman Slave Trade and Its Suppression*. Princeton, N.J.: Princeton University Press, 1982.

Tremearne, A. J. N. *The Ban of the Bori*. 2nd ed. London: Frank Cass, 1968.

Trost, Theodore Louis. *The African Diaspora and the Study of Religion*. New York: Palgrave Macmillan, 2007.

Turner, Richard Brent. *Islam in the African-American Experience*. 2nd ed. Bloomington: Indiana University Press, 2003.

Tweed, Thomas A. *Crossing and Dwelling: A Theory of Religion*. Cambridge, Mass.: Harvard University Press, 2006.

UNESCO. *General History of Africa*. Berkeley: University of California Press, 1989.

Van Aken, Mauro. "Dancing Belonging: Contesting *Dabkeh* in the Jordan Valley, Jordan." *Journal of Ethnic and Migration Studies* 32, no. 2 (March 2006): 203–22.

———. *Facing Home: Palestinian Belonging in a Valley of Doubt*. Maastricht: Shaker Publishing, 2003.

Wadud, Amina. *Qur'an and Woman: Rereading the Sacred Text from a Woman's Perspective*. 2nd ed. New York: Oxford University Press, 1999.

Walker, Bethany J. "The Role of Agriculture in Mamluk-Jordanian Power Relations." *Bulletin d'Etudes Orientales* 57, suppl. (2008): 77–96.

Wallerstein, Immanuel. "The Construction of Peoplehood: Racism, Nationalism, Ethnicity." In *Race, Nation, Class: Ambiguous Identities*, edited by Etienne Balibar and Immanuel Wallerstein, 71–85. Translated by Chris Turner. New York: Verso Press, 1991.

Walvin, James. *Making the Black Atlantic: Britain and the African Diaspora*. London: Cassell, 2000.

Walz, Terence, and Kenneth M. Cuno, eds. *Race and Slavery in the Middle East*. Cairo: American University of Cairo Press, 2010.

Waugh, Earle H. *Memory, Music, and Religion: Morocco's Mystical Chanters*. Columbia: University of South Carolina Press, 2005.

Wesseling, H. L. *The European Colonial Empires, 1815–1919*. Harlow, England: Pearson Longman, 2004.

Wilmore, Gayraud S. *Black Religion and Black Radicalism: An Interpretation of the Religious History of African Americans.* 3rd ed. Maryknoll, N.Y.: Orbis, 1998.

Yimene, Abadu Minda. "African Cavalry Guards: A Place for the Construction of Memory, Identity, and Ethnicity." In *African Communities in Asia and the Mediterranean: Identities between Integration and Conflict,* edited by Ehud R. Toledano, 83–104. Trenton, N.J.: Africa World Press, 2012.

Young, Hershini Bhana. *Haunting Capital: Memory, Text, and the Black Diasporic Body.* Hanover, N.H.: Dartmouth College Press, 2006.

INDEX

Abadás (long white frocks), 117
Abbadi tribe, 41
Abbasid empire, 5
Abd al-Qadir al-Jilani, 33, 37, 104–5
Abd al-Rahman I, 56
Abd al-Rahman Ibrahima, 138–41, 145, 165, 166
Abdullah, Bilaal, 126, 129, 130
Abiad (light or white skin color), 42
'*Abid* (slaves), 42, 48
Abraham (prophet), 2, 104
Abu Bakr (caliph of Islam), 3, 5
Abu Bakr, Yasin, 123, 124, 126–30, 168, 169, 173
Adhan (call to prayer), 1–2, 3, 4, 6, 28, 167
Adoricism, and Zar cult, 26
Adwan tribe, 43
Africa: religions in, 5; Islamization of, 5–6; multiple meanings to Muslim practitioners, 8; as continent, 22, 178 (n. 4); peanuts associated with, 42; trade networks with Europe, 59; European colonization of, 59–60; independence movements in, 60. *See also* Homelands
African American Muslims: Islamic practices of, 19, 74, 112–13, 135, 136, 137, 141–45, 158–64, 165; and African-born Muslim immigrants, 19, 137–38, 147, 156–64, 170–71, 191 (n. 49); and self-determination, 113; and African diaspora, 135–36, 137, 164, 166; ethnic identity of, 136, 155–56, 161, 162, 169; and African-born Muslim slaves, 137, 138–46, 165; and black identity, 137, 148, 149, 172; and material culture, 143; Muslim organizations recruiting, 146; and translocal identities, 157;

and Islamic identity, 161, 165, 166. *See also* Nation of Islam
Africana Muslims: and Bilal, 4; and expansion of early Islamic state, 5; and Sunni Islamic tradition, 5, 11, 50, 169; Islamic practices of, 6–7, 51, 145, 169, 170, 171; Pew poll on five pillars of Islam, 10–11; coding as impure, 12–13; defining of identity, 13–17, 19; and African diaspora, 17, 22, 31, 36, 39, 70, 109, 172, 173, 174; and black liberation, 18, 54; and political Islam, 113
African-Asian solidarity, 18
African-Brazilian Muslims: and Arabic language literacy, 115, 117, 119; *breves* of, 117–18, 121, 122, 132; and Islamic practices, 118, 121; and jihad, 119; religious pluralism of, 121–22; and homelands, 122, 132–33
African-Caribbean Muslims: in Great Britain, 55, 74, 75, 79–80, 81, 82; and African identity, 79–80, 82; and African diasporic identity, 82–83; and ethnic identity, 136, 171
African Cavalry Guards, Hyderabad, 91
African-descended Muslims: and Bilal, 4; and racism, 4, 13, 14, 16–17, 23–24; in Caribbean, 6, 18, 113; defining dispersal of, 9; Islamic practices of, 10, 23, 112–13, 172–74; new religious movements among, 11; and tension between tradition and reform, 12, 64–65, 82, 169–70; and religious blackness, 15; and black saints, 17, 50; and hip-hop, 53–54, 55, 76, 80, 171, 185 (n. 104); and public activism, 54; transnational connections among, 55; and colonial relationships, 60; in Trinidad and

209

Tobago, 126, 130–31, 132, 173. *See also* African American Muslims; British African-descended Muslims

African diaspora: and racism, 4, 92; experience and interpretation of, 6; and Islam, 6, 7, 8, 9, 10, 16, 19, 49, 69, 70, 168–69, 171, 172–75; defining of, 9, 16, 17, 39, 50; and black identity, 14–15, 16, 19, 22, 49; internal diaspora, 17, 22; and Africana Muslims, 17, 22, 31, 36, 39, 70, 109, 172, 173, 174; and ethnic solidarity, 18; multidimensional experiences of, 18; and slavery, 22, 24, 172; metaphysical experience of, 23, 50; and Stambali practices, 34–35; and commercialization of Gnawa practices, 35–36; and boundary marking, 49–50; and Senegalese Murids, 72–73, 163; diversity in, 81; and Siddi practices, 100, 108; and political Islam, 121, 132; and Trinidad and Tobago, 126; and Jama'at al-Muslimeen, 131, 133; and African American Muslims, 135–36, 137, 164, 166; and African American Muslim slaves, 141, 145–46; and Nation of Islam, 154, 155, 156, 164, 172; and African-born American Muslim immigrants, 157–58; and Bilal ibn Rabah, 167, 168

African diasporic identity: and Islamic practices, 9, 22, 50, 73; and African-Caribbean Muslims, 82–83; and Siddis, 87, 94, 108–9, 187 (n. 66)

African identity: strategic use of, 9, 15; and Ghawarna, 43; and Murid Sufi order, 72–73; and African-Caribbean Muslims, 79–80, 82; and hip-hop music, 80–81; and Gori Pir, 94, 108–9; and Siddis, 97, 108, 109

African Moslem Welfare Society of America, 147

African-Portuguese religious mutual aid societies and fraternities, 60

African slave trade, 14, 15, 173
Afrocentrism, 173
Ahl al-bayt (family of Prophet Muhammad), 101, 103
Ahmad, Ghulam, 11, 136, 146
Ahmadiyya group, 146
Ahmadnagar sultanate, 90
Aisha (Prophet Muhammad's daughter), 4
Aisha Qandisha (female jinn), 38
Alcohol abstention, 65, 75, 76, 103, 144, 160
Algeria, 22, 31–32
Ali (caliph of Islam), 5, 11, 101
Ali, Dusé, 148
Ali, Muhammad, 41
Ali, Muhammad (boxer), 137, 151
Ali, Noble Drew, 147–48, 149
Ali Bey I, 27
Almoravid dynasty, 56–57
Alphonso (Christian king), 56
Al-Qaeda, 114, 125, 129
Alufás (religious teachers), 18, 111, 117
Alum, and evil eye, 44, 51
Ambar, Malik, 90
American Colonization Society, 141
American Muslim Mission, 155
American Protestantism, 151
Amulets: and evil eye, 44, 144; and Murid Sufi order, 69, 71; and African-Brazilian Muslims, 117–18, 121, 122, 132; and African-born American Muslim immigrants, 163
Anatolia, 27, 40, 89
Ancient Egyptian Arabic Order of the Nobles of the Mystic Shrine, 147
Andalusia, 56
Andrews, J. B., 31
Angelo 3X, 150
Angola, 60
Ansari, Samuel, 155
Arabian tribal society, 2
Arabic coffee, 46
Arabic language: and African-Brazilian Muslims, 115, 117, 119; and amulets,

117–18; and African American Muslim slaves, 138, 139; and Bilali, 142; and African American Muslims, 146; and African-born American Muslim immigrants, 162
Arabic literature, 23
Arab-Israeli War of 1948, 41
Arab-Israeli War of 1967, 41
Arab League, member states of, 179 (n. 5)
Arabs and Arab world: and black African origin, 23, 24; concept of Arab world, 23, 179 (n. 5); and Stambali practices, 32; and Gnawa practices, 39; and Somalis, 79, 82
Argentina, 113
Arifa (chief priestess): and Bori practices, 28, 29; and Stambali practices, 30, 32, 33, 34
Askia Muhammad, 5
Asmar (dark or black or brown, often referring to skin color), 42
Assimilation, of African-born American Muslim immigrants, 157, 161–62, 191 (n. 49)
Atiba, Kwesi, 129–30
Atlantic slave trade: and Africana Muslims in New World, 6, 112; and racism, 13; and Portugal, 59; and Great Britain, 73; and Caribbean, 79, 112; and Latin America, 112; and black Atlantic, 165
Atlantic world, 7. *See also* Black Atlantic
Austen, Ralph, 89
Austin, Allan, 138
Ayuba Suleiman Diallo. *See* Job Ben Solomon, slave narrative of
Ayyubid era, 40

Baba Farid, 99
Babikir, Babikir Ahmed, 54
Badajoz, Spain, 56
Baghirmi, 28
Bahia, Brazil: and revolt of 1835, 19, 111, 114–16, 118–23, 132, 168; pan-Yoruban consciousness in, 19, 115, 121, 122, 132–33; enslaved Muslims of African descent in, 116; religious diversity in, 122
Bahmani kingdom, 90
Bamba, Ahmadu: followers of, 7, 72, 172; and religious pilgrimages, 17–18; and Touba, Senegal, 55; founding of Murid Sufi order, 66, 88, 109; exile of, 67–68, 138; photographs and images of, 68, 69, 70; descendants of, 69; and African diaspora, 109; and African American Muslims, 163, 164; alternate spellings of name, 183 (n. 42)
Bambara, 28
Bangladesh, 89
Banu Naghrila, 56
Baraka (spiritual power), 12, 29, 67, 69, 88, 102, 103, 121
Basu, Helene, 95, 96, 100
Bava Gor. *See* Gori Pir
Bava Habash: function for Siddis, 87, 95, 97, 108; shrines of, 96; ritual washing of shrine, 98–99
Bawa Muhaiyaddeen Fellowship, 136
Bedouins, 40, 41
Belal, Muslim, 76, 80, 185 (n. 105)
Belali Mahomet. *See* Bilali (slave and overseer)
Belgium, 60, 66
Belize, 126, 154
Ben Ali. *See* Bilali (slave and overseer)
Berbers, 5, 32, 39, 56–57
Berns-McGown, Rima, 76–79
Bible, 149
Bight of Benin, 116, 119
Bilad as-sudan (land of blacks), 23
Bilali (slave and overseer), 141–43, 144
Bilal ibn Rabah: physical appearance of, 1; and call to prayer, 1–2, 3, 4, 6, 28, 167, 175; as former slave, 2, 3, 4, 21, 172; punishment for conversion to Islam, 2–3; Abu Bakr's

Index 211

purchase of bond, 3; burial of, 3; functions performed by, 3, 168; and African presence in Islam, 5, 173; Islamic practices inspired by, 19; as religious exemplar, 21; as patron saint of Gnawa, 21–22, 167, 173; *gumbri* in possession of, 28; as saint of Stambali, 30, 32, 33, 94, 167, 173; Ghawarna not claiming as ancestor, 43; descendants of, 53, 80, 94; and *dhikr*, 86, 94; and Siddis, 94, 109, 173; and Pacífico Licutan, 111–12, 118; and African American Muslims, 135, 136; and Nation of Islam, 135, 155, 156, 164, 168; as ethnic symbol, 167; legacy of, 175

Black African origin, 23–24

Black Atlantic: and music, 36; and Islam as vehicle of self-determination, 54; and transnational connections, 55, 165; and ethnic identity, 136

Black identity: and racism, 13–17, 22; and slavery, 14, 15, 22; and "thin" blackness, 14, 15, 63; and African diaspora, 14–15, 16, 19, 22, 49; and "thick" blackness, 15, 87, 136, 148, 166; and racial consciousness, 22, 23; and **Gnawa**, 35; and Ghawarna, 40, 41, 43, 49; and Moors, 57; and Siddis, 97; and African American Muslims, 137, 148, 149, 172; and Nation of Islam, 148, 149–50, 154, 156, 168, 171

Black liberation, and Africana Muslims, 18, 54

Black Muslims: and lateral diaspora, 9, 17, 109; historiography of, 24

Black nationality, 15

Black power movement, 126, 137

Black saints: and African-descended Muslims, 17, 50; in North Africa, 18; and Ghawarna, 43; and Siddis, 87, 88, 94–100, 107–9; and African diaspora, 109; and African American Muslim slaves, 138; and African-born American Muslim immigrants, 164, 165; and Sufism, 166. *See also specific saints*

Black separatism, and Nation of Islam, 137, 151, 155

Blind Alphabetz, 80

Bluett, Thomas, 58

Blyden, Edward Wilmot, 54, 148

Boddy, Janice, 26

Bori Islam: practices of, 17, 22, 25–29, 34, 38, 39, 50; and lodges or brotherhoods, 27, 28–29; spirits of, 27–28, 30, 122

Bowen, John, 10

Brazil: and revolt of 1835, 19, 111, 114–16, 118–23, 132, 168; Muslim missionaries in, 113; and fear of Muslim revolt, 116; and Islamic practice, 117, 132; Brazilian-born blacks and African-born blacks, 119, 120, 122; racial divisions of, 119–20, 121, 122; and ethnic groups, 120–21; deportation of African-born blacks, 122. *See also* African-Brazilian Muslims

Breves (talismans), 117–18, 121, 122, 132

British African-descended Muslims: influence of, 6; and conversion to Islam, 18, 73–74, 76, 80; and hip-hop artists, 53, 54, 55, 76, 80–81; and Islamic identity, 53–56, 58–59, 75, 76–77, 78, 79; diversity of, 55, 73, 74, 75; and Islamic practices, 55, 75, 76, 77; and East Africa migrants, 73; and prison population, 74, 75, 76, 184 (n. 82); and Nation of Islam, 74–75, 77–78; from Somalia, 74, 76–77, 78, 79, 82, 171; and Qurʾanic education, 77, 78; and religious media, 77–78; and ethnic identity, 78–79, 136

British Merchant Navy, 74

Brown, Katie, 142–43

Bu Allah. *See* Bilali (slave and overseer)

Buffalo Moslem Welfare Society, 147

Buggenhagen, Beth, 70–71

Bu Saʿadiyya, 30–31, 34

Cabra (in reference to skin color, in between black and tan), 119
Camara, Charles, 92–93
Caribbean: African-descended Muslims in, 6, 18, 113; and revolutionaries' understanding of Islamic religion, 18–19; British African-descended Muslims from, 74; and Atlantic slave trade, 79, 112; enslaved Muslims of African descent in, 112; Muslim religious activity in, 125, 126, 131–32. *See also* African-Caribbean Muslims; Trinidad and Tobago
Caroline (queen of England), 59
Carter, Donald, 68, 70
Carter, Emmanuel, 124
Catholicism, 122
Central Africa, 17, 30
Change Institute, 78
Children: as vulnerable to evil eye, 43–44; and Mandinga "writing-on-the-hand" ritual, 62
Chishti Sufi order, 96, 98, 99
Christians and Christianity: and military alliances across religious lines, 56; Muslim relations with, 56, 57, 100, 101, 107; and interventionism of "Christian conscience," 69; and Gori Pir, 95; and Abd al-Rahman Ibrahima, 141; and African American Muslims, 144; and Nation of Islam, 152, 155
Cissé, Hassan, 164
Clarke, Knolly, 124
Clay, Henry, 140
Cleveland Community Islamic School, 164
Clifford, James, 7
Clifton 3X, 152
Cold War, 149, 156
Colonialism: and white superiority, 13; and anticolonial consciousness, 18, 56; and France, 59, 60, 67; and Great Britain, 59, 60, 74, 89, 90, 91; and Portugal, 59, 60–61, 90, 91, 92; and Europe, 59–60, 80–81, 87, 172; and African-descended Muslims, 60; neocolonialism, 80
Colombia, 113
Couper, James Hamilton, 144
Cox, John Coates, 139
Crete, Bori and Zar practices in, 27
Crioulos creoles, 119
Cultural blackness, 15

Daaras (religious communities), 67
Dahiras (religious circles), 67, 68, 69, 72, 183 (n. 44)
D'Alisera, JoAnn, 157, 159, 160, 161, 162, 169
Dalits, 92
Dammal (dance), 99
Dance: and Islamic practices, 17, 22; and Zar cult, 27; and Stambali practices, 32, 33, 34; and Gnawa practices, 35, 37, 38; and Ghawarna practices, 47–49; and hot dancing, 48–49; and Siddi practices, 97, 98, 99, 100, 102, 106; and African American Muslims, 144
Dandará (Muslim scholar), 117
Dan Fodio, Uthman, 53, 54, 119
Dar Barnu, 32–34, 167
Dar Fur, 28
Dar Kofa, 27, 28
Dark-skinned people, Middle East prejudice against, 2, 41–42, 43
Darul Islam, 126–27
Dar Zouzou, 32
Dead Sea salt, and evil eye, 44
Debt peonage, and Ghawarna, 43
Dhikr (religious litanies): and Ramadan, 46; and Murid Sufi order, 70; and Siddis, 94, 97, 98, 99; and African American Muslims, 143, 163; and Tijani Sufi order, 163
Diaspora studies: definitions of diaspora, 7, 8–9, 22; multiple religious dimensions of, 8. *See also* African diaspora

Diop, Cheikh Anta, 53–54
Diouf, Sylviane, 67–68, 71
Divination ceremonies, and Stambali practices, 33, 50
Doli (replica of Husayn's tomb), 101–2
Domestic spaces, and women, 44–45, 64
Dowry, 47
Drissel, David, 185 (n. 110)
Drug trade, 128–29
Drummers: and Zar cult, 26; and Stambali practices, 32, 33; and Gnawa practices, 37; and Siddi practices, 97, 99–100, 101, 102; and African American Muslims, 144
Dubai, Bori and Zar practices in, 27
Dutch, and colonization of South Asia, 91

East Africa: Islam in, 5–6, 17; diaspora communities of, 6, 86; ethnic and geographic labeling of, 24; Zar cult in, 26; and British African-descended Muslims, 73; British importing slaves from, 91; African-born American Muslim immigrants from, 163
Eaton, Richard, 91
Egypt: and guest workers in Jordan, 47; enslaved Africans in, 89; African-born American Muslim immigrants from, 163
El Hamel, Chouki, 35
English-language orientalism, 131
Enlightenment rationality, 45
Essaouira, Morocco, 21, 35, 167
Ethical contemplation, 49
Ethical guidelines: and British African-descended Muslims, 75–76, 77; and Siddis, 103, 107; and Nation of Islam, 153, 155–56
Ethiopia, 26, 163
Ethnic blackness, 15
Ethnic identities: and Mandinga migrants from Guinea-Bissau, 61, 63,

64–65, 81; and Senegalese Muslims, 65; and British African-descended Muslims, 78–79, 136; and African American Muslims, 136, 155–56, 161, 162, 169; and African-Caribbean Muslims, 136, 171; and Islamic practices, 166
Europe: Africana Muslims in, 6, 17, 55–56, 57, 81–83; imperialism of, 13; racial hierarchy in, 14; history of Africana Muslims in, 56–60; enslaved Africans in, 58; trade networks with Africa, 59; colonization of Africa, 59–60, 80–81, 172; immigration patterns in, 66; neocolonialism of, 80; colonization of South Asia, 87; political Islam associated with violence in, 113. *See also specific countries*
Evil eye: women's rituals of healing associated with, 23, 44–45; and Ghawarna, 43–45; and Sunni Islamic tradition, 51; and African American Muslims, 144
Exorcism, 17. *See also* Spirit possession

Faisal, Daoud Ahmed, 147
Fall, Ibrahima, 70
Faqirs (mendicants), 94, 96, 97–98, 100, 101
Fard, W. D., 146, 148, 149, 154, 155
Farrakhan, Louis, 7, 75, 78, 136, 155
Fatima (Prophet Muhammad's daughter), 101
Fez, Morocco, 35
Fiqh (Islamic jurisprudence): and business transactions, 5; authoritative interpretations of, 11, 50; and marriage, 46, 105, 108; and African-descended Muslims, 54, 55; and Mahbub Subhani, 104; and Darul Islam, 127; and African American Muslims, 136, 165; and African American Muslim slaves, 138; Maliki school of, 142

214 Index

France: Africana Muslims in, 6; Senegalese migrants in, 7, 57, 66, 67, 71; Murid Sufi order in, 55; and colonialism, 59, 60, 67

Free black communities, in Morocco, 35, 36

Fruit of Islam, 153

Fullah Progressive Union Islamic and Cultural Center, 161–63, 191 (n. 62)

Fun-Da-Mental, 81

Funerary practices, and Mandinga migrants from Guinea-Bissau, 55, 62–63, 64

Gabon, 67

Gallaudet, Thomas, 140

Galut, 8

Gender: women representing cultural practices associated with African people, 12, 170, 171; and Mandinga migrants from Guinea-Bissau, 55, 64, 82; and Sufi Murid order, 70; gender segregation, 76; and Siddis, 88; and Sierra Leonean refugees, 138; and African-born American Muslim immigrants, 160–61. *See also* Women

George II (king of England), 59

Georgia, 141–45

Georgia Writers Project, 142–43, 144

Germany, 6, 59, 60

Ghana, 11, 163

Ghawarna: Islamic practices of, 17, 23, 40–49, 82; and Ramadan, 17, 43, 45–46; and marriage, 17, 43, 46–48; as African, 40, 180 (n. 67); social status of, 40–43, 48; and Bedouins, 41; dispossession of lands, 42–43; and evil eye, 43–45

Ghor al-Mazraʻa, Jordan Valley, 44–45, 46

Ghor el-Safi, Jordan Valley, 46

Ghusl (bath), 98, 186 (n. 48)

Gilroy, Paul, 7

Global context, of Islamic practices, 10

Globalization: and racial hierarchies, 13; and Siddis, 108; and African-born American Muslim immigrants, 157, 165

Gnawa: and Islamic practices, 21, 35–40, 50, 172–73; night ceremonies of, 21, 37–38, 167, 170; Bilal as patron saint of, 21–22, 167, 173; nonblack participants in, 35; songs of, 35–36, 38; in Morocco, 35–39; and Islamic saints, 37, 38; and blue spirits, 38; and black spirits, 38, 173; scholars on, 38–39; and Sufi practices, 39; and black Muslim identity, 50; and trope of slavery, 172

Goa, India, 91, 92

Goma (dance), 99

Gomez, Michael, 119, 138

Gordon, Lewis, 13

Gordon X, 153

Gori Pir: devotees of, 7, 167; as saint, 18, 94–96; and *dhikr*, 86; function for Siddis, 87, 88, 95, 108; and African identity, 94, 108–9; and songs, 94–95; shrines of, 95, 96, 98, 100, 101; and divination through ordeal, 96–97; and spirit possession rituals, 98; ritual washing of shrine, 98–99; death anniversary of, 98–99, 100, 170; family of, 99–100; and Siddis in Karnataka, 101, 104, 170; rituals performed by devotees, 169, 170; and African diaspora, 173

Gori Pir Hill, India, 100, 109, 170

Granada, Spain, 56

Grant, Rachel, 145, 146

Grant, Rosa, 145

Great Britain: Africana Muslims in, 6, 18, 53–56, 58–59, 73–81; African-Caribbean Muslims in, 55, 74, 75, 79–80, 81, 82; colonization of Africa, 59, 60, 74; and Atlantic slave trade, 73; history of Muslims in, 73; mosques in, 74, 184 (n. 75); Nation of Islam in, 74–75, 77–78;

Index 215

colonization of South Asia, 89, 90, 91. *See also* London, England
Guest workers, 47
Guinea-Bissau: funerary rituals of Mandinga in, 55, 62–63, 64; independence of, 60; civil war in, 61. *See also* Mandinga migrants from Guinea-Bissau
Gujarat, India, 85, 86, 90, 98
Gumbri (stringed instrument), 28, 32, 34, 37

Habshis, 18, 86, 89, 90, 95, 170, 173
Hadith literature: and Bilal's call to prayer, 1, 3; and functions performed by Bilal, 3; and Sunnis, 11; and Muhammad's high regard for Bilal, 21; and evil eye, 44; and reform of Islam, 64; and British African-descended Muslims, 76
Hafla (dance party), 47
Halal (permitted human behavior), 54, 75, 76, 77, 158, 160
Haley, Alex, 155–56
Hall, Shad, 143
Hamas, 129
Hamdushi Sufi order, 39
Hamid, Yusuf Muzaffaruddin, 127
Haram (prohibited human behavior), 54
Hart-Celler Act of 1965, 156
Harun Ar-Rashid (Baghdad caliph), 150
Hasan (Prophet Muhammad's grandson), 3, 101
Hausa, 25–26, 28, 117, 120, 121
Heaven, 22, 50
Henna, and marriage, 47, 105
Hester (Shad Hall's grandmother), 143
Hijab (folded piece of paper), and evil eye, 44–45
Hijab (headscarf), 76, 77, 79, 143, 153, 171
Hindus: relations with Muslims, 85–86, 100, 101, 106; Siddi Muslims' use of rituals and traditions of, 88, 100, 106, 107; and Gori Pir, 95, 108

Hip-hop: and African-descended Muslims, 53–54, 55, 76, 80, 171, 185 (n. 104); Desi hip-hop, 81, 185 (n. 110)
Holloway Prison, Great Britain, 75
Homelands: and diaspora studies, 7; and black European Muslims, 17; and African American Muslims, 19, 137, 165; and classic Gnawa music, 36; and Senegalese Murids, 68, 69, 72–73, 82; and African-Brazilian Muslims, 122, 132–33; and African American Muslim slaves, 140–41, 145–46; and Nation of Islam, 151, 154; and African-born American Muslim immigrants, 157, 159, 160, 165, 166
Horn of Africa, 5
Huggins, Nathan, 156
Hunwick, John, 24
Husayn (Prophet Muhammad's grandson), 3, 101–2, 103, 168
Husaynid rulers, of Tunis, 29, 30
Hyderabad, India, 91
Hydersab Siddi, 104

'*Ibadat* (religious practices), 162
Iberia, 6, 17, 56–57, 112
Ibn Battuta, 89–90
Ibn Hamama. *See* Bilal ibn Rabah
'Id al-Adha, 18, 104, 118
'Id al-Fitr, 3, 80, 88, 103–4
Iftars (evening meals during Ramadan), 103
India: East Africans in, 6, 86; African-descended Muslims in, 18; British Muslims from, 74; Siddis in, 87, 92–93, 108; enslaved Africans settling in, 89; slave trade halted in, 91; social hierarchies of, 92; sectarianism in, 100; and Ahmadiyya group, 146; and Bilal ibn Rabah, 167. *See also* Karnataka, India
Indian Ocean: and migration between Africa and Asia, 6, 18, 86, 87,

88–89; and Gori Pir, 86, 95; trade across, 89
Indonesia, 114
International Monetary Fund, 66
Iran, 27, 114
Iraq, 40
Isawa Sufi order, 39
Ishmael (Abraham's son), 104
Iska (spirit beings), 117
Islam: conversion to, 2–3, 25, 55, 73–74, 76, 136, 172; Muhammad forbidding division between Arab and non-Arab in, 4; African presence in, 5; in African diaspora, 6, 7, 8, 9, 10, 16, 19, 49, 69, 70, 168–69, 171, 172–75; global nature of, 10; five pillars of, 10–11, 50, 55, 75, 76, 77, 168–69; and fundamentalists, 12; reform of, 12, 45, 64–65, 82, 127, 164, 169–70, 171, 173, 174; social construction of Africanness of, 16; and political self-determination, 54; institutionalization of, 117, 156–57, 165; standardization of, 169, 171. *See also* Political Islam
Islamic Center of Washington, 158–59, 161, 170–71
Islamic Circle of North America, 157
Islamic identities: diversity of, 9, 55; of Gnawa, 21, 22; of Ghawarna, 43; of British African-descended Muslims, 53–56, 58–59, 75, 76–77, 78, 79; of Mandinga migrants from Guinea-Bissau, 63, 64–65, 81, 138; of Siddis, 87, 91, 93–94, 100, 103, 107; of African American Muslims, 161, 165, 166; modest dress as symbol of, 171
Islamic Missionaries Guild (IMG), 128
Islamic Party of North America (IPNA), 127
Islamic philosophy, and Sufism, 12
Islamic practices: of Africana Muslims, 6–7, 51, 145, 169, 170, 171; and African diasporic identity, 9, 22, 50, 73; context of, 10; of African-descended Muslims, 10, 23, 112–13, 172–74; and cultural influences, 12, 46, 55, 93–94, 169, 170, 171, 173, 174; impact of racism on, 13; and slavery, 17, 19, 172, 173; of Bori Islam, 17, 22, 25–29, 34, 38, 39, 50; of Ghawarna, 17, 23, 40–49, 82; of African American Muslims, 19, 74, 112–13, 135, 136, 137, 141–45, 158–64, 165; of Gnawa, 21, 35–40, 50, 172–73; of Stambali, 29–35, 170, 171; diversity of, 50, 165, 168, 170, 174–75; of Mandinga migrants from Guinea-Bissau, 55, 60–65; of British African-descended Muslims, 55, 75, 76, 77; of Senegalese Muslims, 68, 70–71, 72, 82, 138, 163, 164; of Siddis, 88, 101–7; and African-Brazilian Muslims, 118, 121; and Nation of Islam, 151, 153, 154, 165, 166; legitimacy of, 170; simplistic representation of, 174–75, 191 (n. 3)
Islamic saints: and Sufism, 12, 29–30; and Gnawa, 37, 38; women lighting candles at tombs of, 45
Islamic Society of North America, 157
Islamic visual art, 12
Islamophobia, 114, 131–32
Ismael (rapper), 53
Italy, 6, 55, 58, 60, 66, 72

Jackson, Jesse, 152
Jakhanke group, 62
Jalal ad-Din Yaqut, 89
al-Jalani, Abd al-Qadir, 33, 37
Jamaʿat al-Muslimeen, 19, 115, 123–25, 127–30, 131, 132, 133, 168
Jamaʿat-i Islami of Pakistan, 127
Jamaica, 74, 126, 154
Jamat (community), 87, 107
Janjira, Maharashtra, India, 90, 91
Jankowsky, Richard, 32–34
Jejes, 120
Jerma. *See* Bilal ibn Rabah
Jews: exile from Roman Palestine, 8; and Stambali rituals, 30; and

Index 217

military alliances across religious lines, 56; expulsion from Iberia, 57
Jihad (struggle): and political Islam, 114, 115, 130, 132, 133; and Bahia revolt of 1835, 116, 119, 121, 122; of Uthman dan Fodio, 119; and Trinidad and Tobago, 123–31, 133; and Pakistan, 127; and nationalist resistance, 129–30
Jinn (spirit beings): and Bori practices, 25–26, 27; and Stambali practices, 30, 31, 32; and Gnawa practices, 35, 38; and Afro-Brazilian practices, 117
Job Ben Solomon, slave narrative of, 58–59
Johnson, Michelle, 61–65
Jones, Charles Colcock, 143–44
Jones, Nero, 144
Jordan: Ghawarna in, 40–49; and clan affiliations, 41; prejudice against dark-skinned people, 41–42, 43; consumer culture of, 42; rural Islamic practices in, 43–49

Kaag, Mayke, 68, 71, 72
Kaʿba: and Bilal's call to prayer, 2, 175; Bilal's planting of spear in direction of, 3; and salat, 98; and Muharram, 101
Kapchan, Deborah, 37
Karachi, Pakistan, 99
Kareemsab Siddi, 105
Karnataka, India: rural Siddi Muslims in, 18, 86, 88, 92–93, 100, 101–7, 121, 170; and religious pluralism, 100, 103, 106, 107, 108; Islamic holidays in Siddi villages of, 101–4, 108, 168; and veneration of Muslim saints, 104–5, 170; and life-cycle rituals, 105–7
Karriem, Anna Burks, 150
Kawar, 28
Kenya, 11, 163
Key, Francis Scott, 140
Khan, Aisha, 130

Khan, Shazard "Teddy Mice," 128
Khawlah bint Azdar, 150
Kinship blackness, 15
Kinship networks, 27
Kinte, Kunta, 156
Kofa Household, 27
KRS-One (rapper), 80
Kunafa (syrupy-sweet pastry with cheese), 45
Kuri spirits, 33
Kuwait, Bori and Zar practices in, 27

Lakshmi (Hindu goddess), 106
Laryea, Masoud, 164
Latin America: enslaved Muslims of African descent in, 112; Muslim religious activity in, 125, 131–32. *See also* South America
Lawih (dance leaders), 48–49
Layla al-Miʿraj, 118
Layla al-Qadr, 32, 46, 115, 132
Lee, Spike, 75
Liberia, 141
Licutan, Pacífico, 111–12, 118, 167–68
Lila (night ceremony of Gnawa), 21, 37–38
Lisbon, Portugal, and Mandinga migrants from Guinea-Bissau, 55, 61, 63, 65, 71, 81
Lobo, Cyprian, 93
Local context, of Islamic practices, 10
Lockman, Zachary, 13
London, England: Somali immigrants to, 18, 54, 55, 56, 74, 82, 171; Nigerian immigrants to, 18, 54, 74, 78; British African-descended Muslims in, 73, 74, 78; mosques in, 78

Maharashtra, India, 90
Mahbub Subhani, 104–5
Mahr (contractually obligated wedding gift), 47
Mai Mishra: and dhikrs, 86, 97; function for Siddis, 87, 88, 95–96, 97, 108, 109; shrines of, 96, 98; ritual

washing of shrine, 98–99; death anniversary of, 99–100; rituals performed by devotees, 169, 170, 171
Majaly tribe, 43
Majid, Baba, 32, 34
Majid, Satti, 146–47
Makhan Devi, 95, 96, 109, 173
Makranis, African-descended Muslims as, 18, 86
Malcolm X, 7, 74–75, 126, 137, 151
Malcolm X (film), 75
Malick, Daud Abdul, 164
Malunga (musical bow), 94, 108
Mamluk era, 40, 89
Mandinga migrants from Guinea-Bissau: and "writing-on-the-hand" ritual, 55, 61, 62, 63, 65; and Lisbon, 55, 61, 63, 65, 71, 81; funerary rituals of, 55, 62–63, 64; and gender, 55, 64, 82; and circumcision ritual, 61; and infant name-taking ritual, 61; and ethnic identity, 61, 63, 64–65, 81; life-cycle rituals of, 61–62, 65; material culture of, 62; and Islamic identity, 63, 64–65, 81, 138
Mansa Musa, 5
Marabouts (Murid Sufi teachers), 67
Maria biscuits, 63
Mauritius, 89
Marques, Antônio, 118
Marrakesh, Morocco, 35
Marriage: and Ghawarna practices, 17, 43, 46–48; and wedding *dabka*, 23, 46–48; and Siddi practices, 94, 105–6
Mashalkha tribe, 41
Masjid al-Haqq, 164
Masjid Aqsa, 163
Masquerades, and Stambali, 30, 51
Material culture: and Islamic practices, 17, 26; trans-Saharan, 26; and Stambali, 30–31; and sub-Saharan Africa, 30–31; and Mandinga migrants from Guinea-Bissau, 62; and Senegalese Muslims, 68, 69, 70, 71; and Siddis, 96; and African American Muslims, 143
Mauritania, 57, 67
Mawdudi, Mawlana, 127
McLeod, John, 187 (n. 66)
Mecca2Medina, 53, 54, 80, 167, 172
Meier, Prita Sandy, 9
Middle Ages, 57
Middle East: multiracial slavery in, 2; dark or black skin synonymous with slavery in, 2, 41; diaspora communities of sub-Saharan Africans in, 6; racial hierarchy in, 14, 23–25, 42; enslaved black Africans of, 24–25, 89; and Sudanic ritual healing, 26; origins of Bori and Zar practices in, 27; and evil eye, 44; British Muslims from, 74
Ministry of Awqaf, 29
al-Misri, Fatima, 27
Modernity: and racial hierarchy, 13; and reform of Islam, 64, 65, 169–70, 174
Mohammed, Wallace D., 75, 135, 154–55, 156, 164, 172
Moorish Science Temple, 147–48, 149, 165
Moors, as identifying term, 57–58
Morocco: racism in, 21, 36, 39; Bori Islam in, 22; Gnawa in, 35–39; and Berbers in Spain, 56
Mosques: men dominating public spaces of, 64; in Great Britain, 74, 184 (n. 75)
Mozambique, 11, 60, 61
Mughal Empire, 90
Muhallabiyya (rice pudding), 45
Muhammad, Elijah: as American prophet, 11; doctrines of, 19, 148, 149, 150–52, 154, 155, 190 (n. 32); and Nation of Islam, 75, 126, 135, 136, 137; on blacks/Muslims as "original man," 136, 149, 150, 166; and black separatism, 151; dietary guidelines of, 151–53; death of, 154; on African diaspora, 172

Index 219

Muhammad, Prophet: and call to prayer, 1–2; Bilal's role as close companion of, 3, 21, 155, 156, 167, 168, 173, 175; on social stigma, 3–4; African religions blending with beliefs in example of, 5; and five pillars of Islam, 10, 11; and Sunna traditions, 11, 47, 50, 51, 65, 136; and Sufism, 12; Bilal as influence on, 21; and Africana Muslims, 23, 25; birthday of, 32, 159, 165; and Layla al-Qadr, 32, 46, 115; and Stambali practices, 33; and Gnawa practices, 37, 38; women lighting candles at tombs of companions of, 45; and *dhikr*, 85, 86; and Medina, 94; and Gori Pir, 95, 99; and Siddis, 95, 101; family of, 101, 103; and Layla al-Miʿraj, 118; and Jamaʿat al-Muslimeen, 131; and Sunni Islamic tradition, 148; and Nation of Islam, 149; and African American Muslim education, 162

Muharram, 18, 88, 101–3

Munkoo (rice flour sweetened with honey), 62, 63

Murid Sufi order: transnational connections of, 17–18, 55, 68, 69, 70–73, 82, 171; and Senegalese Murids, 55, 65, 66–73; and Touba, 55, 67, 68, 69–70, 72, 109; and Ahmadu Bamba, 66, 88, 109; and groundnut economy, 66–67, 68; and *dahiras*, 67, 68, 69, 72, 183 (n. 44); and marabouts/*talibs* relationship, 67–69, 70, 72, 82; and Khalifa General, 69, 70; and religious media, 69, 70–71; and amulets, 69, 71; and United States, 136

Murshids (spiritual masters), 96

Murtada (son of Ahmadu Bamba), 69

Music: and Islamic practices, 17, 22; and Zar cult, 26; and Bori practices, 28; and Stambali practices, 31, 32, 34; and Gnawa practices, 35–38; and African American spirituals, 36, 37; hip-hop, 53–54, 55, 76, 80, 80–81, 171, 185 (n. 104), 185 (n. 110)

Muslim Council of Britain, 80

Muslim Girls Training–General Civilization Class, 152, 153

Muslims: Western stereotypes of, 46, 51; expulsion from Iberia, 57. *See also* Africana Muslims; African-descended Muslims

Muslim Student Association, 157

Nagôs, 120–21

National context, of Islamic practices, 10, 166

Nation of Islam: and Sunni Islam tradition, 19, 148, 155, 156; in Great Britain, 74–75, 77–78; and prison ministries, 75, 152; Muslim missionaries of, 113, 126; and Caribbean, 126; and African American Muslims, 135–36, 137, 146, 165; and black/Muslim self, 137; and black separatism, 137, 151, 155; and black identity, 148, 149–50, 154, 156, 168, 171; and Afro-Asian alliance of color, 149, 150; and Islamic practices, 151, 153, 154, 165, 166; and black uplift, 151–52; and dietary guidelines, 151–53; and manner of dress, 153; and education, 154

Natural/supernatural boundaries, transgression of, 50

New Thought, 147

Niass, Rakin, 80

Niassé, Ibrahim, 164

Nigeria: Nigerian immigrants to London, 18, 54, 78; British African-descended Muslims from, 74, 78; African-born American Muslim immigrants from, 163

9/11 terrorist attacks, 78, 114, 158

Noor, Sukina Abdul, 79–80

North Africa: and Islamization of Africa, 5; diaspora communities of sub-Saharan Africans in, 6, 17; conquest of Iberia, 6, 56; black saints

in, 18; as part of African continent, 22, 178 (n. 4); racial hierarchy in, 23–25; enslaved black Africans of, 24–25, 112; Bori Islam in, 25–26, 34; origins of Bori and Zar practices in, 27; forms of Islamic practice in, 30; Moors from, 57; British Muslims from, 74; and Henry Clay, 140
North America: African-descended Muslims in, 6, 112; racial hierarchy in, 14; and African American spirituals, 36, 37; European conquest of, 57; Muslim missionaries in, 113; and Islamic practice, 188 (n. 22). *See also* African American Muslims; United States
Northrup, David, 57, 58

Obeng, Pashington, 101, 102, 104, 105, 106, 187 (n. 66)
Oglethorpe, James, 58
Omar, Ali, 164
Operation Breadbasket, 152
Orisha religions, 122, 133, 144
Ottoman Empire: slave trade outlawed by, 24, 40; social status of enslaved black Africans in, 24–25, 35; and Sudanic ritual healing, 26
Oxalá (deity), 122

Pakistan: East Africans in, 6, 86; African-descended Muslims in, 18; and guest workers in Jordan, 47; Siddis in, 87, 99; enslaved Africans settling in, 89; and Gori Pir, 98; and jihad, 127; and Bilal ibn Rabah, 167
Palestine: enslaved Africans in, 40; and African Muslim pilgrims, 41; African-Palestinian refugees, 41; *dabka* as symbol of national and cultural identity in, 48; and Hamas, 129
Pan-African unity, 18, 126, 130, 137
Pantin, Raoul, 124

Pan-Yoruban consciousness: in Bahia, Brazil, 19, 115, 121, 122, 132–33; Yasin Abu Bakr's rejection of, 130
Pardos (mulattos), 119, 120
Paris, France, 7, 67
Parsis, and Gori Pir, 95, 108
Patil, Sulemansab, 106
Peanuts, association with Africa, 42
Pearls of Wisdom, 185 (n. 105)
Persian literature, and black African people, 23
Pew Research Center, 184 (n. 75)
Phillip, Lennox. *See* Abu Bakr, Yasin
Phoebe (Bilali's wife), 142–43, 144
Physical healing: and Ghawarna practices, 17; and Stambali practices, 29
Pilgrimages: to Touba, 17–18, 69, 70, 72; migration as religious pilgrimage, 67, 72–73, 171
Pilgrimage to Mecca: and five pillars of Islam, 11; and pious Muslims, 27; pilgrimage to Touba compared to, 70; and Siddis, 104, 108; and Nation of Islam, 155
Poetic Pilgrimage, 79–80
Political Islam: use of, 18–19, 113–14, 169; and Bahia revolt of 1835, 19, 111, 114–15, 119–23; and Siddis, 107, 108; and African American Muslims, 113, 166; violence associated with, 113–14, 115, 131–32; and jihad, 114, 115, 130, 132, 133; and Islamophobia, 114, 131–32; and Noble Drew Ali, 148; and Nation of Islam, 151; and African-born American Muslim immigrants, 157; Bilal ibn Rabah as ethnic symbol of self-determination, 167–68
Poole, Elijah. *See* Muhammad, Elijah
Portugal: colonization of Africa, 59, 60–61; enslaved Africans in, 60; Muslim community of, 64; and colonization of South Asia, 90, 91, 92. *See also* Latin America; Lisbon, Portugal
Portuguese Mandinga, religious practices of, 18

Index 221

Prasad, Kiran, 93
Preto (black skin color), 119
Public Enemy, 80

Qadiri Sufi order, 33, 96, 104, 143
Qasa'ids (poems), 67
Qata'if (cream-stuffed pancakes), 45
Qawwali, 98
Quick, Abdul Hakim, 54
Qur'an: and social stigma, 3–4; and African religions, 5; and angels, 11; and Sunnis, 11, 50; and Zar cult, 27; and Layla al-Qadr, 32, 46, 115; and Stambali practices, 33, 34; and evil eye, 44, 144; and Ramadan, 45–46; Job ben Solomon's knowledge of, 59; and Mandinga "writing-on-the-hand" ritual, 62, 65; and reform of Islam, 64; and Murid Sufi order, 72; and British African-descended Muslims, 75, 76–77; and Gori Pir, 94; and Siddis, 100, 105; and Muharram, 101; and Jama'at al-Muslimeen, 128; and African American Muslims, 136; and African American Muslim slaves, 138; and Bilali, 142; and social and spiritual equality, 146; and Nation of Islam, 149; and African-born American Muslim immigrants, 159, 160, 162
Quraysh, 21

Rabat, Morocco, 37
Race and racism: and African-descended Muslims, 4, 13, 14, 16–17, 23–24; impact on Islamic practices of African-descended people, 13, 23, 112, 172–74; and black identity, 13–17, 22; impact of racism, 14; and stereotypes, 14, 15, 42, 48, 49, 71, 92; in Morocco, 21, 36, 39; in North Africa, 23–25; and Gnawa practices, 39; and Ghawarna, 41, 42, 43, 48; and dance leaders, 48; and European colonization of Africa, 59–60; and Mandinga migrants from Guinea-Bissau, 63–64, 71; and Senegalese Murids, 71, 73; and British African-descended Muslims, 80, 81, 83; and Siddis, 92–93, 109; and African American Muslims, 113, 166; and Trinidad and Tobago, 113, 125; and Brazil, 119, 120, 121, 122; and reform of Islam, 127; and Islam as religion of racial equality, 146
Racial hierarchy: and colonization, 13, 14; in Middle East, 14, 23–25, 42; and dances, 48; in Brazil, 119
Racialization, and colonization, 13
Racialized geography, legacy of, 23–24
Radio Lamp Fall FM, 70
Rajjab, 98
Rakin (rapper), 53
Ramadan: and Ghawarna practices, 17, 43, 45–46; and Siddis, 18, 103–4, 108; and British African-descended Muslims, 77; and African American Muslims, 144; and Nation of Islam, 152, 155
Rashida, Muneera, 79
Rastafarianism, 130
Raziya (queen of Delhi sultanate), 89
Reagan, Nancy, 160
Reagan, Ronald, 160
Reconquista, 57, 116
Reddie, Richard, 75, 80
Regional context, of Islamic practices, 10
Reid, Richard J., 60
Reis, João José, 111–12, 119, 120
Renaissance, 57, 58
Renard, John, 10
Réunion, 89
Riccio, Bruno, 68, 69, 71–72
Rifa'i, Ahmad, 95
Rimini, Italy, 68
Robinson, A. N. R., 123–25
Roderic (king of the Visigoths), 56
Rodinson, Maxine, 179 (n. 17)
Roosevelt, Franklin D., 142

Roots (Haley), 155–56
Royal African Company, 59
Royal spirits, 33
Rumi, 12
Russwurm, John, 140

Sacred space: as component of diasporic practice, 8, 50, 109; aesthetics of, 169
Sacrificial animals: and Zar cult, 26; and Bori practices, 28, 34, 38; and Stambali practices, 31, 32, 33–34; and Gnawa practices, 38; and Siddi practices, 104, 105; and Afro-Brazilian practices, 118
Sadiq, Muhammad, 146, 148
Safran, William, 7
Said, Edward W., 13
Saints. *See* Black saints; Islamic saints; *and specific saints*
Salaam Restaurant, Chicago, Illinois, 152
Salaf (pious ancestors of Muhammad's era), 12
Salafi Muslims, 136
Salat (daily prayers), 1, 11, 98, 100, 104, 105, 158
Salhin (black spirits), 33
Salih Bilali, 144–45, 146, 165
Salt: and evil eye, 44, 51; and Mandinga "writing-on-the-hand" ritual, 62
Sarkin Goda (spirit of Bori pantheon), 27
Saudi Arabia, 114
Sawm (fast), and five pillars of Islam, 11
Scott, Garvin, 128
Senegal: economic changes in, 66, 67; migration trends in, 66, 183 (n. 41); French colonial government of, 67
Senegalese Muslims: and belief in angels, 11; and Murid Sufi order, 55, 65, 66–73, 163; and Job Ben Solomon, 58–59; and ethnic identity, 65; immigration to Europe, 66–68, 71; migration as religious pilgrimage, 67, 72–73; material culture of, 68, 69, 70, 71; and Islamic practices, 68, 70–71, 72, 82, 138, 163, 164; relationship with European host communities, 71–72; tensions between groups, 71–72; diversity of, 71–72, 82; immigration to United States, 163, 164
Senegambia, 61, 138
Sha'ban (Islamic month), 27–28, 32
Shabazz Restaurant, Washington, D.C., 152
Shakir, Zaid, 54
Shams ad-Din Abu Nasr Muzaffar Shah, 90
Shari'a (God's path to salvation), 49
Shaykha (female Muslim religious specialist), 44
Sheff, Rebecca, 68
Shelby, Tommie, 13–14, 15
Shi'a Islamic tradition: and Africana Muslims, 5, 11; and evil eye, 44; and Islamic piety, 49; and British African-descended Muslims, 73; and Muharram, 101, 103; and African American Muslims, 136; and African-born American Muslim immigrants, 158–59; and Islamic practices, 165, 168
Shidis, 99
Shyrock, Andrew, 180 (n. 67)
Siddi Development Society, 86, 93
Siddis: East Africans in India known as, 6, 86; African-descended Muslims as, 18; diversity of, 86–87, 107, 108; and black saints, 87, 88, 94–100, 107–9; history of, 87, 88–94; and Islamic identity, 87, 91, 93–94, 100, 103, 107; and African diasporic identity, 87, 94, 108–9, 187 (n. 66); as biologically and spiritually linked, 87, 103, 108; adaptation of non-Islamic religious traditions, 88; rural Siddi Muslims, 88, 91–92; and Islamic practices, 88, 101–7; and

Index 223

life-cycle events, 88, 105–7, 108; and Christian identity, 91; villages of, 92, 101–7, 109; traditional cultural survival strategies of, 93–94; and endogamous marriage patterns, 94; songs of, 94–95, 101, 102, 108, 109; and material culture, 96; and African identity, 97, 108, 109; and boundary crossing, 99; and religious pluralism, 100; and fire-walkers, 102–3
Sidi Ambar the Little, 90
Sidi Badr, 90
Sidi Frej, 33, 34, 109
Sidi Mubarak Nobi. *See* Gori Pir
Sidi Sa'ad, 29, 30, 31, 34, 88, 109
Sidi Surur, 90
Sierra Leone, African-born American Muslim immigrants from, 138, 157–62, 166, 169, 170–71
Sikhs, relationships with Muslims, 85–86
Sinatti, Giulia, 71, 72
Sirat al-mustaqim (straight path), 75
Slavery: multiracial, in Middle East, 2; dark or black skin synonymous with, 2, 41; and African-descended Muslims, 4; of Africana Muslims, 6, 17, 18, 112; and black identity, 14, 15, 22; and Islamic practices, 17, 19, 172, 173; and African diaspora, 22, 24, 172; in Ottoman Empire, 24–25, 35; and forced conversion to Islam, 25; association with slave past, 42; names of slaveholders given to slaves, 58; and slave narratives, 58–59; and Senegalese Murids, 73; and African-Caribbean Muslims, 79; and Siddis, 87; and Indian Ocean, 89; in Muslim contexts, 89; and preservation of literacy, 112; and Nation of Islam, 152
Slave trade. *See* African slave trade; Atlantic slave trade
Social boundary crossing, and dances, 48

Sokoto caliphate, 54, 119
Somalia: Somali immigrants to London, 18, 54, 55, 56, 78, 82, 171; British African-descended Muslims from, 74, 76–77, 78, 79, 82, 171; refugees from, 74, 82
Songhay, 28
South America: African-descended Muslims in, 6, 18; racial hierarchy in, 14; and revolutionaries' understanding of Islamic religion, 18–19; European conquest of, 57; Muslim missionaries in, 113. *See also specific countries*
South Asia: racial hierarchy in, 14; South Asian mosques in London, 78; and hip-hop music, 81, 185 (n. 110); religious sharing in, 85–86, 88; and European colonization, 87, 89, 90, 91, 92; Asian slaves of, 89; African slaves of, 89–91; South Asian Muslims in Trinidad and Tobago, 130–31; youth taking "black-inflected identities," 185 (n. 110). *See also* Siddis
South Carolina, 141, 144
Southeast Asia, 89
Souza Martins, Francisco de, 115
Space: definitions of, 10, 50; and Gnawa's redemptive reading of black diasporic suffering, 22; diasporic space, 171. *See also* Sacred space
Spain: Islamic conquest of, 55, 56; colonization of Africa, 60. *See also* Iberia; Latin America
Spaulding, Thomas, 141
Spirit possession: and Bori Islam, 22, 25, 28; and Zar cult, 26; and Stambali practices, 30, 32, 33, 34, 170; and Gnawa practices, 35, 37, 38, 39, 170; and Siddi rituals, 97–98, 99, 109
Spiritual healing: and Ghawarna practices, 17; and Bori Islam, 22, 26; and Stambali practices, 29; and Mandinga migrants from Guinea-Bissau, 64

Stambali: and trance states, 7, 30, 33, 170; Bori as black spirits in, 26, 30, 122; as black religious brotherhood, 29–30; lodges of, 29–30, 31, 32–33; and Islamic practices, 29–35, 170, 171; Bilal as saint of, 30, 32, 33, 94, 167, 173; masquerades of, 30–31; change and continuity in, 32–33; multiple imagined communities of, 33; pantheon of, 34; and black Muslim identity, 34–35, 39, 50; and veneration of saints, 104

Sub-Saharan Africa: diaspora communities of, 6; Muslim population of, 6, 175; and belief in evil eye, 11; and black identity, 14, 22, 50; ethnic and geographic labeling of, 24; enslaved peoples' Islamic practices, 24, 25–26, 30–31, 39; culture of, 25, 28, 30–31, 33, 34, 39, 50; and Gnawa practices, 38, 39; Castilian word *negro* referring to people from, 58; migration from, to Europe, 66; British African-descended Muslims from, 74

Sudan, 26, 35

Sudanic Africa, 14, 27, 30, 35

Sufism: role of Sufi masters, 5; orders of, 12, 29; and Sunni Islamic tradition, 12, 164, 166; and internal African diaspora, 17; Gnawa practices distinguished from, 39; brotherhoods of, 71, 72; and British African-descended Muslims, 73; pietistic and mystical practices associated with, 88, 102, 163, 165–66; in United States, 136; and African American Muslims, 164. *See also* Murid Sufi order

Sunna (prophetically sanctioned tradition), 11, 47, 50, 51, 64, 65, 72, 136, 138, 142

Sunni Ali (Songhay emperor), 5, 150

Sunni Islamic tradition: and Africana Muslims, 5, 11, 50, 169; and Sufi and non-Sufi interpretations of Islam, 12, 164, 166; and Nation of Islam, 19, 148, 155, 156; and Islamic piety, 49; and British African-descended Muslims, 73, 74; and Muharram, 103; and Trinidad and Tobago, 127–28; and African American Muslims, 136, 142, 146–47, 163–64; and African-born American Muslim immigrants, 158–59; and Islamic practices, 165, 168–69

Swahili language, 5

Syria, 3, 40, 90

Talismans, and Sufism, 12

Tanzania, 75

Tanzimat reforms, 25

Tapas, 120

Tappan, Arthur, 140

Tappan, Charles, 140

Tariqas (orders), of Sufism, 12, 29

Tariq ibn Ziyad, 56

Temple No. 7 Restaurant, New York, 152

Thomas (Renaissance Islamic man), 58

Tijani Sufi order, 66, 73, 136, 163, 164

al-Timbuktawi, Ahmad ibn Abi Bakr ibn Yusuf, 27–29

Toledano, Ehud, 24

Toledo, Spain, 56

Touba, Senegal: religious pilgrimages to, 17–18, 69, 70; and Murid Sufi order, 55, 67, 68, 69–70, 72, 109

Trance states: and Stambali practices, 7, 30, 33, 170; and Islamic practices, 17, 21; and Zar cult, 26, 27; and Gnawa practices, 35, 38, 39, 170; and Siddi practices, 98, 103

Transjordan, slavery banned in, 40

Translocal identities, 157

Trinidad and Tobago: coup d'état in, 19, 111, 115, 123–31, 132; and Jama'at al-Muslimeen, 19, 115, 123–25, 127–30, 131, 132, 133, 168; and racism, 113, 125; African-descended Muslims in, 126, 130–31, 132, 173;

Indian-descended people in, 126, 130, 173; group tensions in, 126, 173; and Darul Islam, 126–27; and Islamic Party of North America, 127; and drug trade, 128–29; and Nation of Islam, 154
Trinidad and Tobago Television (TTT), 123–24, 129
Truitt, Edward L., 150
Tunis, Tunisia: Bori practices in, 26, 27–28, 29; lodges or brotherhoods in, 27, 30–31; Stambali practices in, 29, 30–31, 32, 33, 35
Tunisia: Muslims' belief in angels, 11; Bori Islam in, 22, 28–29; native-born free blacks in clans, 27; and clan affiliations, 41
Turin, Italy, 67, 68
Turkey, 23, 114
Twelfth Imam, 101

Ulfa Aid, 54
Umar (caliph of Islam), 3, 5, 150
Umayya bin Khalaf, 2, 3
Umayyad empire, 5, 56
Umma (worldwide community of Muslims), 16, 55, 72, 78, 156, 168, 171, 173–74
United Moslem Society, 147
United States: political Islam associated with violence in, 113; and Muslim religious activity in Latin American and Caribbean, 125; African immigration to, 135, 136, 156–64; African American Muslim slaves in, 138–46. *See also* African American Muslims
University of Islam, 154
Urban middle-class Muslims, and Enlightenment rationality, 45
Urdu language, 85, 90, 104, 106
'Urs (death anniversary of saint), 98–99, 105
Uthman (caliph of Islam), 5
Uttara Kannada, India, 91, 92

Van Aken, Mauro, 48
Varella, Antônio Pinto de Mesquita, 111
Vietnamese civil war, 137
Visitation rituals, 45
Voodum, 122

Wadai, 28
Wahhaj, Siraj, 54
Walker, David, 140
War of 1812, 141
Washington, D.C., 157–59, 161, 170–71
Water spirits, 33–34
Waugh, Earle, 21
Wedding *dabka* (dance), 23, 46–49
West Africa: Africana Muslims in, 5, 17; sartorial culture of, 30; Sokoto caliphate in, 54; enslaved soldiers from, 57; Portuguese exploration of, 59; enslaved black Africans of, 112, 139; Islamization of, 139; Islamic practices of, 144, 167; African-born American Muslim immigrants from, 163–64
Weston, Randy, 35
Whites, and racial hierarchy, 13
White supremacy, 148, 149, 154, 166, 172
William E. X, 150
Women: black enslaved women as concubines, 6, 17, 24, 35, 57, 89, 91; rituals of healing associated with evil eye, 23, 44–45; and Zar cult, 26, 27; and Bori practices, 28–29; and Stambali rituals, 30, 31, 33, 34, 170; and Gnawa practices, 37–38, 170; and Ghawarna, 41–42, 44–45; and wedding dances, 46; and Mandinga migrants' funerary rituals, 62–63, 64; discrimination against Mandinga migrant women, 64; and British African-descended Muslims, 76; and Siddis, 88, 92, 93, 95–96, 102, 103, 104, 107, 170; and Muharram, 102; and African American Muslim slaves, 146; and Nation of Islam,

151, 152, 153; and female circumcision, 161, 170–71; Senegalese women migrating to Europe, 183 (n. 41)
Woodson, Carter G., 150
Work Projects Administration (WPA), 142
World Community of al-Islam, 155, 168
World music, and Gnawa music, 36–37
Wudu (ablution), 27, 104, 186 (n. 48)

Yahya, Mohammed, 80
Young, Hershini Bhana, 14–15
Yusuf ibn Tashifun, 56

Zakat (annual alms for the poor and needy), and five pillars of Islam, 11, 104
Zar-Bori complex, 26–27
Zar cult, 26–27, 39
Zawadowski, M. G., 30
Zawiya (Sufi lodge), 29
Ziyara (religious visit or pilgrimage), 30, 34

ISLAMIC CIVILIZATION AND MUSLIM NETWORKS

Edward E. Curtis IV, *The Call of Bilal: Islam in the African Diaspora* (2014).
Sahar Amer, *What Is Veiling?* (2014).
Rudolph T. Ware III, *The Walking Qur'an: Islamic Education, Embodied Knowledge, and History in West Africa* (2014).
Sa'diyya Shaikh, *Sufi Narratives of Intimacy: Ibn 'Arabī, Gender, and Sexuality* (2012).
Karen G. Ruffle, *Gender, Sainthood, and Everyday Practice in South Asian Shi'ism* (2011).
Jonah Steinberg, *Isma'ili Modern: Globalization and Identity in a Muslim Community* (2011).
Iftikhar Dadi, *Modernism and the Art of Muslim South Asia* (2010).
Gary R. Bunt, *iMuslims: Rewiring the House of Islam* (2009).
Fatemeh Keshavarz, *Jasmine and Stars: Reading More than "Lolita" in Tehran* (2007).
Scott A. Kugle, *Sufis and Saints' Bodies: Mysticism, Corporeality, and Sacred Power in Islam* (2007).
Roxani Eleni Margariti, *Aden and the Indian Ocean Trade: 150 Years in the Life of a Medieval Arabian Port* (2007).
Sufia M. Uddin, *Constructing Bangladesh: Religion, Ethnicity, and Language in an Islamic Nation* (2006).
Omid Safi, *The Politics of Knowledge in Premodern Islam: Negotiating Ideology and Religious Inquiry* (2006).
Ebrahim Moosa, *Ghazālī and the Poetics of Imagination* (2005).
miriam cooke and Bruce B. Lawrence, eds., *Muslim Networks from Hajj to Hip Hop* (2005).
Carl W. Ernst, *Following Muhammad: Rethinking Islam in the Contemporary World* (2003).

www.ingramcontent.com/pod-product-compliance
Lightning Source LLC
Chambersburg PA
CBHW020650230426
43665CB00008B/373